Unforgettable AUSSIES

Australian Shepherd Dogs Who Left Pawprints on Our Hearts

Volume II - 1984 to 2000

Paula McDermid

Copyright © 2017 by Paula McDermid
Bainbridge Press

All rights reserved. No part of this book may be reproduced or utilized in any form or by any means, electronic or mechanical, including photocopying, recording, or by any information storage and retrieval system, without written permission from the author.

First edition
First printing October 2017
Book design by Paula McDermid
Edited by Kate Johnson

Companion book:
Unforgettable Aussies
Volume I: 1970-1984

Even though the information in this book has been researched as carefully as possible, there may be a few errors. If you notice a mistake, please let me know.
Contact me
MyAussie2@gmail.com
www.Facebook.com/UnforgettableAussies

ISBN 978-0-9975534-2-0

Front cover: AKC CH McMatt's EZ Victor USASA HOFX-ASCA HOF
Photo courtesy of Tina Beck, Goldcrest

Back cover: Propwash Jessey
Photo courtesy of Saskia Snoeck

Contents

Dedication to Kutabay's Blue Chip Toby iv

Foreword vi

Preserving the Health of Our Aussies vii

Finding "Mr. Right" for Your "Princess." Public-Access Canine Health Databases xii

Beauwood's Rustlin' In The Sun 1

Bayshore's Lucy In The Sky 18

Broadway's Blaze of Glory 30

Peppertree's Magic by Moonlight 56

Cobbercrest Propwash Obla-De 72

Bluestem's Man of Firethorne 90

McMatt's EZ Going 110

McMatt's EZ Victor 136

Briarbrooks Silver Sequence 154

Oprah Winfree of Heatherhill 166

My Main Man of Heatherhill 182

Blended Bloodlines 196

Abbreviations of Titles 214

About the Author 216

Acknowledgements

Thank you to the breed fanciers who inspired me to create Unforgettable Aussies. Special recognition goes to the breeders and owners of the influential dogs in this book, and to people who shared their knowledge and historic photos. With deep appreciation I thank Kate Johnson for her editing and research, which were vital to the accuracy of this book.

Listed in the order their dogs appear in this book:
Debra Pardridge St. Jacques, Beauwood; J. Frank Baylis, Bayshore; Jane Firebaugh and Nora Porobic, Paradigm; Sheila Hall, Peppertree; Kate Johnson, Rainyday; Tim Preston, Cobbercrest; Flo McDaniel, McMatt; Tina Beck, Goldcrest; Linda Wilson, Briarbrook; Alan McCorkle, Heatherhill.

Dedicated to
Kutabay's Blue Chip Toby
February 2002 - November 2009

Within this book are the shared memories and photos of dogs who made a lasting impact on the Australian Shepherd breed, and whose legacy extends to the dogs who are dear to our hearts today.

Kutabay's Blue Chip Toby left a legacy that is permanently etched on our breed. He became the face of epilepsy. This disease was buried in shame and silence until Toby's owner, Pam Douglas, bravely and publicly announced his illness.

In 2002 Pam and her husband Jim fell in love with a little blue puffball they named Toby. He was an adorable and loveable puppy who developed normally. When he was ten months old, Toby had a partial seizure. At thirteen months old he experienced his first Grand Mal seizure, with many more to follow. He was diagnosed with Idiopathic Epilepsy. Although he had the best possible care, Toby succumbed to the disease and its complications after a nearly seven year battle. He was brave and loved life until the end.

Toby's legacy to the canine world is Toby's Foundation, a lifeline of inspiration and information for people with epileptic dogs of all breeds. Established in 2004, Toby's Foundation seeks to increase awareness of canine epilepsy and to help eliminate it by supporting the research to find a gene marker and develop a screening test for this disease.

Toby's Foundation website: http://www.tobysfoundation.org

Toby was one of the most significant Aussies of the past decade.

He never attended a dog show, didn't do obedience or agility and may never even have seen a cow or sheep. Even so, his impact has been tremendous and will continue long after his recent death.

Epilepsy was once this breed's dirty little secret. Few would discuss it, and those that did often found themselves hounded into silence. Then Pam Douglas and her husband, Jim bought a puppy who started seizing. Pam sought help, but the breeder and stud owner stonewalled. When Pam realized this was often standard operating procedure, she launched a very public campaign to raise epilepsy awareness and work toward a DNA screening test.

Today we have a large international study of epilepsy in Aussies underway because Pam buttonholed the researcher at a conference and convinced him to accept our breed into his study. The breed community has acknowledged we have a problem and many will now speak openly and honestly about the disease. People have contributed thousands of dollars to support research and education efforts. We probably would have reached this point eventually, but we got there a lot quicker because of Toby.

C.A. Sharp
Australian Shepherd Health & Genetics Institute
News Release, December 2009

"You can lose your shadow... but not your memories."

Foreword

"If you don't have your health, you don't have anything."
"The greatest wealth is health."

The above quotes are true for both ourselves and our dogs. No matter what activities you do with your dogs, their health has a profound impact on your life.

The dog I loved most was so arthritic by age 10 that he had to stay home when the other dogs and I went on our daily hikes. A few weeks after his 11th birthday he died of cancer.

My heart ached. I wanted many more years with him and still miss him deeply.

Aussies can live active, healthy lives well into their late teens. Breeders who prioritize health and longevity can increase the life expectancy of their litters by choosing sires who remain in good health as they age. Long-time breeder Paula Waterman said, "For me, longevity has same level of importance as structure, movement, and temperament."

In the following pages are stories of Aussies who have lived full lives well into their senior years, showing what is possible.

AKC CH-Multiple Premier ASCA CH Milwin's Silver Ribbon at Inkwell ROM X-I "Ribbon" turned 13 in May. She's in great condition, still chasing balls, and imposing "Granny Law" on her kids and grandkids. This breed should be able to go strong well into its teens. Part of making that happen is looking at longevity in the pedigrees we are interested in adding to our programs. - Paula Waterman. Photo credit: Olivia Frost.

Sharing Knowledge about Health

Because Australian Shepherds have become popular world-wide, we need to work together with Aussie fanciers internationally to ensure we all build health and longevity into our breeding programs. Robust Aussie health databases have been developed in both the U.S. and several European countries. They were designed to preserve health records and provide breeders with resources for making knowledgeable decisions when choosing breeding stock.

A list of those resources are on pages xiii-xvi. It's our responsibility to think long-term and use those resources because our choices determine the destiny of our breed.

- Paula McDermid

On the left is DreamCatcher's Sendoa of Zoriah "Zori." On the right is Milwin's Blue Summer Pleasure "Summer" who is 14 years and 4 months old now. She's been my best friend through some of the most difficult times in my life. Her health and longevity are so important to me because I want her to have the best, most comfortable, and most-loved life she can possibly have. - Pamela Mason White.

Preserving the Health of Our Aussies
"It takes a village...."

"Without proper health clearances, good breeding programs, and conscious breeders, we would not have healthy pups to start with. It takes a healthy diet, proper exercise, and mental stimulation to raise an Aussie that will be in your life for many, many years. It's not just the breeders or just the environment the dog is raised in...it takes all of us to come together to make all the right things happen. It takes a village." - Kathy Kellogg

"There's nothing like having an old dog who is just happy to see you come home and cuddle on the couch." - Lizette Durrschmidt

"Health and longevity are important because my dogs are first and foremost my family members and best friends, and I want them around as long as possible. They are too special and too important in our lives to not strive for longevity and good quality of life." - Marcy Rauch

"I want my dog to have the best, most comfortable, and most-loved life she can possibly have." - Pamela Mason White

"Health and longevity are really important for breeders to pay attention to. We can make smart choices by selecting dogs from pedigrees with good longevity and health, and cross our fingers that we do right by each future generation we produce." - Pat Zapf

A-CH Dutch-Lux CH Moorea's Wild Adventure CD STDs "Sasha" lived to 15½ years old. - Geneviève Chomé.

W.Z. Wild Blue Yonder OTDc ATDds with many agility titles "Corky." Pictured on Advanced cattle at 12 years old, competitive in agility until 14. Lived life to the fullest until 15½. - Kelly Gann.

"At 15 years of age 'Emma' came with me to herding camp. We need to keep our dogs as long as possible with continuous quality of life. Our broken hearts will heal more completely knowing that they lived their FULL life, and we can enjoy their old years as much as we enjoy their puppy years." - Raine Lutz

"I love that my 14-year old 'pup' Kylie still acts like her much younger self, just a little slower and with more naps. I know she's happy and that makes my heart sing. That, to me is the epitome of healthy aging. She's still sharp as a tack, gives her younger brother heck every day and is thriving. I give credit to very conscientious breeding and good genes. Thanks to the breeders for making this a priority in their programs." - Kathy Dukinfield

"My foundation girl CH Bayshore's American Pie 'Cookie' lived 16 years and 20 days, and my heart dog CH Propwash Northern Dancer 'Andy' lived 17 years and 3 months. We still have their sons who are almost 16 years old." - Gabriella Lovati

MACH ATCH NATCH CH Show Me Howe to Highland Fling AKC-ASCA RA MXP MJP2 MXB MJS JV-E-SP S-EJC O-TN-E WV-E TG-E HP-N HIC NADAC Elite Versatility Award ASCA HOF "Merlin" is 16 years and 3 months old and still going strong. I am beyond lucky that Merlin is still here with me, to love and enjoy every day. - Diana Hefti. Photo credit: Nina Sage.

PCH WTCH ADCH-B NATCH ATCH-SP MACH2 APD Arboretum's Masked Bandit AKC-ASCA CDX RN AKD-S ASD AJD S-EAC S-EGC TN-O TG-E LAA-Bronze "Z" lived to 17. He was healthy all the way to 16, and because of that was able to have many wonderful years of retirement. - Lizette Durrschmidt.

AKC-ASCA CH County-Ways Mattina STDc OTDs ATDd RA HSAds USASA versatility certificate "Maddie" is 14 and still with me. - Kim Herness Buffum. Photo credit: Nancy Gaffney.

Horizon's No Trouble At All "Trouble" at almost 13 years of age, playing with a 10-week old puppy. - Georgianne Balcas Doyle.

My ASCA CH Copper Hill's Aurora Borealis ASCA HOF "Ayr" is 14 years old and is going strong. She swims in the ocean everyday and loves it! - Kathy Kellogg. Photo credit: Robin Mulligan.

My heart dog MACH NATCH ATCH-IV A-CH Casa Blanca's Lancia CD RN HSAs OTDs ATDd MXG MJG TDI "Lancia" lived to be 15! In the +13 Veterans class at the Bakersfield Nationals she entertained the crowd leaping and barking and showing she still had her "attitude." - Janet Colby

CKC CH Hemlocks All A Flame CGC TKN ACT1 "Flame" earned her CGC TKN and ACT1 titles at 12½ years young! Good health and longevity are one of the most important hallmarks of a successful breeding program. - Karen Bachelle.

ASCA CH Diamond Aire Silver Lace "Lace" lived to be 17 years and 1 week old. Our dogs are with us such a comparatively short time as it is. The healthier they are, the longer they can live a quality life at our side, out in the sporting rings or working on the farm. - Kathi Schwengel.

Ziggy lived 13½ years. Photo credit: Jim Geiser.

CH Rainyday's Ziggy Stardust NA FD60K

*"Ziggy." Born 2004. By AKC CH Briarbrooks Quicksilver x
AKC-ASCA CH Rainyday GirlsJusWannaHavFun ROM X-III ROM O-I ROM P-I.*

Ziggy loved flyball, he loved everyone he met, and he loved to "kiss."

He and I were at a flyball tournament with an audience of special needs spectators. These individuals were always supervised and they seemed to enjoy watching the dogs race. During a break in the action, one of the special needs people, a scruffy-looking man in his late 50s, shuffled out of the building. He was very upset and crying. His helper, a middle-aged woman, tried to comfort him. I heard the man say, "They won't kiss me." The woman patted the man's back and explained, "The dogs are just too focused to want to play with you." But the scruffy man kept repeating, "They won't kiss me!"

I had some time before my next race, so I asked the helper if the man REALLY wanted to be kissed by a dog. The woman nodded. I quickly went to my van and returned with Ziggy. Now, Ziggy LOVED men and he LOVED LOVED LOVED men with facial hair. Ziggy saw the scruffy-looking man and thought he was in heaven! He tried to lick every whisker off the man's face. The man laughed and exclaimed, "He loves me, he loves me!"

Most of the time I was annoyed that Ziggy preferred hairy men over me, but at that moment I was very proud to be his owner.

- Mary Mynaugh

Tropical Blue Sea of Surf Paradise "Dise" turned 15 years old in September 2017. - Alain-Louis Aymard.

Taiji du Temple de Palés "Taiji" lived to 14½ years. - Bénédicte Palés.

"These dogs are athletes! Structure is important! Health is important! I have a friend who runs the Iditarod and has purebred Siberian huskies that run 1,100 miles at age 9." - Tish Brockmire

"My Copperhill Stunning N Silver 'Jackfrost' is 15 years and 8 months old and still loving life! We take four to five short daily walks, probably totaling two miles. Health and longevity are quality of life issues. Good diet, much exercise, affection, boundaries, stimulation, calm and clean environment are all factors. Taking care of our little buddy is what we do." - Sandy Winsor Clark

"Longevity is important because it shows we are doing something right in our breeding programs and care of our dogs. We need to try our best to create the healthiest animals possible." - Diana Hefti

"My girl Milwin's Blue Summer Pleasure 'Bonnie' lived almost until her 16th birthday. She was my heart. Together we did agility, obedience, rally, herding, conformation, and she was certified therapy dog. She lived a full life and we had lots of fun together. Miss her every day."- Shari Dodson

"Longevity and health are important because it takes a long time and a lot of money to train a good dog. If you put years of training into a dog, ideally you should have a partner for the next 10+ years." - Danielle McJunkins

"The heart of the matter is that I just plain love my dogs. I want them to be healthy and comfortable and to be with me for a very long time." - Tish Brockmire

A-CH Imagineer Ashlyn Dreams CGC TT "Megan" lived to 15. She decided that she liked the show ring when she was 10 years old and became one of the first ASCA Altered Champions. Many judges asked why she was altered and complimented her on being such a sound bitch at her age. - Amy Hiscock. Photo credit: Mike Gorecki.

WTCH Winslows Eye Candy ASCA HOF "Courtney" passed away last year at age 16. Her parents passed when they were 15 and great-grandma passed at 16. Most of her progeny from her first litter are in their teens as well. Courtney worked all her life and finished her WTCH at 12. - Margi Floyd.

Photo courtesy of Alain-Louis Aylmard. Photo credit: Christophe Hermelinne. (FRANCE)

Finding "Mr. Right" for Your "Princess"
Public-Access Canine Health Databases

By C.A. Sharp, President
Australian Shepherd Health & Genetics Institute, Inc.

The decision to breed dogs brings with it many responsibilities. Dedicated breeders take care of their dogs' physical needs, properly socialize their puppies, and screen prospective buyers. They place their puppies in good homes and maintain a lifelong commitment to the animal.

Another area of responsibility assumed by the dedicated breeder is a commitment to the health of their breeding stock and puppies. Conformation traits, working ability, and temperament are routinely factored into deciding on breeding pairs. Health concerns need to have an equally important role in choosing the best sire for your next litter.

Health problems can reduce lifespan, limit or end competition or working careers, cause misery for the dog, and create heartache for the owner. Breeders now have tools to help them avoid some genetic health pitfalls, so they can produce the healthiest puppies possible.

Tracking our breed's major health issues, as well as less common ones that may occur in specific bloodlines, is vital. There's tremendous value in knowing not only the qualities of your own dogs, but also those of their offspring, siblings, parents, and extended families. For example, if a dog has good hips but three littermates are dysplastic or produced dysplastic offspring, a breeder may choose not to use that dog in a breeding program. Gathering this information requires effort, but there are tools available that will help.

Fifteen years ago, researching the health of dogs on a pedigree was no easy matter. Often a breeder had to depend on whatever information people were willing to share—if they were willing to share. Today, breeders have online access to U.S. and European canine health databases that contain tremendous amounts of health information on thousands of dogs. Now it's possible to work hand-in-hand with Aussie breeders across the ocean to protect the health of our breed.

Aussies became popular in Europe in the mid-1980s and U.S. and Canadian exports to Europe are still common. Most European dogs are within a few generations of North American dogs, so all resources can be pertinent wherever you live.

There are a number of major health data sources that can help you on the path to your own pedigree-based health research.

Orthopedic Foundation for Animals (OFA) – The major U.S. health registry, OFA has been in existence since the 1960s. It initially focused on hip dysplasia and other orthopedic screenings. Today they include an eye registry and registries for a variety of other diseases and defects. For Aussies, this includes orthopedic, eye, heart, and thyroid screening as well as some DNA test results. A flexible search page allows you to select individual dogs, groups of dogs, particular health screenings, or a combination of these. This registry is semi-open so non-passing results are shown only with the owner's permission. https://www.ofa.org

Svenska Kennelklubben (SKK) – The Swedish kennel club has been at the forefront of proactive management of genetic diseases in dogs for decades. Their registry is open (all results) and includes orthopedic and eye exams. The site is in Swedish, but Google Translate can get you where you want to go. Once you locate a dog that interests you there's a button that takes you to its health information. hundar.skk.se/hunddata/Hund_sok.aspx

"Salka" and "Kiljan." Born 2017. By ISCh Östra Greda Guccio Gucci x ISCh Östra Greda Bloody Mary. Photos courtesy of Svava Björk Ásgeirsdóttir. Photo credit: Pétur Alan Gudmundsson. (ICELAND)

AKC-UKC-ASCA CH Peppertree's Stars Go Blue STDc OTDds JHD HTADIS "Billy." Born 2007. By ASCA CH Melody's The Beat Goes On x AKC-INT-ASCA CH Rainyday's You Made Me Love U. Photo courtesy of Tina Miller. Photo credit: Evelyn Vinogradof.

Finska Kennelklubben (FKK) – The Finnish kennel club has a website offering similar features to the SKK site but they also have an English language version. All information on a dog (pedigree, health results, competition results, offspring and sibling lists) appears on a single page. One advantage this site has is the ability to move between pages for related individuals by simply clicking on their names. jalostus.kennelliitto.fi

L'Ente Nazionale della Cinofilia Italiana (ENCI) - The Italian Kennel Club offers pedigrees and owner-provided screening results. It is only in Italian, so keep Google Translate handy until you learn where to click. You search using the dog's registered name and breed or one other identifier. Health results, if available, can be reached via a button above the pedigree.
www.enci.it/libro-genealogico/libro-genealogico-on-line

The Kennel Club (KC) – The English Kennel Club offers a health information search service. You must enter the dog's full registered name exactly or the KC registration number. That will take you to a page listing the dog's orthopedic and eye screening results plus certain DNA tests. They offer several reports comparing the dog's test results with those of near relatives.
www.thekennelclub.org.uk/services/public/mateselect/test/Default.aspx

Club Francais Berger Australien (CFBA) – The French FCI club posts PDF listings of hip, elbow, eye and DNA test results, passing or not. The reports are in need of updating, but contain thousands of individual records on French-registered dogs. They are in French but should be relatively easy to understand even if you don't read the language. CFBA is also, to my knowledge, the first and only national breed club to develop an epilepsy registry. Participation is voluntary and only cases supported by veterinary documentation will have their names and pedigrees displayed (over two dozen as of this writing).

Epilepsy registry:
> http://www.epi-cfba.com/la-base-de-donneacutees-franccedilaise.html

Health reports:
> HD, ED, Eyes, CEA, HSF4, PRA: http://secretaire.cfba.free.fr/cte/PUBLICATION%20SANTE%20par%20ALPHA.pdf
> CD: http://secretaire.cfba.free.fr/cte/PUBLICATION%20ADN%20CDm.pdf
> MDR1: http://secretaire.cfba.free.fr/cte/PUBLICATION%20ADN%20MDR1.pdf
> NBT: http://secretaire.cfba.free.fr/cte/PUBLICATION%20ADN%20QC.pdf

International Directory for Australian Shepherd Health (IDASH) - There is a publicly available, Aussie-specific health registry. IDASH is a program of the Australian Shepherd Health and Genetics Institute (ASHGI), a U.S.-based organization that is international in scope. One segment of IDASH is its Open Health Database (OHD) which contains data on health screenings, DNA test results, inherited diseases, dental faults, and disqualifying colors on over 25,000 Aussies. The data comes from other health registries as well as submissions by owners and breeders. It also offers a pedigree service, including a "health

Multi BIS-OH Multi RBIS-OH AKC Bronze GCH-ASCA CH Lk Michigan RU Ready to Rumble CA CGC AKC-ASCA RN CA CGC "Thunder." Photo courtesy of Barb Hoffman & Marcie Boomsliter. Photo credit: Mary Huff.

pedigree" with links any OHD records available. A pedigree analysis service for dog owners that issues reports including the dog's coefficient of inbreeding and relative risk scores for over two dozen health, dental and disqualifying color traits. www.ashgi.org/open-health-database-search/idash

Other kennel clubs – Kennel clubs in some other countries, including Germany and Switzerland, require breed clubs to collect certain health information so that it may be printed on pedigrees. Every official pedigree shows the information on each dog that was available at the time the pedigree was printed.

Australian Shepherd Klub Austria (ASK) – Once a regular breed club, ASK has morphed into a health organization. They work with the Austrian FCI club and serve as an ASHGI liaison for German-speakers in Europe who aren't fluent in English. Their website offers health information and resources. It's a good example of what health-conscious groups in small countries can do to keep Aussie owners and breeders informed. ask.or.at

Australian Shepherd Club Nederland (ASCN) – ASCN maintains a pedigree and health database for its members that currently holds over 18,000 dogs. It includes Dutch-bred Aussies and their ancestors, pedigrees up to 10 generations, behavior tests, conformation evaluations, and health records that have been voluntarily submitted by members—including evaluations of some entire litters. The data includes hip and elbow dysplasia grades, eye health, MDR1 status, DNA results, inbreeding coefficient, bites and teeth, excessive white, tail length, and date of death.

The purpose of the database is to preserve health records and provide breeders with a resource for making knowledgeable decisions about choosing breeding stock. While not available to the general public, ASCN's database is a shining example of what a motivated club and its members can accomplish for the good of the breed.

The Club for Australian Shepherd Germany e.V. (FCI) established a database that stores the health test results required for breeding allowances on over 5,000 Aussies. Other health problems that are reported to the club, such as epilepsy, are also recorded. Life span is documented, health surveys can be generated, and analysis of inbreeding coefficients is offered. Health statistics are documented in the yearly official stud book and health clearances are published in the club newsletter.

The club also established a health fund to provide financial support to owners of puppies who develop serious illnesses. For each puppy bred by a club member, the breeder donates money to the fund. Documented illnesses from this fund are stored in the database and are made official in the club newsletter.

MACH ADCH-Bronze PDCH ATCH3 NATCH Top Rail's Keeper of the Stars "Echo." She's 16 years and 10 months old! - Marcy Rauch.

Inoby Urban Chaos, Beg.Ex, AW (B) "Steiff." Now 14 yrs old and still going strong. He'd like to go round an agility course if he could. - Catherine Fuller. Photo credit: Pixel Photoz.

"My 'Jade' is 16 years and 4 months old. She is still as determined as ever, even though her body is failing. As our foundation bitch, her longevity is essential to our breeding program. Jade is the dog that taught us all about Australian Shepherds. At 10 years of age she earned her STDs title and her daughters are our first WTCH, PCH and VCH." - Donna Burdick

"Our 'Dove' is 15½. She made the move with our family to Mexico at age 13+, and still likes to gallop through a flock of chickens every once in a while just to ruffle some feathers." - Amanda Burgner Valtierra

"My almost 14-year old 'Pelar' was playing with a tennis ball this morning. Tossing it in the air and pouncing on it. Slightly deaf and a tad slower getting up, but still rules the roost." - Elizabeth McIntosh

AKC-ASCA CH Terra-Blue Kalispell HSAs STDds JV-N "Pelar" turned 18 years old on October 22, 2017! She is still holding her own and is a very happy dog. Every day with her is such a blessing!
- Maggie O'Neil. Photo credit: JT PawPrints

Ahh...Raina! My first Aussie, Wyewury Ewe Know I Reign UDX RE HSAds HIAs CGC. Took me from Novice A to UDX. Gathered some OTCH points and a few herding titles too. Going on 14 years now and still going strong. Such a blessing and a life well lived! - Heidi Streeval. Photo credit: Dawn Spivey.

In your winter you reflected...
Humbly watching your progeny...
Carrying on the tradition...
Of versatility.
A look, a manner, a way of moving...
The attitude, the presence.
It is seen in many...
A bit of Bear continues on.

The seasons do change...
And the leaves will always fall...
Appearances deceive the end...
Then again the trees will bud...
Forever promising new life in spring.
Your legacy is certain.
Thank-you, Bear.
All will miss you.

Sierra-Echo
Jan. 2000

Photo credit: Dave Ashbey

SVCH WTCH AKC-CKC-ASCA CHAMPION
Beauwood's Rustlin' In The Sun
AKC-ASCA UDT RD TT HI HTD2s NA RV-N CKC-CD CGC TT
ASCA HOF Sire #19

Call name: Bear
Born: 1986
Sire: ASCA CH Sunspot of Windermere
Dam: ASCA CH Pepper's Special K
Breeder: Debra St. Jacques, Beauwood
Owner: Debra St. Jacques, Beauwood

From the time he was little, Bear was a dog who had the desire to do it all. He always wanted to please, and excelled at stock work, tracking, conformation, and obedience. He especially loved utility. He had the ideal Aussie temperament—highly intelligent, eager to please, lovable, and a pleasure to live with. He had a lot of drive, but also had an "off" switch, and would come into the house and lie down. He passed those desireable traits to his offspring.

Bear was easy-going, good with puppies and children, liked almost everyone, and was incredibly loyal to his family. He had a special quirk: he would walk over and sit on people's feet, which made them think they were special to him. However, Bear never forgot a person he didn't like and he let them know it.

Bear was particularly keen on stock work. His owner, Deb, recalled, "One day I got a call from a nearby farmer who had a dozen Holstein heifers get loose. He'd been looking all over but couldn't find them. He'd heard that Bear was a good stock dog as well as a tracking dog so he asked for our help.

First, Bear had to track the cattle. He and I hiked on a mountainside that was dense with trees and brush, and finally found the heifers. They were not dog broke, so when Bear went on an outrun, they repeatedly split into two or three groups and scattered among the trees. He worked and worked to gather them, and after six long and difficult hours we finally got them to a farm where they had grain and water waiting and were confined. We were exhausted, and the farmer was very happy to have his livestock safe."

Bear was also an excellent school dog. Deb said, "He was my go-to dog when I gave herding lessons. He never got me into trouble and he made sure the sheep were under control. I had a Bear son, Tucker, who needed to learn how to be a school dog. It was hard for me to change dogs because Bear was so dependable. But Tucker did become a wonderful farm and lesson dog."

Bear had strong conformation traits that he passed to his offspring. He had an excellent shoulder assembly, topline and headpiece, and had perfect feet. He was a moderate-sized dog at 21" tall and 50 lbs. He carried a dark red, correct, dense coat that shed dirt and mud easily—he would shake, get dry, and the dirt would fall off.

Bear was successful in all areas of competition. He competed in herding, tracking, obedience, and conformation at many National Specialties. He was awarded Most Versatile Aussie at the Texas National Specialty from the Started Herding classes. He placed in the stud dog class at the 1988 ASCA National Specialty and showed at Westminster the first year that Aussies were recognized. Whatever he was asked to do, Bear gave 100%.

Bear and Debra. Spring 1986. Photo courtesy of Debra St. Jacques. Photo credit: Mark St. Jacques.

Bear's daughter Beauwood's No Contest "Tess." Born 1989. By Bear x Snowy River T.B. ASCA STDdsc JJ-N AKC-NA AHBA-HTDI. Best friend of Renee St. Jacques. Photo courtesy of Debra St. Jacques.

Pedigree

```
                                                  CH Dutchman of Flintridge CDX HOF
                                 CH Windermere's Sunshine of Bonnie-Blu CDX HOF
                                                  Thistle of Flintridge HOF
                ASCA CH Sunspot of Windermere
                                                  CH Papillon of Meshlacon
                                 CH Best Wishes of Windermere CD STDd
                                                  Winter Wishes of Windermere
SVCH WTCH Multi CH Beauwood's Rustlin' In The Sun UDT RD NA ASCA HOF
                                                  George's Red Rustler
                                 CH Beauwood's Out Rustlin' Bear UDT STDsc OTDd
                                                  Beauwood's Caligari Bear
                ASCA CH Pepper's Special K
                                                  CH Coppertone's East of the Sun
                                 CH Pepper's Grapenuts at Dawn CD
                                                  Pepper's Kiss Me Kate
```

Bear's sire ASCA CH Sunspot of Windermere "Spotter." Born 1982. Photo courtesy of Debra St. Jacques.

Bear's dam ASCA CH Pepper's Special K "Sunny." Born 1982. Photo courtesy of Debra St. Jacques. Photo credit: Susan Rossy.

Bear's grandsire ASCA CH Beauwood's Out Rustlin Bear UDT STDsc OTDd ASCA HOF "Rus." Born 1977. Photo courtesy of Debra St. Jacques. Photo credit: LM Gray.

Bear's granddam ASCA CH Pepper's Grapenuts at Dawn CD "Grapenuts." Born 1979. Photo courtesy of Debra St. Jacques.

Some of the finest bitches in the country were brought to him, and as a result, he sired many outstanding puppies. Because of their quality, Bear and his progeny helped bring the red gene into modern conformation bloodlines.

Some of Bear's most notable offspring were:

› VCH AKC-ASCA CH Beauwood Sierra-Echo Yogiber OTDc ATDds RJ-E JJ-E GV-E AX AXJ HSs AHBA JHDs ASCA HOF, 1999 ASCA National Specialty Winners Dog and Best of Winners. Sire of:
  › VCH ATCH CKC-OTCH CKC CH ASCA A-CH Beauwood Cleared For Takeoff AKC-NA NAJ ASCA-UD RE OTDc RG-O RJ-O CKC-RE HA AAC AGMCH AREas-RS-O
  › MACH5 PACH2 Chukker's Orso of Beauwood CD RAE2 HSAsd HSBd HIAsd HXAd MXS2 MJB2 MXP6 MXPS MJP6 MJPS PAX2 MXF MFB TQX MFP T2BP
› AKC-ASCA CH Sierra-Echo Stokin' the Fire ASCA HOF, 2000 ASCA National Specialty Winners Dog and Pre-Show Winners Dog
› AKC-ASCA CH Sierra-Echo Hazardous Glow STDs HSAs RS-N NAC JS-N NJC, Reserve Winners Dog 2000 ASCA National Pre-Show
› SVCH WTCH PCH AKC-ASCA CH Beauwood's Bear Foote Rustler AKC-ASCA CDX HS AX AXJ RV-E JV-E GV-E RD
› ATCH-III NATCH-3 Beauwood's Rustlin' Sunpiper CDX
› AKC-ASCA CH Hearthside and Terrablue's Beauwood CD CGC. Sire of:
  › AKC-ASCA CH Hearthside Surfin' In The Sun
  › AKC CH Hearthside Unforgettable CGC
› Multiple Premier AKC-ASCA CH Cimarron's Here Comes The Sun
› ASCA CH Irish Eyes of Imagineer CD NA STDds CGC
› Jan-Mar Scarlet O'Ara STDdsc ASCA HOF

Bear with Beauwood's Rustlin' At Dawn AKC CD ASCA CDX STDdsc AX RS-N RJ-N CGC ASCA HOF "Sassy." Born 1993. Together they produced the three Beauwood offspring in the photo on next page. Photo courtesy of Debra St. Jacques. Photo credit: Melissa Hammond.

Bear with Beauwood's Rustlin' At Dawn AKC CD ASCA CDX STDdsc AX RS-N RJ-N CGC ASCA HOF "Sassy" (center) and their son SVCH WTCH PCH AKC-ASCA CH Beauwood's Bear Foote Rustler AKC-ASCA CDX HS AX AXJ JV-E GV-E RD "Tucker" (left). Pictured with owner Debra St. Jacques. Photo courtesy of Debra St. Jacques. Photo credit: Melissa Hammond.

Bear (lying down) with his sons at the 1998 USASA National Specialty. (Left to right) CH Cimarron's Reason To Believe. SVCH WTCH PCH CH Beauwood's Bear Foote Rustler CDX RD RV-E JV-E GV-E. Beauwood's Rustlin' In The Wind CDX RS-O JS-O. Blue merle on right not identified. Beauwood's Bright Arrow STDd RS-O. Photo courtesy of Debra St. Jacques. Photo credit: JC Photo.

- AKC-ASCA CH Propwash St. Elmo's Fire USASA HOFX-ASCA HOF. Sire of:
    - WTCH AKC CH Gold Nugget's Contender CD ASCA HOF. Foundation sire for Spring Fever
    - AKC CH Gefion's Kissing Bandit ASCA HOF
    - ASCA CH Mystery Girl of Heatherhill ASCA HOF
- AKC CH Propwash Flounce, BOB 1992 ASCA National Specialty; BOS 1994 USASA National Specialty; BOS Westminster Kennel Club 1994, 1995, 1997
- Propwash Motion Carried. Dam of:
    - Cobbercrest Propwash Obla-De USASA HOFX-ASCA HOF. Matriarch of the Rainyday dynasty of Aussies
- Propwash Flying Colors. Dam of:
    - AKC-ASCA-CRO-ESP-GIB-ITA CH Propwash Syzygy 3 x WW 2000, 2001, 2003, EW 2001 3 x CACIB, 1 x CAC, 3 x BOB 1 x BIS, 1 x BIG
- ASCA CH Propwash Phantom of the Sky. Sire of:
    - AKC-ASCA CH Propwash Remarque TT ASCA HOF
    - AKC-CKC-ASCA CH Propwash Manape Ghostrider ROM X-I ROM C-III ASCA HOF
    - AKC-ASCA CH Manape Griffen
- ASCA CH Propwash Pocket Full of Miracles ASCA HOF

Bear will be remembered as an outstanding, versatile dog. His offspring were exceptionally intelligent, talented, and trainable, and had Bear's "do it all" attitude.

Many thanks to Debra Pardridge St. Jacques for these highlights about Bear.

CONVERSATIONS

Cathy Lowe · Bear was such a contributor to our breed!

Cynthia Hokes · It's neat to read about a dog farther back in my pup's pedigree. Some of his traits remind me of my guy, too.

Christine Pouliot · I would recognize Bear anywhere.

Gail Karamalegos · Bear's son Multiple Premier AKC-ASCA CH Cimarron's Here Comes The Sun "Travis" was also an ASCA Top 10 Merit Award winner.

Pepe Rosas · Wow! Gorgeous!

Janet Walden-West · Bear was a lovely dog.

Karyne Gagné · I have Bear in the seventh generation of my litter by CKC GCH-ASCA CH Cedarpaws Lasting Impresion CA "Koda." Bear is exactly what I search for in an Aussie. Thank you for the memories!

Christine Porter-Holler · My Bear granddaughter CH Porter's Sierra Spice "Robin" was sired by VCH AKC-ASCA CH Beauwood Sierra-Echo Yogiber OTDc ATDds RJ-E JJ-E GV-E AX AXJ HSs AHBA JHDs ASCA HOF "Yogi." Robin will be 14 in April. She is from my first litter and all of my dogs go back to her.

Ada Nowek · I feel blessed and honoured that I had a son of Bear, Beauwood's The Big Cheese "Nacho." He was a great dog in a little, plain packet. I was so happy that I could meet Bear at the 1999 Nationals in Longview. At that time Nacho already lived with us in Germany.

Shawna Wiebe · I had a Bear son, too. He was a littermate to Ada Nowek's Nacho.

Bear's son SVCH WTCH PCH AKC-ASCA CH Beauwood's Bear Foote Rustler AKC-ASCA CDX HS AX AXJ RV-E JV-E GV-E RD "Tucker." Versatility Award 1999 ASCA National Specialty. By Bear x Beauwood's Rustlin' At Dawn AKC CD ASCA CDX STDdsc AX RS-N RJ-N CGC ASCA HOF Photo courtesy of Debra St. Jacques. Photo credit: Animal World Studio.

Bear's son VCH AKC-ASCA CH Beauwood Sierra-Echo Yogiber OTDc ATDds RJ-E JJ-E GV-E AX AXJ HSs AHBA JHDs ASCA HOF "Yogi." Born 1997. Winners Dog and Best of Winners 1999 ASCA National Specialty. By Bear x A-CH Sierra-Echo Firedancer NA NAJ HIC ASCA HOF. Pictured with owner-handler Renee St. Jacques. Photo courtesy of Debra St. Jacques. Photo credit: Animal World Studio.

Bear's son AKC-ASCA CH Hearthside and TerraBlues Beauwood CD OA RS-E JS-E GS-E "Woody." Born 1991. By Bear x AKC CH Brightwood's Society Page. Photo courtesy of Debra St. Jacques. Photo credit: JC Photo.

Bear's daughter ASCA CH Gefion's Cloverhill Jitterbug "Tag." Born 1986. By Bear x ASCA CH Gefion Flashdance. Photo courtesy of Debra St. Jacques. Photo credit: LM Gray.

Stud dog class 1988 ASCA National Specialty. (Left to right)
› SVCH WTCH AKC-CKC-ASCA CH Beauwood's Rustlin' In The Sun AKC-ASCA UDT RD TT HI HTD2s NA RV-N CKC-CD CGC TT ASCA-HOF "Bear" with Debra St. Jacques.
› ASCA CH Gefion's Cloverhill Jitterbug CD STDs "Tag" with Robin Prouty.
› ASCA CH Propwash Phantom of the Sky ASCA HOF "Repo" with Leslie Frank.
Photo courtesy of Debra St. Jacques.

Ulla Patzek · Ja, lach, kann mich da an einiges erinnern. (Yes, I can remember a lot of things.)

Ada Nowek · Ich auch. (Me too.)

Peggy Albertson · Bear was a great dog!

Gia Coppi · So lucky to have Bear behind my dogs!

Sierra Echo Aussies · My Bear son AKC-ASCA CH Sierra-Echo Hazardous Glow HSAs STDs RS-N JS-N NAC NJC "Hazard" was Reserve Winners Dog at the 2000 ASCA Nationals Pre-Show. He also won a Herding Group 1.

Bear's son AKC-ASCA CH Sierra-Echo Stokin' the Fire ASCA HOF "Stoker" was the 2000 ASCA National Specialty Winners Dog and Pre-Show Winners Dog.

Bear's son VCH AKC-ASCA CH Beauwood Sierra-Echo Yogiber was the 1999 ASCA National Specialty Winners Dog and Best of Winners. His owner and handler was Renee St. Jacques.

Bear's great-granddaughter A-CH Sierra-Echo Firedancer NA NAJ HIC ASCA HOF won the 2000 ASCA National Specialty Brood Bitch class. Her offspring, sired by Bear, were CH Sierra-Echo Sanburg CeeVee, AKC-ASCA CH Sierra-Echo Stokin' the Fire ASCA HOF, and VCH AKC-ASCA CH Beauwood's Sierra-Echo Yogiber OTDc ATDds RJ-E JJ-E GV-E AX AXJ HSs AHBA JHDs ASCA HOF.

Dancin Eyes Aust Shep · Dancin' Eyes' foundation sire was a Bear son. Every dog in my Hall of Fame Kennel goes back to him. My current one-year-old pups are seven generations down from Bear.

Mary Mynaugh · My Teddy was from one of Bear's last litters. He was titled in conformation, obedience, herding, agility, and flyball. Ted also had a quirk.

Bear's daughter AKC-ASCA CH Propwash Flounce "Flounce." Born 1989. BOB 1992 ASCA National Specialty. BOS 1994 USASA National Specialty. BOS Westminster 1994, 1995, 1997. By Bear x Propwash Bayshore Fogbow ASCA HOF. Photo courtesy of Robin Prouty. Photo credit: Laurie Shuren. Flounce was 14 years old in this photo.

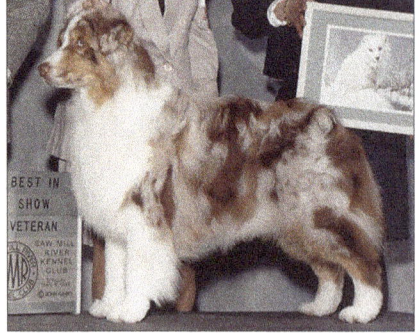

Bear's son MBIS BISS AKC-ASCA CH Propwash St. Elmo's Fire USASA HOFX-ASCA HOF "Elmo." Born 1989. BOB Westminster 1995. BOB at first USASA Nationals. By Bear x Propwash Bayshore Fogbow ASCA HOF. Photo courtesy of Leslie Frank. Photo credit: John Ashbey.

Bear's littermate ASCA CH Beauwood's Touch The Sun "Sunny." Born 1986. By ASCA CH Sunspot of Windermere x ASCA CH Pepper's Special K. Photo courtesy of Debra St. Jacques.

Bear's daughter AKC CH Sierra-Echo Christmas Cotton "Cotton." Born 1997. By Bear x A-CH Sierra-Echo Firedancer NA NAJ HIC ASCA HOF. Photo courtesy of Debra St. Jacques. Photo credit: John Ashbey.

Bear's son Multiple Premier AKC-ASCA CH Cimarron's Here Comes The Sun "Travis." Born 1996. ASCA Top 10 Merit Award. By Bear x AKC-ASCA CH Cimarron's Gotcha Number. Photo courtesy of Gail Karamalegos. Photo credit: Luis Sosa.

Bear's son CH Charisma's Mi-T's Eliminator PT STDsc OTDd NA NAJ "Eli." Born 1994. By Bear x Charisma's Little Sis. Photo courtesy of Kym Base. Photo credit: Rinehart.

Bear's son AKC-ASCA CH Sierra-Echo Stokin' the Fire ASCA HOF "Stoker." Born 1999. Winner's Dog 2000 ASCA National Specialty and Pre-Show Winner's Dog. By Bear x A-CH Sierra-Echo Firedancer NA NAJ HIC ASCA HOF. Photo courtesy of Sierra Echo Aussies. Photo credit: Kohler.

Bear's son AKC-ASCA CH Sierra-Echo's Hazardous Glow HSAs STDs RS-N JS-N NAC NJC "Hazard." Born 1997. Reserve Winner's Dog 2000 ASCA National Pre-Show. By Bear x A-CH Sierra-Echo Firedancer NA NAJ HIC ASCA HOF. Photo courtesy of Sierra Echo Aussies. Photo credit: Tom Nutting.

He would only walk on leash if I was at the other end of it. If I handed over the leash to the person I was walking with, Ted would immediately sit down and not move until I was holding the leash again. He also liked to sing along with me on road trips. Teddy was the spitting image of his daddy.

Helen Ferguson · I'm proud that four of my Aussies past and present go back to Bear: Archie, Taxi, Wikki, and Feisty. All (except Feisty because she's too young) have multiple breed and performance titles.

Nancy Elizabeth · My Bear granddaughter was Meri Mors Ray-Nan's Shelby CD CGC. She was a special girl! Her sire was Bear's son AKC CH Propwash St. Elmo's Fire USASA HOFX-ASCA HOF.

Kym Base · I loved Bear! He was the sire of my foundation dog CH Charisma's Mi-T's Eliminator PT STDsc OTDd NA NAJ "Eli." Eli was also ASCA's first Started Sheep Merit winner!

Kathy Fretz · My Bear grandson ATCH NATCH CH Beauwood's Kole Black Rustler CD "Kolby" was sired by AKC-CKC-ASCA CH Summertime Gemini of MontRose CD ROM X-III ROM C-II ROM O-I ROM P-I ASCA HOF and out of ASCA CH Sierra-Echo's Christmas Cotton. He is my foundation sire and all the dog's of Sunpiper are his descendants. What a great dog he was! Kole passed away last year at 15 years old. Bear's daughter ATCH-III NATCH-3 Beauwood's Rustlin' Sunpiper CDX "Piper" was born in 1997. She's by Bear x Beauwood's Rustlin' At Dawn AKC CD ASCA CDX STDdsc AX RS-N RJ-N CGC ASCA HOF. She was my heart dog and I named my kennel in her honor "'Sunpiper." She was the greatest dog and Debra St. Jacques has been the greatest friend and mentor since 1997. I am humbled and honored to carry on the Bear and Beauwood line. Piper helped to make her mother a HOF and Beauwood Kennel a HOFX Kennel.

Bear's daughter Propwash Motion Carried "Mojo." Born 1991. By Bear x Propwash Bayshore Fogbow ASCA HOF. Photo credit: Tim Preston.

Bear's son AKC-CKC CH Lazy L's Dennis The Menace CKC-ASCA CD RN HIT CGC "Denny." Born 1994. By Bear x Bayshore's Sierra Girl. Photo courtesy of Debra St. Jacques. Photo credit: JC Photo.

Bear's grandson ATCH NATCH CH Beauwood's Kole Black Rustler CD "Kolby." Born 2001. By AKC-CKC-ASCA CH Summertime Gemini of MontRose CD ROM X-III ROM C-II ROM O-I ROM P-I ASCA HOF x ASCA CH Sierra-Echo's Christmas Cotton. Photo courtesy of Kathy Fretz.

Bear's daughter AKC-ASCA CH Propwash Flying Colors CD "Mandy." Born 1989. By Bear x Propwash Bayshore Fogbow ASCA HOF. Photo courtesy of Laura Kirk.

Bear's great-great-grandson VCH RTCH2 A-CH Sunpiper Beauwood Flyin' Finish CD OTDsc ATDd RAs REA RX AX AXJ RS-E JS-E GV-E "Finn." Born 2010. By AKC CH Legacy's Fly Right x ATCH CH Kylin's Ice Blue Eaglett CDX RE RNX RA AX AXJ NF RS-E-OP JS-E-SP GS-E-SP. Photo courtesy of Debra St. Jacques.

Bear's offspring and their dam won the Brood Bitch class at the 2000 ASCA National Specialty. (Left to right)
› AKC-ASCA CH Sierra-Echo Sanburg Cee Vee CDX RS-O with Col. John Eckert.
› AKC-ASCA CH Sierra-Echo Stokin' The Fire ASCA HOF with Debra St. Jacques.
› Dam: Bear's great-granddaughter A-CH Sierra-Echo Firedancer NA NAJ HIC ASCA HOF "Tabu." Born 1995. By Sierra-Echo's Firewalker x Spring Fever's Cocksure Ideal with Sara Elhoffer.
› VCH AKC-ASCA CH Beauwood Sierra-Echo Yogiber OTDc ATDds RJ-E JJ-E GV-E AX AXJ HSs AHBA JHDs ASCA HOF with Renee St. Jacques.
Photo courtesy of Debra St. Jacques. Photo credit: Liz Eckert.

Alison Smith · Bear was the sire of my very first litter ever. A great producer!

Karen Roesner · Bear was the first beau of my AKC-INT-ASCA CH Show-Me's Shadow Dancer CGC. Very consistent litter.

Diane Dodge · I was Deb's Maid of Honor at her wedding and it was our Aussies that got us connected. Such great memories.

Diana Hefti · I loved Bear when I saw pictures of him, and considered using him for my (one and only) girl Di, a LONG time ago. Things didn't work out, so I waited and saw Bear's son VCH AKC-ASCA CH Beauwood's Sierra-Echo Yogiber HOF "Yogi" at Nationals in 1999. When my Andy died unexpectedly of hemangiosarcoma in 2000, I started my search for a new puppy with Debra St. Jacques. She had nothing out of Yogi coming up soon, so I kept looking, then checked back with her in June of 2001. She told me about a litter just born, out of Yogi and a Hearthside bitch. I talked to the breeder and loved the pedigree. In September, on Labor Day weekend, my Merlin came to me all the way from New York to Seattle, Wash. My darling Merlin is still with me and has followed in the footsteps of his father and grandfather. I am so very honored to have a piece of these great dogs in my boy. Merlin is MACH ATCH NATCH CH Show Me Howe to Highland Fling AKC-ASCA RA MXP MJP2 MXB MJS JV-E-SP S-EJC O-TN-E WV-E TG-E HP-N HIC NADAC Elite Versatility Award ASCA HOF.

Bear's grandson MACH ATCH NATCH CH Show Me Howe to Highland Fling AKC-ASCA RA MXP MJP2 MXB MJS JV-E-SP S-EJC O-TN-E WV-E TG-E HP-N HIC NADAC Elite Versatility Award ASCA HOF "Merlin." Born 2001. By VCH AKC-ASCA CH Beauwood Sierra-Echo Yogiber OTDc ATDds RJ-E JJ-E GV-E AX AXJ HSs AHBA JHDs ASCA HOF x Hearthside Too Hot to Dance. Photo courtesy of Diana Hefti. Photo credit: Amber Jade Aanensen.

Bear's grandson CH Sierra-Echo Firewalker "Flint." Born 1993. By ASCA CH Sankano Whisper of Hope x Hearthside Rustlin' Up Ransom. Photo courtesy of Sierra-Echo Aussies.

Bear's daughter ATCH-III NATCH-3 Beauwood's Rustlin' Sunpiper CDX "Piper." Born 1997. By Bear x Beauwood's Rustlin' at Dawn. Photo courtesy of Kathy Fretz.

Bear's daughter Propwash Beauwood Jessey. Born 1989. By Bear x Propwash English Muffin. One of the first Aussies in the Netherlands. Photo courtesy of Saskia Snoeck. (NETHERLANDS)

SVCH WTCH AKC-CKC-ASCA CH Beauwood's Rustlin' In The Sun AKC-ASCA UDT RD TT HI HTD2s NA RV-N CKC-CD CGC TT ASCA-HOF "Bear." Photo courtesy of Debra St. Jacques. Photo credit: Carol Goozy.

Bear's granddaughter CH Porter's Sierra Spice "Robin." Born 2003. By VCH AKC-ASCA CH Beauwood Sierra-Echo Yogiber OTDc ATDds RJ-E JJ-E GV-E AX AXJ HSs AHBA JHDs ASCA HOF x Eaglerun's Fletcher. Photo courtesy of Christine Porter-Holler.

Bear's grandsire ASCA CH Beauwood's Out Rustlin' Bear UDT STDsc OTDd ASCA HOF "Rus." Born 1977. By George's Red Rustler ASCA HOF x Beauwoods Caligari Bear. Photo courtesy of Debra St. Jacques. Photo credit: LM Gray.

Sierra Echo Aussies · Bear's grandson CH Sierra-Echo Firewalker "Flint" was a certified therapy dog who made weekly visits to children's hospital and nursing homes with Becky Scrivener.

Martina Naffien · Bear is in my Sly's pedigree on his dam's side. He is Blue Sunnycreek's Try 2 Beat This RS-N JS-E GS-N.

Sherrie A. Scott · Everything we have goes back to Bear through our WTCH CH Gold Nuggets Contender CD ASCA HOF, who was a son of AKC-ASCA CH Propwash St. Elmo's Fire USASA HOFX-ASCA HOF.

Pamela A. Gagnon · So much of what I have goes back to Bear.

Kathleen Haley · It's nice to be reminded of dogs I was fortunate enough to see in person.

Bear's grandson AKC CH Gefion's Coup D'Etat "Ta Da." Born 1995. By MBIS BISS AKC-ASCA CH Propwash St. Elmo's Fire USASA HOFX-ASCA HOF x AKC CH Gefion's Revolution. Photo courtesy of Georjean Hertzwig.

Bear' great-great-granddaughter CH Spring Fever's Standing Ovation ASCA HOF "Carson." Born 1998. By AKC-ASCA CH Caledonia's Crowd Pleaser USASA HOFX-ASCA HOF x WTCH ASCA CH Spring Fevers Whoopi Gal ASCA HOF. Photo courtesy of Spring Fever.

Bear earned his ASCA Utility title. Photo courtesy of Debra St. Jacques.

Bear's grandsire CH Beauwood's Out Rustlin' Bear UDT STDsc OTDd ASCA HOF "Rus." Born 1977. By George's Red Rustler ASCA HOF x Beauwood's Caligari Bear. Photo courtesy of Debra St. Jacques.

Bear passed his Tracking Dog test in 1993. Photo courtesy of Debra St. Jacques.

Bear was awarded Most Versatile Aussie at the 1988 ASCA National Specialty. Photo courtesy of Debra St. Jacques. Photo credit: LM Gray.

Bear's grandson CH Beauwood Black Russian Bear STDdsc RS-N JS-N HS "Dmitri." Born 2003. By VCH AKC-ASCA CH Beauwood Sierra-Echo Yogiber OTDc ATDds RJ-E JJ-E GV-E AX AXJ HSs AHBA JHDs ASCA HOF x AKC CH Shamrock Sure As It Gets. Photo courtesy of Debra St. Jacques. In Motion Photos.

Bear's granddaughter VCH ATCH CKC-OTCH CKC CH ASCA A-CH Beauwood Cleared For Takeoff AKC-NA NAJ ASCA-UD RE OTDc RG-O RJ-O- CKC RE HA AAC AGMCH AREas-RS-O "Taxi." Born 2003. By VCH AKC-ASCA CH Beauwood Sierra-Echo Yogiber OTDc ATDds RJ-E JJ-E GV-E AX AXJ HSs AHBA JHDs ASCA HOF x CH Shamrocks Sure As It Gets. Photo courtesy of Debbie St. Jacques.

Bear's granddaughter SVCH SPCH PCH WTCH A-CH Sierra-Echo Shadow Canyon AKC-VCD1 CDX RE HIAs OAJ NA ASCA-UD TD RTDs GS-E JV-E RV-E RMX REM "Echo." Born 2003. By AKC-ASCA CH Sierra-Echo Stokin' the Fire ASCA HOF x Mistretta's Shadow Painting ASCA HOF. Photo courtesy of Melanie Magamoll. Photo credit: In Motion Photos.

(Left to right) ASCA CH Linerider's Imagineer of Dakota ASCA CD "Maggie" with Diane Peters. Bear's daughter ASCA CH Irish Eyes of Imagineer ASCA CD STDds NA "Kirby" with handler Gemi Sasson-Brickson. Bear's son ASCA CH Advantage of Imagineer "Dylan" with handler Eric Brickson. Kirby and Dylan were sired by Bear and out of Maggie. Born 1990. Photo courtesy of Debra St. Jacques.

Bear's grandsire ASCA CH Beauwood's Out Rustlin' Bear UDT STDcs OTDd ASCA HOF won the Stud Dog class at an ASCA show with two puppies bred by Georjean Hertzwig. Photo credit: LM Gray.

Second from the left is Bear's son Beauwood's The Big Cheese "Nacho," at 12 years old. (Left to right) "Connor," "Nacho," Touchstone Heart of Thunder "Oya," and Georgia Rose von Preussen's Gloria "Georgia." Photo courtesy of Ada Nowek. (GERMANY)

Bear's great-grandson AKC-ASCA CH PennYCaerau Kinetic Red Alert STDs ASCA HOF "Scanner." Born 1996. By AKC-ASCA CH Heatherhill Sweet Talkin Dude CD HS STDs OA OAJ ASCA HOF x Striderite's Head Over Heels. Photo courtesy of Debra Johnson.

Bear's great-grandson UKC CH Buff Cap Caught Red Handed "Pete." Born 2005. By BIS AKC-ASCA CH Elite's Sailing on Sunshine x CH Buff Cap Bayberry Bustle. Photo courtesy of Francine Guerra.

Bear's granddaughter AKC CH Striderite's Head Over Heels ASCA HOF "Kasha." Born 1993. By ASCA CH Sankano Whisper of Hope x Hearthside Rustlin' Up Ransom. Photo courtesy of Leida Jones.

Bear's son KC CH Sazbrat Here's the Deal AKC-ASCA CD STDs HT HCT ONYX OA NAJ NAC PD1 CGC RA "Teddy." Born 1998. By Bear x AKC CH Merribrook Testarosa of Windogo ROM X-II. Photo courtesy of Mary Mynaugh.

Bear's granddaughter AKC-ASCA CH Propwash Confidence "Connie." Born 1990. By MBIS BISS AKC-ASCA CH Propwash St. Elmo's Fire USASA HOFX-ASCA HOF x Propwash Lo And Behold CD.

Bear's great-great-great-grandson RTCH Toffee's Creed of Rosecreek CD GS-O JV-E RV-E RAX RMX REX REMX "Creeden." Born 2008. By Mi-T's Brilliant Black Rapper x CC Earlybird of Rosecreek. Photo courtesy of Claudia Römer. (GERMANY)

Bear's great-granddaughter Meri-Mors Simon Sez Dodge ASCA CD "Dodgee." Born 1996. By AKC CH Silvertone Simon Uproar Mermor x Meri-Mors Blazing Bows CDX. Photo courtesy of Diane Dodge.

Lucy was a phenomenal producer. Her sons and daughters became foundation sires and dams for many kennels, and through them, she played a significant role in the development of Aussies in the United States, Europe and Australia.

Photo courtesy of Leslie Frank

ASCA Champion
Bayshore's Lucy In The Sky CD
ROM X-II ROM C-I - ASCA HOF Dam #76

Call Name: Lucy
Born: 1984
Sire: ASCA CH Winchester's Three Cheers
Dam: ASCA CH Sitting Pretty of Sunnybrook ASCA HOF
Breeder: J. Frank Baylis, Bayshore
Owner: Leslie Frank, Propwash

From the very beginning of his involvement with dogs, Lucy's breeder, J. Frank Baylis, had focused on breeding the finest quality show dogs. In 1984, his goal was to produce a stud dog with big sidegait, nice bone, a long cresty neck, and showdog attitude. Frank crossed ASCA CH Winchester's Three Cheers and ASCA CH Sitting Pretty of Sunnybrook ASCA HOF, and he struck gold. The litter contained three outstanding puppies who were stamped with the qualities he desired.

The male in the litter was just what Frank was looking for. He became Multi CH Bayshore's Three To Get Ready CD TT STDd ROM C-I ASCA HOF. One of the females became CH Bayshore's Cloud Nine and the other female became CH Bayshore's Lucy In The Sky CD ROM X-II ROM C-I ASCA HOF "Lucy."

Lucy had a wonderfully sweet temperament. She was a pretty blue color with a lot of merling on her face and lighter tan points. She was well-angulated, and had long sidegait, good bone, a lovely neck, and that desirable showdog attitude.

When Lucy was a puppy, Frank Baylis sold her to Leslie Frank of Propwash Farm, where she had a successful show career and was an exceptional brood bitch.

Lucy was an outstanding producer and the dam of:
- AKC-ASCA CH Propwash Two Up CD
- AKC-ASCA CH Propwash Hey Jude, foundation sire for Thornapple Aussies and sire of:
    - Cobbercrest Propwash Obla-De USASA HOFX-ASCA HOF, foundation for Rainyday.
    - AKC CH Thornapple White Diamonds. Dam of:
        - AKC CH Thornapple Diamonds N Spurs
        - AKC CH Thornapple Climate Controlled, top-winning dog in the U.K.
- ASCA CH Propwash Phantom of the Sky ASCA HOF. Sire of:
    - AKC-CKC-ASCA CH Propwash Manape Ghostrider ROM X-I ROM C-III ASCA HOF. Sire of:
        - AKC CH Bayshore's Propwash Balderdash USASA HOFX-ASCA HOF
        - AKC CH Thornapple What It Takes
        - AKC-ASCA CH CH Elite's Eisen On the Cake ASCA HOF
        - AKC-CKC CH Thornapple Sweethearts Dance
        - AKC-IT-INT CH Elora Danan's Ticket to Ride
    - AKC-ASCA CH Manape Propwash Griffen
    - AKC-ASCA CH Propwash Remarque ASCA HOF
- ASCA CH Propwash Marshmallow Pies
- Propwash Lo and Behold CD. Grandam of:
    - BISS AKC-ASCA CH Ferncroft's Ball of Fire CD RN AX OAJ CGC ROM X-III ROM P-I, National Specialty Best of Breed titleholder

Lucy's son AKC-ASCA CH Propwash Two Up CD "Tupper." Born 1986. By ASCA CH Windhill's Take A Chance x Lucy. Photo courtesy of Leslie Frank.

Lucy's son AKC-ASCA CH Propwash Hey Jude "Jude." Born 1992. By ASCA CH Topper's Levi Blues x Lucy. Photo courtesy of Thornapple. Photo credit: Booth.

Pedigree

ASCA CH Bayshore's Lucy In The Sky CD ROM X-II ROM C-I ASCA HOF
- ASCA CH Winchesters Three Cheers
  - ASCA CH Hot Toddy of Emerald Isle ASCA HOF
    - CH Sunshine of Bonnie Blu CDX HOF
    - Hopscotch of Emerald Isle
  - Meshlacon's Trilogy
    - Heard's Salt of Flintridge
    - Evan's Flower Blue Chips
- ASCA CH Sitting Pretty of Sunnybrook ASCA HOF
  - ASCA CH Fieldmaster of Flintridge HOF
    - The Herdsman of Flintridge
    - Heard's Savor of Flintridge
  - ASCA CH Summer Breeze of Sunnybrook
    - CH Little Abner of Flintridge HOF
    - CH Fromer's Free Breeze

Lucy's maternal grandsire ASCA CH Fieldmaster of Flintridge ASCA HOF "Sage." Born 1969. Photo courtesy of Marcia Hall Bain. Photo credit: Rubin.

Lucy's dam ASCA CH Sitting Pretty of Sunnybrook ASCA HOF "Pretty." Born 1977. Photo courtesy of Frank Baylis.

Lucy's daughter ASCA CH Propwash Marshmallow Pies "Marcie." Born 1988. By WTCH SVCH AKC-CKC-ASCA CH Beauwood's Rustlin' In The Sun AKC-ASCA UDT CKC CD RDa RV-E NA HTD-2s TT CGC ASCA HOF x Lucy. Photo courtesy of Tammy Flaga.

Lucy's son ASCA CH Propwash Phantom of the Sky ASCA HOF "Repo." Born 1987. By WTCH SVCH AKC-CKC-ASCA CH Beauwood's Rustlin' In The Sun AKC-ASCA UDT CKC CD RDa RV-E NA HTD-2s TT CGC ASCA HOF x Lucy. Photo courtesy of Leslie Frank.

Lucy's great-grandson AKC CH Bayshore's Propwash Balderdash USASA HOFX-ASCA HOF "Balderdash." Born 1993. By AKC-CKC-ASCA CH Propwash Manape Ghostrider ROM X-I ROM C-III ASCA HOF x AKC CH Bayshore Propwash Lalapalooza. Photo courtesy of Frank Baylis.

Lucy's grandson AKC-CKC-ASCA CH Propwash Manape Ghostrider ROM X-I ROM C-III ASCA HOF "Gucci." Born 1991. By ASCA CH Propwash Phantom of the Sky ASCA HOF x ASCA CH Propwash Boomerang Tangrey ASCA HOF. Photo courtesy of Laura Kirk.

◆

CONVERSATIONS

J Frank Baylis · I remember when the litter was born. Leslie Frank flew into Washington D.C. and picked Lucy out at my best friend's house. That was a lifetime ago!

Kelly Menear English · What a lovely girl! Almost all of my current dogs go back to Lucy's grandson AKC-CKC-ASCA CH Propwash Manape Ghostrider ROM X-I ROM C-III ASCA HOF "Gucci." Love seeing these old photos.

Sandie Penn · Lucy looks so much like her dam ASCA CH Sitting Pretty of Sunnybrook ASCA HOF.

Lucy's grandson AKC CH-BISS CKC CH Pintado's Mr Right HC "Bob." Born 1995. By AKC-ASCA CH Propwash Hey Jude x CH Silver Screen Leading Lady FDCH NA OAC RV-O TT CGC HC. Photo courtesy of Virginia Hills. Photo credit: JC Photo. (CANADA)

Lucy's great-grandson OTCH BISS CKC CH Pintado's Bohemian Rhapsody AKC CDX-ASCA CD AG-N CGC CGN "Moja." Born 1997. By AKC CH-BISS CKC CH Pintado's Mr Right HC x CH Ebbtide I Showed Up In Boots. Photo courtesy of Sally McKay. Photo credit: Alex Smith. (CANADA)

Lucy's great-grandson RBIS BISS AKC CH Thornapple Climate Controlled "Lorenzo." Born 1998. By AKC-ASCA CH Heatherhill Sweet Talkin Dude CD HS STDs OA OAJ ASCA HOF x AKC CH Thornapple's White Diamonds. Photo courtesy of Jayne Holligan.

Lucy's great-grandson BIS AKC CH Thornapple Diamond Rio "Bubba." Born 1995. By AKC CH Bayshore's Propwash Balderdash USASA HOFX ASCA HOF x AKC CH Thornapple's White Diamonds. Photo courtesy of Jayne Holligan. Photo credit: Wayne Cott.

Sarah Bowdish · All of my dogs trace to Lucy through her son ASCA CH Propwash Phantom of the Sky crossed with my foundation bitch Serena. A couple of my dogs also have Lucy through her great-grandson AKC CH Bayshore's Propwash Balderdash USASA HOFX-ASCA HOF.

Heather Mee · Lucy was the best foundation for me!

Jessica Doty · My Drcral Dreamquest "Tucker" was Lucy's great-great-grandson through Ghostrider and Balderdash. Woobie, my new pup, is Tucker's cousin.

Jeff Margeson · I love seeing a foundation dog or bitch that could easily be competitive today. It speaks to the strong genetics passed down from that individual, and Lucy fits that description.

I owe much to this line in my own foundation dog, Group Winning AKC CH Bayshore's Bravado "Bravo," who was Best in Sweepstakes and Winner's Dog at the 2001 USASA National Specialty. He also produced some outstanding get. He goes back to Lucy through both his sire, the great AKC CH Bayshore's Propwash Balderdash USASA HOFX-ASCA HOF, and his dam, AKC CH Bayshore's Jones New York.

Lucy's influence can also be seen in our AKC-INT-UK-LUX-IR CH Bayshore Stonehaven Cat Burglar "Prowler," who is a grandson of AKC CH Bayshore's Propwash Balderdash USASA HOFX-ASCA HOF. Prowler was the Top Producing Aussie Sire in the U.K. for 2015.

Becky Wyant · My boy AKC CH Gemfire's Ours is the Fury CGC "Renly" traces back to Lucy through AKC-CKC-ASCA CH Propwash Manape Ghostrider ROM X-I ROM C-III ASCA HOF.

Penny Jipson · My CH Shadow Fox's Capt'n Morgan CD RAE "Capt'n" is by AKC CH Bayshore Shadow Fox (Lucy's great-great-grandson) and out of AKC CH Bayshore Ralph Lauren. He was my first Aussie. He is behind all four of my Aussies now.

Mona Persson · My boy AKC CH ThundeRun Rough and Ready CA CGC "Trace" goes back to Lucy and London.

Jodie Strait · Lucy is in all of my dogs multiple times. AKC-ASCA CH Bayshore's House of Blues "Memphis" is by AKC GCH Fiann Silver Sabre of Myshara x CH Bayshore's Bumble Bee RN CGC TDI. Memphis traces to Lucy through AKC CH Bayshore's On The Catwalk on the dam's side of his pedigree, and Lucy's granddaughter Cobbercrest Propwash Obla-De USASA HOFX-ASCA HOF through his sire's side.

Jess Flossie Simpson · My Rannaleroch Chilaca at Applecreek BEG EX "Morgen" is from Scotland. She's from Thornapple lines with Lucy's great-grandson RBIS BISS AKC CH Thornapple Climate Controlled in her pedigree a couple of times. She's my heart and soul, a wonderful companion and showdog.

Barbara Klausz · My Tanmark's Arctic Ice Fighter "Vito" has four lines that trace to Lucy. He's a son of Thornapple Iced Latte who traces to Lucy through AKC CH Bayshore's Propwash Balderdash USASA HOFX-ASCA HOF and AKC-ASCA CH Propwash Hey Jude, and grandson of AKC-INT-IT CH Elora Danan's Ticket to Ride (Lucy's great-grandson).

Diane Taylor · Fraytal Sirius Wins Via Auziway (imp. Russia) is a son of RUS CH Thornapple Black Strap Rum who traces back to Lucy through AKC-ASCA CH Propwash Hey Jude. Lucy is the great-great-great-grandmother of my Black Satin Topaz For Auziway.

Allmark Rheddy To Rumble "Jet." Born 2013. His pedigree has several lines tracing to Lucy. By AKC GCH-INT-UK-LUX-IR CH Bayshore Stonehaven Cat Burglar (Imp USA) x CH Allmark Careless Whisper. Photo courtesy of Mel Harris. (UNITED KINGDOM)

Lucy's great-granddaughter BISS AKC-ASCA CH Ferncroft's Ball of Fire AKC-ASCA CD RN AX OAJ CGC ROM X-III ROM P-I "Haley." Born 1995. BOB 1998 USASA National Speciality. By AKC-ASCA CH Caledonia's Crowd Pleaser USASA HOFX-ASCA HOF x AKC-ASCA CH Propwash Confidence. Photo courtesy of Donalee McElrath. Photo credit: Kenneth Reed.

Lucy's great-great-granddaughter INT CH Saussurea Spellbound "Paige." Born 2009. By VWW 2010, EW 2006, AKC-FIN-DAN CH Thornapple Oh Brother x Res.WW 2008, Multi CH Sunnyrain The Star At Saussurea. Photo courtesy of Leeandra Mifsud Mizzi. Photo credit: Dennis Mifsud. (MALTA)

Heather Mee · Applefire Wishes Come True for Lamintone BEG EX "Reva" is linebred on ASCA CH Bayshore's Lucy in the Sky ROM X-II ROM C-I ASCA HOF. She was the foundation of the Lamintone kennel. Lucy's name appears twice in the fourth generation of her pedigree and several times beyond that. Reva has a very strong resemblance to Lucy. She competed successfully in the breed ring, as well as wining in agility and obedience in the U.K. She has two sons that each have one Challenge Certificate and one Reserve Challenge Certificate, and a daughter with three Reserve Challenge Certificates, and

AKC-ASCA CH Samwise Never Say Never "Vaughn." Born 2013. His pedigree traces to Lucy on both sides. By BIS AKC GCH-CKC-ASCA CH Hearthside's Standing Ovation CGC TDI ROM X-I ASCA HOF x AKC-ASCA CH Rainyday's You Took Me By Surprise AKC-ASCA CD RE HIT. Photo courtesy of Star Mathis. Photo credit: Marco Rosetti.

Lucy's great-great-grandson UKC CH Sazbrat Shindig OA AD OJ FD60K "Archie." Born 2001. By AKC-ASCA CH Poinsett's Heartbeat x AKC CH Merribrook Testarosa of Windogo ROM X-II. Photo courtesy of Mary Mynaugh.

Applefire Wishes Come True for Lamintone "Reva." Born 2007. She is linebred on Lucy. By AKC CH Thornapple Climate Controlled x Thornapple Baja Blast. Photo courtesy of Jayne Holligan. Photo credit: Lamintone. (UNITED KINGDOM)

Lucy's granddaughter AKC-ASCA CH Propwash Beardom Zizanie HT ASCA HOF "Zanie." Born 1998. By ASCA CH Jimmee Blue of Adelaide ASCA HOF x Propwash Lo And Behold CD. Photo courtesy of Laura Kirk.

another with wins in obedience. Some of her grandchildren, sired by AKC-ASCA CH Rainyday's I'm On Fire HT ROM X-III ROM C-I ROM P-I ASCA HOF, will soon be entering the show rings in the U.K.

Cheryl Shick · Lucy was a pretty girl.

Jayne Holligan · AKC-ASCA CH Propwash Confidence's sire was AKC-ASCA CH Propwash St. Elmo's Fire USASA HOFX-ASCA HOF and her mum was Propwash Lo and Behold CD, a daughter of Lucy.

Laura Kirk · Propwash Lo and Behold CD was the dam of my foundation bitch AKC-ASCA CH Propwash Beardom Zizanie HT AKC HOF "Zanie." My girl and her offspring were outstanding producers. Lo and Behold was a littermate

Lucy's granddaughter AKC-ASCA CH Propwash Remarque ASCA HOF "Remy." Born 1989. By ASCA CH Propwash Phantom of the Sky ASCA HOF x ASAC CH Propwash Positively CD ASCA HOF. Photo courtesy of Alison Smith.

AKC-ASCA CH ThundeRun Rough and Ready CD CGC "Trace." Born 2013. His pedigree traces to Lucy through Balderdash and Hey Jude. By AKC GCH- ASCA CH Hearthside Master of Disguise x BIS CKC CH ThundeRun That's the Spirit. Photo courtesy of Mona Persson. Photo credit: Amber Jade Aanensen.

AKC CH Bayshore's House of Blues "Memphis." Born 2011. His pedigree traces back multiple times to Lucy. By AKC GCH Fiann Silver Sabre of Myshara x AKC CH Bayshore's Bumble Bee RN CGC TDI. Photo courtesy of Jodie Strait.

Champagne Lili Des Mazellieres "Lili." Born 2007. Her pedigree traces back to Lucy, Ara, and Bear. By Uruck Black Magic x Victoria Des Chemins Cathares. Photo courtesy of Isabelle Guillot. (FRANCE)

sister of AKC-ASCA CH Propwash Two Up CD. They were out of Lucy and ASCA CH Windhill's Take a Chance.

Jayne Holligan · I loved Lucy's son AKC-ASCA CH Propwash Two Up CD "Tupper."

Laura Kirk · I loved Tupper too! I saw his picture on the front cover of the Aussie Times and called his breeder, Leslie. I had been thinking about getting a second Aussie and I wanted to show my next one. Leslie invited me to her farm for an afternoon and I was very fortunate. She gave me an outstanding bitch and has remained an amazing friend. All because of Tupper. I showed Tupper and finished his AKC Championship in 1993. I also showed him to Best Veteran at the USASA Nationals in Pennsylvania the following year. He was stunning to look at and had an outstanding temperament.

Lucy's great-grandson AKC-INT-IT CH Elora Danan's Ticket to Ride "Trip." Born 1998. BOS 2006 USASA Nationals. By AKC-CKC-ASCA CH Propwash Manape Ghostrider ROM X-I ROM C-III ASCA HOF x Elora Danan Propwash Tell Me Story. Photo courtesy of Richard Hellman. (ITALY)

Lucy's great-granddaughter ASCA CH Dewmoor Work of Art Afterall ASCA HOF "Doodle." Born 1998. By AKC-ASCA CH Manapé Propwash Griffen x Manape Propwash Turtle Dove. Photo courtesy of Melinda Vinson.

My boy AKC-CKC-ASCA CH Propwash Manape Ghostrider ROM X-I ROM C-III ASCA HOF "Gucci" was Lucy's grandson. He sired AKC-IT-INT CH EloraDanan's Ticket to Ride "Trip" who was BOS at the USASA Nationals. Gucci also sired AKC CH Bayshore's Propwash Balderdash USASA HOFX-ASCA HOF.

Virginia Hills · My boy BISS AKC-CKC CH Pintado's Mr Right "Bob" is a son of AKC CH Propwash Hey Jude, and is Lucy's grandson. He was the first Canadian bred dog to win a CKC BISS in 1996, and he sired another CKC BISS winner, BISS CKC CH Pintado's Bohemian Rhapsody Multi HIT AKC-CKC CDX-ASCA CD AG.N CGN "Moja." Moja won the 2000 ASCO CKC Specialty, and was half a point off from HIT at that show.

Star Mathis · It has been such a treat seeing these foundation dogs in photos and reading about them. Many thanks to those who laid the way. My boy AKC-ASCA CH Samwise Never Say Never is by BIS AKC GCH-CKC-ASCA CH Hearthside's Standing Ovation CGC TDI ROM X-I ASCA HOF and out of AKC-ASCA CH Rainyday's You Took Me By Surprise AKC-ASCA CD RE HIT. Lucy is in his pedigree several times by way of Lucy's granddaughter Cobbercrest Propwash Obla-De USASA HOFX-ASCA HOF and Lucy's grandson AKC-CKC-ASCA CH Propwash Manape Ghostrider ROM X-I ROM C-III ASCA HOF. He's from my first litter and I enjoy looking over the breed history and finding bits and pieces of his history in him.

Lidija Glusica · Multi CH Thornapple Twist of Fate "Fate" is by AKC GCH-DAN CH Thornapple Cuba Blue "Cuba" and out of Thornapple Euphoria "Maya." Her pedigree traces back to Lucy through AKC-ASCA CH Propwash Hey Jude and AKC-CKC-ASCA CH Propwash Manape Ghostrider ROM X-I ROM C-III ASCA HOF.

Lucy's great-great-great-grandson Tanmark's Arctic Ice Fighter "Vito." Born 2006. By HUN CH Silver Dream Aussie's Cabriolet x CH Thornapple Iced Latte. Photo courtesy of Barbara Klausz.

Lucy's great-grandson AKC-ASCA CH Elite's Eisen On The Cake ASCA HOF "Eisen." Born 1998. By AKC-CKC-ASCA CH Propwash Manape Ghostrider ROM X-I ROM C-III ASCA HOF x AKC-ASCA CH Rosewood's Summertime Romance. Photo courtesy of Jackie Bayes. Photo credit: Photos by Kit.

IR CH JCH Mistyholly Red Peril "Koda." Born 2015. Annual Champion 2016 of Ireland. By IR-HUN-INT CH Allmark Muffin Muncher x UK CH Allmark Join the Clan at Mistyholly. His pedigree traces back to Lucy through AKC-CKC-ASCA CH Propwash Manape Ghostrider ROM X-I ROM C-III ASCA HOF. Photo courtesy of Aidan Bourke. (IRELAND)

Fate's daughter GCH Kamerado Legacy Beauty Extraordinaire "Belle" and her litter brother Kamerado Legacy Beating the Odds "Oddie" trace back to Lucy through their sire's side too. They are by Thornapple Dream for Austria and out of Multi CH Thornapple Twist of Fate.

AKC CH Gemfire's Ours Is The Fury CGC "Renly." Born 2014. His pedigree traces back multiple times to Lucy. By AKC-ASCA CH XSell's The Drums Are Drumming x Bayshore's Ali McGraw. Photo courtesy of Becky Wyant. Photo credit: Cary Manaton.

Lucy's great-great-granddaughter AZE-BIH-SMR CH Thornapple Twist of Fate "Fate." Born 2011. By AKC GCH-DAN CH Thornapple Cuba Blue x Thornapple Euphoria. Photo courtesy of Lidija Glusica. (MONTENEGRO)

"Blaze was an awesome dog to live with and he loved everyone he met. He not only enjoyed every activity he tried—he excelled at it. It was partly because of his tremendous desire to please his people, but mostly because he just had so much fun doing every activity he was introduced to. We were honoured to have Blaze in our lives and are extremely proud of him and all of his amazing descendants!"

- Jane Firebaugh and Nora Porobic

Photo credit: Nora Porobic

AKC-ASCA Champion
Broadway's Blaze of Glory
Certified Therapy Dog and Hearing Dog
RE OA OAJ CGC ROM X-II ROM C-II
ASCA HOF Sire #220

Call Name: Blaze

Born: 1999

Sire: AKC-ASCA CH Heatherhill Sweet Talkin' Dude CD HS STDs OA OAJ ASCA HOF

Dam: Broadway's Bonnie Blue ROM X-II ROM P-III ROM C-I

Breeders: Maggie Pryor, Broadway, and Heather C. Septer, Free Spirit

Owners: Jane Firebaugh and Nora Porobic, Paradigm

As luck would have it, Blaze was born into a litter of 10 puppies from a "golden" cross. The overall quality was so excellent that seven of the pups finished their championships, and some went on to have impressive show careers.

Jane Firebaugh and Nora Porobic acquired three of the males from that litter: Zip, Riley, and Blaze. AKC-ASCA CH Broadway's One Fine Day RA OA OAJ "Zip" became a multiple group winner as well as winning an Award of Excellence at the first AKC Invitational in 2001. AKC CH Broadway's Life of Riley RE OA OAJ "Riley" finished his championship and earned agility titles. AKC-ASCA CH Broadway's Blaze of Glory RE OA OAJ CGC ROM X-II ROM C-II "Blaze" finished from the puppy class with Best of Breed wins over specials and group placements. He won Best of Breed at the first AKC Invitational in 2001 under Mr. J. Donald Jones. He became a multiple group winner in his career and finished as the #1 male Aussie all systems in 2002.

An interesting sidenote from Blaze's handler was that his owners, Jane and Nora, traveled to every show where their dogs were shown. Regardless of where in the country the show was held, they drove their truck and travel trailer.

Author: What traits made Blaze influential to the breed?
Jane and Nora: His rock-solid front and rear, and his ability to pass those traits down to his offspring.

Author: Which ancestors contributed the most to this dog's genetic prepotency?
Jane and Nora: He inherited excellent genes from both sides of his family.

Author: What were his structural strengths?
Jane and Nora: His rear was probably his best structural feature, although he also had a great front. His headpiece wasn't as broad as some people preferred, but for us it was enough. Blaze consistently produced offspring with beautiful fronts, rears, and great sidegait.

Author: Describe Blaze's temperament.
Jane and Nora: He had a huge desire to please and was super sweet with all people. He loved rally, agility, and conformation. Although he only tried herding once, he loved it too. He got along well with the other five intact males living with us.

(Left to right) Blaze's son AKC-ASCA CH Paradigm's Red Storm Rising RE OA OAJ "Clancy," Blaze, and Blaze's litter brother AKC CH Broadway's Life of Riley RE OA OAJ "Riley." Photo credit: Nora Porobic.

Pedigree

```
                                                          CH Arrogance of Heatherhill HOF
                                    ASCA CH Brigadoon's One Arrogant Dude HOFX- HOF
                                                          CH Patch-Work's River Fog
                 AKC-ASCA CH Heatherhill Sweet Talkin Dude CD HS STDs OA OAJ HOF
                                                          CH Agua Dulce Final Option HOF
                                    AKC-ASCA CH Oprah Winfree of Heatherhill HOF
                                                          Moonspinner of Brigadoon HOF
AKC-ASCA CH Broadway's Blaze of Glory RE OA OAJ CGC ROM X-II ROM C-II ASCA HOF
                                                          CH Briarbrooks Broadway Joe
                                    The Spirit of Broadway
                                                          Broadway's Waltzin N Hi-Cotton
                 Broadway's Bonnie Blue ROM X-II ROM P-III ROM C-I
                                                          Broadway's Blue Moon Jones
                                    Broadway's Pistols and Roses
                                                          CH Darts Pandoras Surprise
```

Blaze's sire AKC-ASCA CH Heatherhill Sweet Talkin Dude CD HS STDs OA OAJ ASCA HOF "Shooter." Born 1993. Photo courtesy of Leida Jones.

Blaze's dam Broadway's Bonnie Blue ROM X-II ROM P-III ROM C-I "Bonnie." Born 1995. Shown with Blaze and his littermates. Photo courtesy of Nora Porobic.

Author: Did he have any special personality quirks?

Jane and Nora: Blaze always knew if someone was upset. He tried to comfort them by attempting to lick their tonsils.

Author: Is there an interesting story you can tell about him?

Jane and Nora: Blaze always got excited about agility. At his very first trial, Nora put him in a "stay" at the start line. She led out and told him to jump the first jump. He ran the whole course forward, backward and sideways before she made it to the second obstacle. He got a laughing, clapping ovation from the entire crowd, though, of course, he didn't get a ribbon.

Blaze's son BIS AKC GCH-CKC-ASCA CH Bayouland Creme Brûlée CGC USASA HOFX-ASCA HOF "Keegan." Born 2003. By Blaze x AKC CH Lil' Creeks Hug Me Tight ROM C-III. Photo courtesy of Martha Gisselbeck and Brandy Dirksen. Photo credit: John Beals.

Blaze's son BIS AKC-ASCA CH Bayouland Flamin Glory "Logan." Born 2007. By Blaze x AKC CH Lil' Creeks Hug Me Tight ROM C-III. Photo courtesy of Krista Denman-Keel. Photo credit: Luke Allen.

Blaze sired 31 champions including six Best In Show winners.

BLAZE and AKC CH LIL' CREEKS HUG ME TIGHT ROM C-III

One of Blaze's early litters was out of AKC CH Lil' Creeks Hug Me Tight ROM C-III. That cross was so successful it was repeated three more times and produced a total of eighteen champions and four Best in Show winners.

Blaze's daughter BIS AKC-ASCA CH Bayouland's Dazzle Me Razz ASCA HOF "Razz." Born 2003. By Blaze x AKC CH Lil' Creeks Hug Me Tight ROM C-III. Photo courtesy of Flo McDaniel. Photo credit: Nugent.

BIS AKC GCH-ASCA CH Paradigm's Bayouland on Broadway ASCA HOF "Cash." Born 2007. By Blaze x AKC CH Lil' Creeks Hug Me Tight ROM C-III. Photo courtesy of Maggie Pryor. Photo credit: Kerr.

Those four Best In Show winners are shown on these two pages.
› BIS AKC GCH-CKC-ASCA CH Bayouland Creme Brûlée CGC USASA HOFX-ASCA HOF
› BIS AKC-ASCA CH Bayouland Flamin Glory
› BIS AKC-ASCA CH Bayouland's Dazzle Me Razz ASCA HOF
› BIS AKC GCH-ASCA CH Paradigm's Bayouland on Broadway ASCA HOF

Blaze's son MBIS AKC GCH-CKC GCHEx-ASCA CH TreeStarr's Billion Dollar Baby CD HIC ASCA HOF "Jackpot." Born 2007. By Blaze x AKC-ASCA CH McMatt's Too Good To Be Blue CD NA NAJ CGC ROM X-II ASCA HOF. Photo courtesy of Ayella Grossman. Photo credit: Amber Jade Aanensen.

BLAZE and AKC-ASCA CH MCMATT'S TOO GOOD TO BE BLUE CD NA NAJ CGC ROM X-II ASCA HOF

This cross produced three outstanding littermates including one BIS winner.

› MBIS AKC GCH-CKC GCHEx-ASCA CH TreeStarr Billion Dollar Baby CD HIC ASCA HOF (above)
› AOM Select AKC GCH-CKC-ASCA CH TreeStarr Rmzcrk's I'm on Fire CGC TDI ROM X-I ROM C-II ASCA HOF (below)
› AKC GCH-CKC-ASCA CH TreeStarr's Northwind Breeze ROM X-I (below)

Blaze's son AOM Select AKC GCH-CKC-ASCA CH TreeStarr Rmzcrk's I'm on Fire CGC TDI ROM X-I ROM C-II ASCA HOF "Fire." Born 2007. By Blaze x AKC-ASCA CH McMatt's Too Good To Be Blue CD NA NAJ CGC ROM X-II ASCA HOF. Photo courtesy of Becky Rowan Androff. Photo credit: Amber Jade Aanensen.

Blaze's daughter AKC GCH-CKC-ASCA CH TreeStarr's Northwind Breeze ROM X-I "Breeze." Born 2007. By Blaze x AKC-ASCA CH McMatt's Too Good To Be Blue CD NA NAJ CGC ROM X-II ASCA HOF. Photo courtesy of Laurie Thompson. Photo credit: Jeffrey Hanlin.

Blaze's daughter MBIS AKC-ASCA CH Windypine Winter Willow "Willow." Born 2006. Winner of nine Best In Show awards, #1 Aussie and #4 Herding dog in 2006. By Blaze x Windypine Heaven Cent. Photo courtesy of Carolyn Asquith. Photo credit: Tammie.

BLAZE and WINDYPINE HEAVEN CENT

Blaze's very successful daughter, MBIS AKC-ASCA CH Windypine Winter Willow "Willow," won nine Bests in Show and was #1 Aussie and #4 Herding dog in 2006.

Blaze sired many other offspring who passed on his legacy of exceptional quality and prepotency. Some of his outstanding descendants were:

› AKC GCH Windypine Autumn Storm
› AKC-ASCA CH Windypine Kinetic Banner
› AKC GCH Bayouland's I'm Your Huckleberry
› AKC CH Bayouland's Tight Squeeze
› AKC GCH-ASCA CH Bayouland's Hug Me Forever CD
› AKC-ASCA CH Bayouland's Touched By An Angel RN
› AKC-ASCA CH Paradigm's Red Storm Rising RE OA OAJ
› AKC-UKC-ASCA CH De Abajo Ledgerock JnD's Rumor HIC
› AKC-ASCA CH Bayouland's Big EZ
› AKC-ASCA CH Bayouland's Kiss Ana Hug
› AKC CH Bayouland's Hug Me Forever
› BIS MBISS AKC GCH-CKC-ASCA CH CopperRidge Fire N Bayouland ASCA HOF

Many thanks to Jane Firebaugh, Nora Porobic, and David Stout for providing these highlights about Blaze.

Blaze and his offspring won the Stud Dog Class at the 2007 USASA National Specialty. (Left to right)
› MBIS AKC-ASCA CH Windypine Winter Willow with Pat Stout.
› AKC-UKC-ASCA CH De Abajo Ledgrock JnD's Rumor HIC with Morgan Higgins.
› AKC-ASCA CH Broadway's Blaze of Glory RE OA OAJ CGC ROM X-II ROM C-II with Jamie Orr.
› BIS AKC GCH-CKC-ASCA CH Bayouland Creme Brûlée CGC USASA HOFX-ASCA HOF with Sarah Patterson Kalkes.
› AKC-ASCA CH Paradigm's Red Storm Rising RE OA OAJ with handler Barry Elliot.
Photo courtesy of Nora Porobic and Jane Firebaugh. Photo credit: Downey.

Blaze's granddaughter AKC GCH-ASCA CH Wedgewood's Sunset On The Miramar AKC-ASCA CD-AKC CGC RN ASCA RA RS-O GS-O JS-E "Havana." Born 2011. By BIS AKC GCH-CKC-ASCA CH Bayouland Creme Brûlée CGC USASA HOFX-ASCA HOF x AKC-ASCA CH Sazbrat She's The One For Kebrea. Photo courtesy of Martha Gisselbeck. Photo credit: Amber Jade Aanensen.

Blaze's granddaughter ASCA CH Wedgewood's Every Day I Need Attention CGC "Edina." Born 2014. By BIS AKC GCH-CKC-ASCA CH Bayouland Creme Brûlée CGC USASA HOFX-ASCA HOF x AKC CH CopperRidge Written in Blue at Lil' Creek. Photo courtesy of Martha Gisselbeck. Photo credit: Amber Jade Aanensen.

Blaze's offspring and their dam won the Brood Bitch class at the 2009 USASA Nationals. Dam (lying down) AKC-ASCA CH McMatt's Too Good To Be Blue ASCA-AKC CD NA NAJ CGC ROM X-II ASCA HOF with owner/handler Becky Rowan Androff. (Back row left to right)
› AKC GCH-CKC-ASCA CH TreeStarr's Northwind Breeze ROM X-I with Laurie Thompson.
› AOM Select AKC GCH-CKC-ASCA CH TreeStarr Rmzcrk's I'm on Fire CGC TDI ROM X-I ROM C-II ASCA HOF with Lana Williams Schultz.
› MBIS AKC GCH-CKC GCHEx-ASCA CH TreeStarr's Billion Dollar Baby CD HIC HOF with Ayella Grossman.
Photo courtesy of Becky Rowan Androff. Photo credit: Mike Fine.

Blaze's grandson AKC-ASCA CH Paramount's Organized Chaos "Ruckus." Born 2013. Multiple National Specialty placements. Winner's Dog 2015 Eukanuba Pre-show. By AKC GCH-CKC-ASCA CH TreeStarr Rmzcrk's I'm on Fire CGC TDI ROM X-I ROM C-II ASCA HOF x Paramount's Proof Is In The Pudding CGC. Photo courtesy of Valerie Blevins Yarber. Photo credit: Amber Jade Aanensen.

Blaze's grandson BIS-OH Multi RBIS-OH AKC Bronze GCH-ASCA CH Lk Michigan RU Ready to Rumble AKC-ASCA RN CA CGC "Thunder." Born 2014. By AKC GCH-CKC-ASCA CH TreeStarr Rmzcrk's I'm on Fire CGC TDI ROM X-I ROM C-II ASCA HOF x AKC-ASCA-UKC CH UAG1 Bayouland Don't Stop Believin ASCA RN CGC. Photo courtesy of Barb Hoffman & Marcie Boomsliter. Photo credit: Amber Jade Aanensen.

Three generations of Blaze descendants.
- (Right) Blaze's son MBIS CKC GCHEx-AKC GCH-ASCA CH TreeStarr Billion Dollar Baby CD HIC ASCA HOF "Jackpot."
- (Center) Jackpot's son AKC GCH-CKC-ASCA CH Paradox Pickwick HIC "Pike."
- (Left) Pike's son BIS UKC CH-AKC-CKC-ASCA CH Oracle's Pick Me Up of Eweturn HIC "Kohen."

Photo courtesy of Ayella Grossman. Photo credit: Amber Jade Aanensen.

◆

CONVERSATONS

Karen Roesner · I bred and own a Blaze grandson, CH Show-Me's Midnite Rambler "Jag." Born 2011. By BIS AKC GCH-CKC-ASCA CH Bayouland Creme Brûlée CGC USASA HOFX-ASCA HOF x Roundabout's Walking In Memphis.

Kirstie Venton New · Blaze is great-great-grandad to Little Red-Cap Du Chemins Des Korrigans "Ember" through Creme Brûlée. I was lucky enough to visit the USASA Nationals when they were held in Colorado. As I watched judging I noticed dogs I liked, and when I checked the catalogue I found nearly all were by Keegan or Blaze. I knew that one day I wanted something from their lines, and now I have Ember!

Dianne Kent · Blaze's son AKC GCH Bayouland's I'm Your Huckleberry "Doc" was born in 2007. He's by Blaze x AKC CH Lil' Creeks Hug Me Tight ROM C-III. "Doc" is a gentleman farmer in his retirement. He makes sure the chickens stay where they belong, the cows stay back from the fence, and any strangers are watched very carefully!

Blaze's great-great-grandson MBIG UKC CH URO1 Hearthside On The Rocks RN CA CGCA "Wyatt." Born 2013. By AKC GCH Impact's Pop Rocks x AKC-ASCA CH Hearthside Naughty Messages NAC TN-N TG-N. Photo courtesy of Krista Myers.

Blaze's son AKC GCH Bayouland's I'm Your Huckleberry "Doc." Born 2007. By Blaze x AKC CH Lil' Creeks Hug Me Tight ROM C-III. Photo courtesy of Dianne Kent.

Blaze's grandson BIS AKC Bronze GCH Broadway's Canyon Lake Cruisen RN "Cruis." Born 2011. By BIS AKC GCH-ASCA CH Paradigm's Bayouland on Broadway ASCA HOF x BIS AKC CH Ramsey- Rush Creek Talk Of The Town. Photo courtesy of Maggie Pryor. Photo credit: Garden Studio.

Blaze's daughter AKC-ASCA CH Bayouland's Hug Me Forever TDI "Chloe." Born 2003. Award of Merit 2006 USASA National Specialty. By Blaze x AKC CH Lil' Creeks Hug Me Tight ROM C-III. Photo courtesy of Yvette LeBlanc. Photo credit. Downey.

Blaze's great-granddaughter MBIS UKC CH-CKC GCH-AKC-ASCA CH Ninebark Make A Wish ASCA-CKC RN CGN "Dove." Born 2012. By AKC GCH-ASCA Premier CH Meadowlawns Night To Remember CD ROM X-I x AKC-CKC-ASCA CH Ninebark Wishing Well. Photo courtesy of Alaina Sarah Anthon. Photo credit: K. Booth.

Blaze's granddaughter AKC GCH-BIS ASCA CH Northwind's Singin in the Rain "Raine." Born 2010. By BIS AKC GCH-CKC-ASCA CH Whidbey's Moonlight Frost RA x AKC GCH-CKC-ASCA CH TreeStarr's Northwind Breeze ROM X-I. Photo courtesy of Laurie Thompson. Photo credit: Jeffrey Hanlin.

Blaze descendants in Europe

Aussie breeders in the United States began to export dogs to other countries beginning in the 1970s. Quarter Horse fanciers from Europe took Aussies with them when they went back to their home countries. Aussies were sent to a ranch in Germany in the early 1980s. The Kennel Club of the United Kingdom recorded the importation of a blue merle dog in 1985. Since then, many Aussies have made their way to Europe. American and European breeders are working together to improve the breed on both continents and elsewhere around the world. Blaze's legacy is an important part of those advancements.

Blaze's son CH Rafter Creek's EZ Valentine Day "Chase." Born 2012. German Club Champion, VDH Champion, Swiss Show Champion, VDH European Winner, CASD Club Winner, Most Versatile Australian Shepherd 2017. By Blaze x CH Mill Creek's American Express. Photo courtesy of Claudia Bosselmann.

My CH Rafter Creek's EZ Valentine Day "Chase" is a Blaze son. He was produced via frozen semen sent to Germany and was born Feb. 14, 2012. His dam is CH Mill Creek's American Express (CH McKay Terbo Trix of the Trade x CH McMatt's Megapup of Mill Creek). Chase has three Champion titles and several working titles. He is a truly versatile dog. He has beautiful herding talent, is a great rally dog, is running agility like a maniac. I enjoy training and showing for performance events, and Chase is everything I could ask for. He has an incredible will to please, is very focused, obedient, cooperative and always motivated. He is calm in every environment and loves people. A wonderful dog who was worth the risk. I had only one puppy in this litter, but what a puppy!

- Claudia Bosselmann
(GERMANY)

Blaze's great-great-granddaughter Little Red-Cap Du Chemins Des Korrigans "Ember." Born 2015. By AKC GCH Northbays Who Toad U Tryfecta x Sonrise Million Dollar Baby. Photo courtesy of Kirstie Venton New. (UNITED KINGDOM)

Blaze's great-granddaughter JRBIS AKC-ES-LUX CH Caufosca Your Coupit Name "Eva." Born 2015. By BIS BISS AKC GCH-CKC-ASCA CH CopperRidge's Fire in Bayouland ASCA HOF x BIS AKC GCH Bayouland Fleur de Lea. Photo courtesy of Cristina Friexes. Photo credit: Jeffrey Hanlin. (SPAIN)

Blaze's great-granddaughter Happy Spark Dragon Princess "Xena." Born 2016. By MBISS AKC-CKC-ASCA CH Blue Isle's Bourrée ASCA HOF x BISS ASCA-INT- NL-BE-DE-Dt CH Happy Spark Apple Blossom JS-N NL-BE-DE-Dt-JCH-W'16-BEW'14-ES'14-NL-DE-BE JW'13. Photo courtesy of Karin Dekker. Photo credit: Jill Foreman. (NETHERLANDS)

Blaze's great-grandson MBIS-World Winner 2016-Multi CH-INT CH Risingstar Royal Flash DCD Energies CACIB CAC "Magnum." Born 2009. By Multi CH-INT CH Risingstar's Heaven Sent RN x Outlaws Million Dollar Baby. Photo courtesy of Ludovic Gerona and Kerstin Patzold. Photo credit: Martin Svec. (GERMANY)

Blaze's granddaughter Picture Perfect Of The Mighty Crown " Dazzle ." Born 2015. By AKC GCH-CKC-ASCA CH TreeStarr Rmzcrk's I'm on Fire CGC TDI ROM X-I ROM C-II ASCA HOF x ASCA CH Northbays Incognito. Photo courtesy of Martina Naffien. Photo credit: Günter Naffien. (GERMANY)

Blaze's grandson Bayouland's Catch Me If You Can R.CACIB R.CAC "Joshua." Born 2012. By BIS BISS AKC GCH-CKC-ASCA CH CopperRidge's Fire in Bayouland ASCA HOF x AKC-ASCA CH Bayouland's Kiss Ana Hug. Photo courtesy of Fabio Cardea. Photo credit: Marco Rosetti. (ITALY)

Blaze's grandson AKC-CKC-ASCA CH Eminence of the Mighty Crown "Uno." Born 2010. By AKC-ASCA CH Windypine's Autumn Storm x ASCA CH Northbay's Incognito. Photo courtesy of Tina Wilk. Photo credit: Fabian Sollereder. (GERMANY)

Blaze's great-grandson INT-SP-HR-CH I Master de Zecchinetta des Terres de Laumeneel RN JS-N "Zecchi." Born 2013. By CH Harmony Hill's Arrivederci x CH CauFosca Here Ace of Clover. Photo courtesy of Vanessa Soler. Photo credit: Margot Guillet. (FRANCE)

Blaze's granddaughter AKC-CKC-ASCA CH JnD's Live Wire "Izzy." Born 2004. By AKC GCH-UKC-ASCA CH De Abajo Ledgerock JnD Rumor x AKC CH Bayshore's Uptown Girl x Photo courtesy of Julie Ostberg. Photo credit: Susan & Lennah LLC.

Blaze's grandson CH Show-Me's Midnite Rambler "Jag." Born 2011. By BIS AKC GCH-CKC-ASCA CH Bayouland Creme Brûlée CGC USASA HOFX-ASCA HOF x Roundabout's Walking In Memphis. Photo courtesy of Karen Roesner. Photo credit: Booth.

Blaze's granddaughter ASCA CH Paramount TreeStarr Hot Little Number "Paris." Born 2013. By AKC GCH-CKC-ASCA CH TreeStarr Rmzcrk's I'm on Fire CGC TDI ROM X-I ROM C-II ASCA HOF x Paramounts Proof Is In The Pudding CGC. Photo courtesy of Valerie Blevins Yarber. Photo credit: Amber Jade Aanensen.

Blaze's granddaughter Premier AKC-ASCA CH Paramounts Perfectly Scandalous "Ember." Born 2013. By AKC GCH-CKC-ASCA CH TreeStarr Rmzcrk's I'm on Fire CGC TDI ROM X-I ROM C-II ASCA HOF x Paramounts Proof Is In The Pudding CGC. Photo courtesy of Valerie Blevins Yarber. Photo credit: Amber Jade Aanensen.

Blaze's granddaughter AKC-ASCA CH RedEarth Adelaide Cadeau des Rouge CGC "Adelaide." Born 2010. By BIS AKC GCH-CKC-ASCA CH Bayouland Creme Brûlée CGC USASA HOFX-ASCA HOF x CH NiteStar's Rosemary Clooney. Photo courtesy of Lauren Wright. Photo credit: Amber Jade Aanensen.

Blaze's grandson AKC GCH-ASCA CH Heartland's Creme De La Creme CD STDc OTDds JHD HATDs1 PT HSAS HT "Fenn." Born 2007. By BIS AKC GCH-CKC-ASCA CH Bayouland Creme Brûlée CGC USASA HOFX-ASCA HOF x AKC-CKC-INT-ASCA CH Woodlake's Abby of Canyon Oaks CD. Photo courtesy of Katie Johnson. Photo credit: M. Fine.

Brittany Greendeer · AKC GCH-UKC BIS CH URO1 Impact's Golden Ray CA CGCA Total Dog "Rhea" is Blaze's great-great-granddaughter.

Pat Zapf · AKC GCH Shadomoons I'm All The Buzz HT CA DN "Minx" is a Blaze great-great-granddaughter.

Krista Myers · I have a Blaze great-great-grandson (and a great-great-great-grandson) UKC MBIG CH URO1 Hearthside On The Rocks RN CA CGCA.

David Stout · My mom, Pat Stout, and I enjoyed every minute with Blaze! She was his main handler throughout his show career.

Karin Dekker · I have a Blaze great-grandson and daughter. Love them!

Jillayne Karras · Our boy is linebred on Blaze. He's a paternal great-grandson and maternal great-great-grandson. He is AKC GCH-BISS IT CH Stormridge Hightide Bolero of Fire at G.Jorasses "Kindle."

Maria Neff · Blaze is one of my all time favorites! I'm so blessed to own a beautiful Blaze grandson!

Kimberly J Welton · Multi Group Placing AKC GCH-UKC BIS CH Bayouland's Act of True Love CA RATI "Truly" is a Blaze great-granddaughter and great-great-granddaughter. He's on both sides of her pedigree. We are honored to have her and hope to have her first litter this summer.

Susan Landry Whiticar · I have a lovely Blaze grandson, AKC-ASCA CH Rondolay's Moonglow Mystique "Tique." He's out of Carolyn Asquith's Blaze daughter MBIS AKC-ASCA CH Windypine Winter Willow, who won nine Bests In Show. Tique is producing well in his own right.

Alaina Kugel Holstege · My girl AKC CH Tryfecta This'll Make Ya Whistle! "Whistle" is a great-granddaughter of Blaze. She was sired by the 2013 ASCA

Blaze's grandson BIS BISS AKC GCH-CKC-ASCA CH CopperRidge's Fire in Bayouland ASCA HOF "Rowan." Born 2006. BOB 2008 Eukanuba show. By BIS AKC GCH-CKC-ASCA CH Bayouland Creme Brûlée CGC USASA HOFX-ASCA HOF x AKC CH Fiann's Silver Sweet Sound. Photo courtesy of Yvette LeBlanc. Photo credit: Tom Weigand.

Blaze's grandson AKC CH Lk Michigan Journey Through Fire at Airam "Ashton." Born 2014. By AKC GCH-CKC-ASCA CH TreeStarr Rmzcrk's I'm on Fire CGC TDI ROM X-I ROM C-II ASCA HOF x AKC-ASCA CH Bayoulands Dont Stop Believing. Photo courtesy of Maria Neff. Photo credit: Amber Jade Aanensen.

Nationals Best of Breed winner BIS MBISS AKC GCH-CKC-ASCA CH CopperRidge's Fire N Bayouland ASCA HOF "Rowan" and is out of the 2014 ASCA Nationals Best of Breed winner AKC GCH-CKC CH-UKC CH-BISS ASCA CH Northbay's Who's That? "Marlo." I have high hopes that Whistle will be top-winning and top-producing like her parents. She's truly from a very royal pedigree. She won the very competitive Bred By Exhibitor bitches class at the 2015 USASA National Specialty.

Laurie Thompson · I LOVE Blaze! I enjoy life with his beautiful daughter AKC GCH-CKC-ASCA CH TreeStarr's Northwind Breeze ROM X-I "Breeze" (Blaze x Carly). I also have his beautiful granddaughter AKC GCH-BIS ASCA CH Northwind's Singin in the Rain "Raine" (Tucker x Breeze) and his great-granddaughter "Hailey" AKC GCH-CKC-ASCA CH Northwind's Proudly we Hail (Sydney x Rain).

Heather Parson Herron · AKC-ASCA CH Northbay's Who Dat N Bayouland "Drew" is a Blaze great-grandson sired by BIS MBISS AKC GCH-CKC-ASCA CH CopperRidge's Fire N Bayouland ASCA HOF "Rowan." His dam is linebred on BIS AKC-ASCA CH Northbay's Captain Morgan HT. Drew is carrying on the family tradition of producing Multi BIS and BISS winning kids who excel in all types of competition.

Chris Chloe Rattigan-Lemar · ASCA CH Navrock Some Like It Hot "Pyro" is a Blaze granddaughter sired by BIS AKC GCH-CKC-ASCA CH Bayouland Creme Brûlée CGC USASA HOFX-ASCA HOF "Keegan."

Heather Chris Hertrich-Septer · Blaze, along with his littermates, were born in my bedroom. He was a wonderful dog, as were his siblings. It was an amazing litter all the way around. That litter, plus one other breeding, gave his dam

Blaze's great-grandson AKC GCH-ASCA CH Casa Blanca's Zippity Doo Dah "Zippo." Born 2014. Winner's Dog 2016 ASCA Nationals. Best Opposite Sex Sweepstakes 2015 ASCA Nationals. By BIS AKC GCH-CKC-ASCA CH Bayouland Creme Brûlée CGC USASA HOFX-ASCA HOF x Casa Blanca's Shimmer's Magic ASCA HOF. Photo courtesy of Judy Chard. Photo credit: Jeffrey Hanlin.

Blaze's grandson UKC CH-ASCA A-CH Casa Blanca From The Ashes CGC TKN "Phoenix." Born 2014. By BIS AKC GCH-CKC-ASCA CH Bayouland Creme Brûlée CGC USASA HOFX-ASCA HOF x Casa Blanca's Shimmer's Magic ASCA HOF. Photo courtesy of Kathy Dukinfield. Photo credit: Jeffrey Hanlin.

Blaze's great-grandson AKC GCH-UKC-ASCA CH JnD's Bare Necessities AKC RE CD-ASCA RM CD "Baloo." Born 2011. By MBIS AKC CH Dreamstreet's Season Ticket ROM X-II ROM C-II x AKC-CKC-ASCA CH JnD's Live Wire. Photo courtesy of Julie Ostberg.

Blaze's great-granddaughter ASCA RTCH 2 A-CH Risingstar's Fire 'N Ice CD GS-O JS-O RS-E REMX "Halley." Born 2008. By Multi CH Rising Star's Heaven Sent RN x RisingStar's Divine Outlaw. Photo courtesy of Karen Souza. Photo credit: Jeffrey Hanlin.

Blaze's granddaughter ASCA CH Navrock Some Like It Hot "Pyro." Born 2012. By BIS AKC GCH-CKC-ASCA CH Bayouland Creme Brûlée CGC USASA HOFX-ASCA HOF x Thornapple Warning Shot. Photo courtesy of Chris Chloe Rattigan-Lemar. Photo credit: Jerrad Miller.

Blaze's grandson ASCA-INT CH Casa Blanca's Creme de Amoure "Beau." Born 2015. By BIS AKC GCH-CKC-ASCA CH Bayouland Creme Brûlée CGC USASA HOFX-ASCA HOF x CH Casa Blanca's Victoria's Secret. Photo courtesy of Cara Hales-Jensen. Photo credit: Jillian Ward.

Blaze's grandson AKC GCH-ASCA-UKC-INT CH Cattail Ridge Three's Company CGC "Tripper." Born 2006. By BIS AKC GCH-CKC-ASCA CH Bayouland Creme Brûlée CGC USASA HOFX-ASCA HOF x INT-ASCA CH Koala-T's I'm Not The Girl OA NAJ RJ-O JJ-O JS-N CGC TDI ASCA HOF. Photo courtesy of Kathy Dukinfield. Photo credit: Downey.

Blaze's grandson BIS-OH AKC GCH-ASCA CH UR01 Malpaso Keep the Fire Burning RA RL1 CWZ1 "Torch." Born 2009. By AKC GCH-CKC-ASCA CH TreeStarr Rmzcrk's I'm on Fire CGC TDI ROM X-I ROM C-II ASCA HOF x AKC-CKC-ASCA CH Taisho Final Impact At Malpaso. Photo courtesy of Angelica DeMont. Photo credit: Phyllis Ellis.

Blaze's great-grandson CKC CH Ninebark Boldly Go "Karson." Born 2016. By AKC-ASCA CH Calais Carolina First In Flight STDs x AKC-CKC-ASCA CH Ninebark Wishing Well. Photo courtesy of Valerie Yates. Photo credit: Booth.

Blaze's grandson AKC CH Impact's Jokers Wild "Joker." Born 2012. By BIS MBISS AKC GCH-CKC-ASCA CH CopperRidge's Fire N Bayouland ASCA HOF x Bayouland's Uptown Girl. Photo courtesy of Gayle Kukulka. Photo credit: Jeffrey Hanlin.

Blaze's great-grandson BISS Italian CH-AKC GCH Stormridge Hightide Bolero of Fire at G. Jorasses "Kindle." Born 2014. By AKC GCH-BISS ASCA CH Crofton Fat Chance STDds x AKC-ASCA CH Stormridge's Light My Fire. Photo courtesy of Jillayne Karras. Photo credit: Jeffrey Hanlin.

Blaze's great-grandson AKC-ASCA CH Northbay's Who Dat N Bayouland "Drew." Born 2012. By BIS MBISS AKC GCH-CKC-ASCA CH CopperRidge's Fire N Bayouland ASCA HOF x AKC GCH-CKC CH-UKC GCH-BISS ASCA CH Northbay's Who's That? Photo courtesy of Heather Parson Herron. Photo credit: Amber Jade Aanensen.

Blaze's great-granddaughter AKC GCH-CKC-ASCA CH Northwind's Proudly We Hail "Hailey." Born 2013. By AKC-ASCA CH Ivory Isles Meets The Criteria ASCA HOF x AKC GCH-BIS ASCA CH Northwind's Singin in the Rain. Photo courtesy of Laurie Thompson. Photo credit: Jeffrey Hanlin.

Blaze's great-granddaughter AKC CH Tryfecta This'll Make Ya Whistle! "Whistle." Born 2013. By BIS MBISS AKC GCH-CKC- ASCA CH CopperRidge's Fire N Bayouland ASCA HOF x AKC GCH-CKC CH-UKC GCH-BISS ASCA CH Northbay's Who's That? Photo courtesy of Alaina Kugel Holstege. Photo credit: Jeffrey Hanlin.

Bonnie ROM X-II ROM P-III ROM C-I. It proved to be a fabulous cross.

Kathy Dukinfield · Group-placing AKC GCH-INT-UKC-ASCA CH Cattail Ridge Three's Company CGC "Tripper" was sired by BIS AKC GCH-CKC-ASCA CH Bayouland Creme Brûlée CGC USASA HOFX-ASCA HOF and out of INT-ASCA CH Koala-T's I'm Not The Girl OA NAJ RJ-O JJ-O JS-N CGC TDI ASCA HOF. Tripper was a Blaze grandson out of Keegan's first litter in 2003. Bubbly, happy personality, athletic and successful in the conformation ring, he also competed in Rally and Agility until he succumbed to hemangiosarcoma in 2014 at 8½ years old.

UKC CH-ASCA A-CH Casa Blanca From The Ashes CGC TKN "Phoenix" was sired by BIS AKC GCH-CKC-ASCA CH Bayouland Creme Brûlée CGC USASA HOFX-ASCA HOF x Casa Blanca's Shimmer's Magic ASCA HOF. He also has a bubbly, happy personality and is so athletic!

Yvette LeBlanc · Blaze was one of the great ones! Always in my heart. The Blaze and Whitney cross produced 18 champions!

Jane Firebaugh · Blaze's daughter AKC-ASCA CH Windy Pine Winter Willow was also a multiple BIS winner. I believe she had nine Bests in Show.

Kelly McIntosh · My AKC CH Lunar Ridge's Special Edition "Marley" is a Blaze great-granddaughter on her sire's side and great-great-granddaughter on her dam's side.

Becky Rowan Androff · I adore my three truly amazing Blaze kids. AOM Select AKC GCH-CKC-ASCA CH TreeStar Rmzcrk's I'm on Fire CGC TDI ROM X-I ROM C-II HOF "Fire," MBIS AKC GCH-CKC GCHEx-ASCA CH Treestarr's Billion Dollar Baby CD HIC ASCA HOF "Jackpot," and AKC GCH-CKC-ASCA CH Treestarr's Northwind Breeze ROM X-I "Breeze."

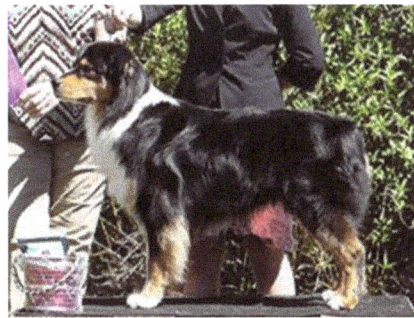

Blaze's great-great-grandson WCK's It Wasn't Me RN CGCA TKP ATD TDI "Wyatt." Born 2015. By AKC-ASCA CH Marabil's Shoot To Thrill STDs PT x Meadowlawns A Night In Victory Lane STDs RATO RATN PT CGC. Photo courtesy of Melonie Stemick Eso. Photo credit: Mari Bryan.

Blaze's great-grandson AKC GCH-ASCA CH Lil' Creek's Moves Like Jagger UCD-AKC UD-ASCA CDX "Jagger." Born 2011. By AKC GCH Equinox The Edge Of Reason RE x CopperRidge's No Ordinary Olive ROM C-III. Photo courtesy of Eileen Wilson.

Blaze's great-grandson ASCA CH Trilogy's Captured By Perfection "Rhett." Born 2015. By AKC Silver GCH-RBIS BISS MEX-INT-LatAm CH Bayoulands Capture The Flag CGC x ASCA CH Iron Rose Once Upon A Time. Photo courtesy of Carol Morgan. Photo credit: Amber Jade Aanensen.

Blaze's grandson RBIS MBISS AKC Gold GCH- CKC-ASCA CH Blue Isle's Bourrée ASCA HOF "Junior." Born 2008. By BIS AKC GCH-CKC-ASCA CH Bayouland Creme Brûlée CGC USASA HOFX- ASCA HOF x AKC-ASCA CH Bayshore's Dance With Me ASCA HOF. Photo courtesy of Barbara Hager. Photo credit: Nancy Gaffney-Gaff Photography.

They were the offspring that earned their dam First Place in the Brood Bitch class at the 2009 USASA National Specialty. Their dam was AKC-ASCA CH McMatt's Too Good To Be Blue ASCA-AKC CD NA NAJ CGC ROM X-I ASCA HOF "Carly."

Bára Drahonovská · Blaze's great-great-granddaughter CH Bayouland's Who'd Have Known BIG II BOB CACIB res.CACIB CAC CAJC "Brittany" was born in 2015. She was by AKC-ASCA CH Northbay Who Dat N Bayouland and out of AKC CH Bayouland Set Fire To The Rain CD.

Fabio Cardea · Blaze's great-grandson Bayouland's Catch Me If You Can "Joshua" was born in 2012. By BIS MBISS AKC GCH-CAN-ASCA CH CopperRidge's Fire N Bayouland ASCA HOF x AKC-ASCA CH Bayouland's Kiss Ana Hug.

Lyndy Jacob · I remember seeing Blaze when I first got into conformation. I got to know him and his brothers quite well, as I would camp out with Jane and Nora quite a bit. They were like a second family to me! I knew I just had to have one of Blaze's offspring because they were so pretty.

I got a Blaze son, Paradigm's Talk of the Circuit "Rumor." He was from Blaze's first litter with CH De Abajo's Little Red Rodeo. After Rumor, I got Montana, who was Blaze's nephew. And then came my Elan who is a granddaughter of Blaze's sister Jewel.

I don't know how many people know this, but seven out of 10 puppies in Blaze's litter finished their championships. Blaze and his brothers and sisters were all lovely examples of the breed and I am proud to have owned progeny of them. I would agree that Blaze definitely stamped a good rear, his rear was a 10!

Blaze's great-granddaughter AKC GCH-ASCA CH Ninebark Wish Me Well "Della." Born 2014. WB and BOW 2016 USASA Nationals. By AKC GCH-CKC-MEX-INT-ASCA CH Hearthside Riveredge Sure Is Summum x AKC-CKC-ASCA CH Ninebark Wishing Well. Photo courtesy of Sarah Kalkes. Photo credit: Amber Jade Aanensen.

Blaze's great-great-granddaughter AKC GCH-BIS UKC CH Impact's Golden Ray CA CGCA URO1 Total Dog "Rhea." Born 2014. By AKC GCH Northbay's Bee-Cuz You're Mine x AKC CH JnD's You Can Fly. Photo courtesy of Brittany Greendeer. Photo credit: Amber Jade Aanensen.

Blaze's great-great-grandson WCK's Ushookmeallnitelong@Shellbluff "Bonn." Born 2015. By AKC-ASCA CH Marabil's Shoot To Thrill STDs PT x Meadowlawns A Night In Victory Lane STDs RATO RATN PT CGC. Photo courtesy of Melonie Stemick Eso. Photo credit: Don Meyer.

Blaze's great-granddaughter RBIS AKC GCH-ASCA CH CopperRidge's Little Black Dress AKC RA ASCA RN NA NAJ NAP NJP RS-N JS-O CGC "Gabby." Born 2009. By BIS AKC Gold GCH-ASCA CH CopperRidge's One Time Offer x CopperRidge's No Ordinary Olive ROM C-III. Photo courtesy of Mari Jebens. Photo credit: Garden Studio.

Maria Neff · Blaze is one of my all time favorites! I'm so blessed to own a beautiful Blaze grandson! My boy AKC CH Lk Michigan Journey Through Fire at Airam "Ashton" is by AKC GCH-CKC-ASCA CH TreeStar Rmzcrk's I'm on Fire CGC TDI ROM X-I ROM C-II ASCA HOF "Fire" x AKC-ASCA CH Bayouland's Don't Stop Believing "Journey." Ashton is a joy to live with and is so willing to please.

Angelica DeMont · I LOVE Blaze and search for him in pedigrees! My foundation stud UR01 AKC GCH-ASCA CH Malpaso Keep the Fire Burning RA RL1 WZ1 is a Blaze grandson sired by AKC GCH-CKC-ASCA CH TreeStar Rmzcrk's I'm on Fire CGC TDI ROM X-I ROM C-II ASCA HOF "Fire."

Julie Ostberg · My AKC-CKC-ASCA CH JnD's Live Wire "Izzy" is a Blaze granddaughter. She's by Blaze's son AKC-UKC-ASCA CH De Abajo Ledgerock

JnD's Rumor and out of AKC CH Bayshore's Uptown Girl. My Blaze great-grandson is AKC GCH-UKC-ASCA CH JnD's Bare Necessities AKC RE CD-ASCA RM CD "Baloo." He was born in 2011. He's by MBIS AKC CH Dreamstreet's Season Ticket ROM X-II ROM C-II and out of AKC-CKC-ASCA CH JnD's Live Wire.

Brandy Dirksen · Keegan is co-owned and resides with us. We have upcoming grand kids of Keegan's and seven Keegan offspring that we either own or bred.

Barb Hoffman · I love Blaze and consider myself very lucky to own a beautiful Blaze grandson! He is Multi Group Placing BIS-OH Multi RBIS-OH AKC GCH-ASCA CH Lk Michigan RU Ready to Rumble AKC-ASCA RN CGC "Thunder." His sire is AKC GCH-CKC-ASCA CH TreeStar Rmzcrk's I'm on Fire CGC TDI ROM X-I ROM C-II ASCA HOF "Fire" and he's out of AKC-ASCA CH Bayoulands Don't Stop Believing "Journey." Thunder was bred by co-owners Marcie Marcie Barron Boomsliter and Maria Neff.

AKC CH Impact's Jokers Wild "Joker" is a Blaze grandson, owned by Gayle Kukulka of Y-not Aussies. He's by BIS MBISS AKC GCH-CAN-ASCA CH CopperRidges's Fire N Bayouland ASCA HOF and out of Bayouland's Uptown Girl. I have shown Joker for Gayle. He was bred by Judy Flynn Vandersteen.

Reninca Lenting · ASCA Premier CH-German CH KoKo Blue is a granddaughter of Blaze, sired by Keegan and out of Love is Xtreme at Snowcrest. She's the foundation bitch for Deguellos. Amazing mother and grandmother, always happy, loves every other human and dog.

Blaze's granddaughter RedEarth's Sweetheart Rose "Pip." Born 2011. By BIS AKC GCH-CKC-ASCA CH Bayouland Creme Brûlée CGC USASA HOFX- ASCA HOF x NiteStar's Rosemary Clooney. Pip partnered with her junior handler the last three years of her Junior career. Photo courtesy of Shannon Wynne Hoppmann Jackson.

Blaze's grandson "Cash" AKC-CKC-UKC-ASCA CH Wedgewood's Walk the Line at Silvermoon RN JS-E RS-O GS-N-OP "Cash." Born 2012. By BIS AKC GCH-CKC-ASCA CH Bayouland Creme Brûlée CGC USASA HOFX-ASCA HOF x AKC-ASCA CH Halfmoon She's a Brick House. Photo courtesy of Kelli Manthey.

Blaze's great-great-granddaughter CH Bayouland's Who'd Have Known CACIB res. CACIB CAC CAJC "Brittany." Born 2015. By AKC-ASCA CH Northbay Who Dat N Bayouland x Bayouland's Set Fire to the Rain. Photo courtesy of Bára Drahonovská. (CZECH REPUBLIC)

Blaze's great-granddaughter AKC CH Lunar Ridge's Special Edition "Marley." Born 2014. By AKC-ASCA CH Rondolay's Moonglow Mystique x AKC GCH Lunar Ridge's Riverdance. Photo courtesy of Kelly McIntosh. Photo credit: Rick Meyer.

Blaze's great-granddaughter FCI GCH Harmony Hill's The Search Is Over BH Certified Therapy dog and Agility dog USDAA "Misha." Born 2014. By AKC GCH Harmony Hill's Main Squeeze x AKC CH Harmony Hill's L'Attitude. Photo courtesy of Carole Ares. (COSTA RICA)

Blaze's son AKC-ASCA CH Paradigm's Red Storm Rising RE OA OAJ "Clancy." Born 2003. Group winner, multi BOB winner. By Blaze x AKC CH Lil' Creeks Hug Me Tight ROM C-III. Photo courtesy of Jane Firebaugh. Photo credit: Bill Meyer.

Blaze's grandson Wedgewood Infinite Treasure "Pi." Born 2014. By BIS AKC GCH-CKC-ASCA CH Bayouland Creme Brûlée CGC USASA HOFX-ASCA HOF x AKC CH CopperRidge's Written in Blue at Lil' Creek. Photo courtesy of Beth Lynn.

Blaze's son BIS AKC GCH-CKC-ASCA CH Bayouland Creme Brûlée CGC USASA HOFX-ASCA HOF with his daughter ASCA Premier CH-German CH KoKo Blue "Koko." She was born in 2009 and is out of Love is Xtreme at Snowcrest. Photo courtesy of Reninca Lenting. Photo credit: Heidi Erland. (GERMANY)

Photo credit: Nora Porobic   Photo credit: Veni Harlan

On the left is Blaze. On the right is his great-grandson AKC CH Cadeau des Rouge Etouffée.

"My red merle boy, AKC CH Cadeau des Rouge Etouffée, bears a remarkable resemblance to his great-grandsire Blaze, especially the eyes! Etouffée was born in 2016 and is by BIS AKC GCH-ASCA CH Bayouland's Capture the Flag out of AKC-ASCA CH RedEarth Adelaide Cadeau des Rouge CGC, who is a Keegan daughter."

- Lauren Wright

Florida Australian Shepherd Association with Judge Heidi Mobley. (Left to right)
- Best of Breed was AKC-ASCA CH Broadway's Blaze of Glory RE OA OAJ CGC ROM X-II ROM C-II ASCA HOF "Blaze" with Jane Firebaugh.
- Best of Opposite Sex was Blaze's daughter AKC-ASCA CH Windypine Kinetic Banner "Glory" with Deb Johnson.
- Winner's Bitch and Best of Winners was Blaze's daughter AKC-ASCA CH Bayouland's Touched By An Angel RN "Angel" with Nora Porobic.
- Winner's Dog was Blaze's son AKC-ASCA CH Paradigm's Red Storm Rising RE OA OAJ "Clancy" with Lyndy Jacob.

Fun times! Great dogs! All in the family! Photo courtesy of Lyndy Jacob.

Blaze's granddaughter AKC GCH-ASCA CH Navrock Pardon My French "Burke." Born 2012. By BIS AKC GCH-CKC-ASCA CH Bayouland Creme Brûlée CGC USASA HOFX-ASCA HOF x Thornapple Mercury Rising. Photo courtesy of Brandy Dirksen.

AKC-ASCA CH Broadway's Blaze of Glory RE OA OAJ CGC ROM C-II ROM X-II. Blaze sired 31 champions including six Best In Show winners. His litter out of AKC CH Lil' Creeks Hug Me Tight ROM C-III contained four of those Best In Show winners. Photo courtesy of Nora Porobic.

Blaze's granddaughter AKC GCH-ASCA CH Navrock Rodeo Queen "Sheridan." Born 2012. By BIS AKC GCH-CKC-ASCA CH Bayouland Creme Brûlée CGC USASA HOFX-ASCA HOF x Thornapple Mercury Rising. Photo courtesy of Brandy Dirksen.

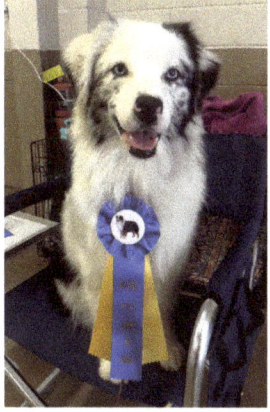

Blaze's great-granddaughter Treestarr BZ Be'N Blue@Oracle STDs JS-N RS-N RAX RE Service Dog "Velvet." Born 2013. By AKC GCH-CKC-ASCA CH Paradox Pickwick HIC x PCH RTCH CH TreeStarr's 1SlickChick AKC CD ASCA CDX AKC RE ASCA RTX ATDds RS-O JS-O GS-N DS. Photo courtesy of Sara Swanson.

Blaze's great-granddaughter AKC Multi Group Placing AKC GCH-UKC BIS CH Bayouland's Act of True Love CA FDC RATI "Truly." Born 2014. By Multi CH Bayouland's Big EZ x CH Bayouland's Set Fire To The Rain CD. Photo courtesy of Kimberly J. Welton. Photo credit: Mari Bryan.

I stood by your bed last night, I came to have a peep.
I could see that you were crying...you found it hard to sleep.
I whined to you softly as you brushed away a tear.
"It's me, I haven't left you...I'm well, I'm fine, I'm here."
I was close to you at breakfast, I watched you pour the tea.
You were thinking of the many times your hands reached down to me.
I was with you at the shops today, your arms were getting sore.
I longed to take your parcels, I wish I could do more.
I was with you at my grave today, you tend it with such care.
I want to reassure you that I am not lying there.
I walked with you toward the house, as you fumbled for your key,
I gently put my paw on you. I smiled and said, "It's me."
You looked so very tired, and sank into a chair.
I tried so hard to let you know that I was standing there.
It's possible for me to be so near you every day.
To say to you with certainty, "I never went away."
You sat there very quietly, then smiled, I think you knew...
In the stillness of that evening, I was close to you.
The day is over...I smile and watch you yawning
And say, "Goodnight, God bless, I'll see you in the morning."
And when the time is right for you to cross the brief divide,
I'll rush across to greet you and we will stand, side-by-side.
I have so many things to show you, there is so much for you to see.
Be patient, live your journey out...then come home to be with me.

- Author Unknown

Photo courtesy of Sheila Hall

Peppertree's Magic By Moonlight
USASA HOFX Sire #14 - ASCA HOF Sire #175

Call name: Merlin
Born: 1999
Sire: MBISS AKC-INT-ASCA CH Moonlight's Must Be Magic NA RS-E-OP JS-E-OP GS-E RTD ROM X-II ASCA HOF
Dam: Flo Sonya Red Marie
Breeders: Sheila Hall, Peppertree; Charmaine Melton and Tammy Gaboury, Moonlight
Owners: Sheila and Don Hall, Peppertree

Merlin was a handsome dog who turned heads wherever he went. He was perfectly balanced, with an ideal profile, excellent structure, effortless sidegait, and a rock-solid temperament. Merlin had an attractive headpiece with correct planes and proportions, which created his sweet expression. A jet black coat and bright copper trim were the icing on the cake.

Merlin possessed a beautiful front assembly with nice width and depth of chest, well layed-back shoulders and correct length of upper arm. His rear quarters were equally nice, with excellent turn of stifle and short hocks. Merlin was strong-boned with absolutely straight front legs and tight feet. He had a well-arched neck and his back was level and solid.

He began his ASCA show career with a five-point major from the 6-9 month class. The following weekend he took Winner's Dog and Best of Winners in AKC. Sadly, Merlin's show career ended when he was injured at just under two years of age. He suffered a ruptured disc in his neck that damaged his spinal cord. Although he underwent surgery, his head was permanently tilted, and his left shoulder and the left side of his neck were permanently paralyzed. Through it all, he maintained his sweet, happy, loving personality.

Despite Merlin's injury, his neurologist said, "Let him be a dog." He enjoyed going to the gate and bringing the daily paper back to the house. He also had an opportunity to gather sheep in a round pen. He loved it, and had a natural outrun and fetch.

Merlin had a special personality quirk. He could find and squeak any number of squeakers in any toy. When he went to a show, he was always given a new toy. After the injury ended his show career and he no longer went along to shows, he still expected to receive a new toy!

Merlin was intelligent and very easy to train. He was brave, loyal, sweet, and loved people and other animals. He adored little puppies and slept by the whelping box when a litter was born. He passed his wonderful temperament to his offspring.

Merlin was a sixth-generation ASCA Hall of Fame sire on his sire's side, going back to ASCA CH Starstruck of Bainbridge STDds ASCA HOF. Merlin's descendants were outstanding conformation dogs that also excelled in obedience, rally, agility, herding and tracking.

A prepotent sire, he consistently passed on his outstanding physical qualities and wonderful temperament to his offspring.

Merlin at 11 weeks old. Best of Opposite Sex Puppy, Texas Australian Shepherd Association show. Photo courtesy of Sheila Hall.

Merlin at five months old winning Best in Sweepstakes at the Mastino Association of Southern States show. Photo courtesy of Sheila Hall.

Pedigree

```
                                              CH Moonlight's Hottest Thing Goin HOF
                          ASCA CH Moonlight's Against All Odds HOF
                                              CH Jazz of Bainbridge
             MBISS AKC-INT-ASCA CH Moonlight's Must Be Magic ROM X-II HOF
                                              CH Sunshine's Action Jackson HOF
                          Sunshine's Flyin High
                                              CH Cheyenne Autumn of Woodhaven
Peppertree's Magic By Moonlight USASA HOFX-ASCA HOF
                                              CH Siena's Sock It To Em
                          Riveroak's Mr. Custom Made
                                              Woodland's Bright Rivermede
             Flo Sonya Red Marie
                                              CH Amberwood's Red Hot Conversation
                          Bluecrest Caldonia del Oro
                                              CH Bluecrest 3Xs a Lady
```

Merlin's sire MBISS AKC-INT-ASCA CH Moonlight's Must Be Magic NA RS-E-OP GS-E RTD ROM X-II ASCA HOF "Wizard." Born 1997. Photo courtesy of Kathy Austin. Photo credit: Photos by Kit.

Merlin's dam Flo Sonya Red Marie "Flo." Born 1994. Photo courtesy of Sheila Hall.

Merlin's paternal grandsire ASCA CH Moonlight's Against All Odds ASCA HOF "Squeak." Born 1993. Photo courtesy of Moonlight Aussies. Photo credit: Photos by Kit.

Merlin's paternal great-grandsire AKC CH-MBISS ASCA CH Moonlight's Hottest Thing Goin ASCA HOF "Tucker." Born 1989. Photo courtesy of Moonlight Aussies.

Merlin received the AKC 2007 Australian Shepherd Sire of the Year Award.

He was the sire of:

› Three AKC Best In Show Champions, two UKC Best in Show Champions, and one Altered Best in Specialty Show Champion
  › BIS AKC-ASCA CH Rainyday's Bend It Like Beckham
  › MBIS MBISS AKC Platinum GCH-ASCA CH Catalina's Master of Illusion
  › BIS AKC CH Rainyday's Pandemonium
  › UKC GCH BIMBS-AKC-ASCA CH Callisto BadaBingBadaBoom
  › UKC GCH BIMBS-ASCA CH Callisto's Ziggy Stardust ASCA HOF
  › A-BISS A-CH Rainyday's Howdoyoulikemenow? AKC-ASCA CD AKC-ASCA RA OA OAJ NAP NJP RS-E JS-E GS-E NAC NGC NJC TG-N WV-N
› Five AKC Grand Champions in Conformation
› Twenty-four AKC Conformation Champions
› Twenty-seven ASCA Conformation Champions
› Two AKC Master Agility Champions
› One AKC Master Agility II Champion
› Seventeen AKC Agility/Herding and twenty-eight AKC Obedience/Rally titled offspring
› Ten ASCA Conformation Altered Champions
› Two ASCA Working Trial Champions
  › WTCH Rainyday's C Ya' at Da' Top ASCA CD HSAds HIAs JS-N CGC
  › SVCH PCH ATCH WTCH AKC-ASCA CH Rainyday's Remember When AKC-ASCA CDX AKC RAE ASCA REM HIAs HSAcd RTDs AX AXJ NF NAP NJP RS-E-OP JS-E-OP GS-E-SP EAC NGC NJC TG-O WV-O TN-N
› Multiple ASCA Obedience, Rally, Agility and Herding titled offspring

Merlin at seven months old. He began his ASCA show career with a five-point major win from the 6-9 month class. Photo courtesy of Sheila Hall.

Merlin's son Peppertree's Make Believe At Madalay "Hex." Born 2016. By Merlin x Madalay's Good Vibrations. Photo courtesy of Adrianne Tullier.

Merlin's son MBIS MBISS AKC Platinum GCH-ASCA CH Catalina's Master of Illusion "Copperfield." Born 2011. By Merlin x AKC-ASCA CH Catalina Come Sail Away. Photo courtesy of Joyce Siddall. Photo credit: Amber Jade Aanensen.

Winners Dog and Best of Winners 2013 ASCA National Specialty. Select Dog 2014 Eukanuba National Championship show. Best Opposite Sex 2015 Eukanuba National Championship show. Ended 2016 as the #1 Male Australian Shepherd - Breed and All Breed #5 Herding Dog. In 2016, Copper earned six Bests in Show, 94 Group placements, and 110 Best of Breed wins. As of August 31, 2017 Copper was the #1 Australian Shepherd - All Systems - and #2 Herding Dog (CC 8/17), earning nine Bests In Show, 10 Reserve Bests In Show, 90 Best of Breed awards, and 81 Group placements.

Some of Merlin's other beautiful and talented offspring were:

› AKC-ASCA CH Rainyday's Perro Rojo ROM X-II ROM P-I ASCA HOF
› AKC-ASCA CH Rainyday's Awesome Blossom ROM X-II ROM P-III ROM O-III ASCA HOF
› AKC GCH-UKC BIS CH-ASCA RTCH CH Mpossible Magic Victory CD RE THD CGCA CGCU ASCA-CD ASCA-REX ASCA-RMX ASCA-REMX TDIA
› UKC-ASCA CH Jail House Magic Serenade AKC RN CGCA RATI-ASCA RNC RNX
› AKC GCH-UKC-ASCA CH Catalina's Knight of Peppertree CGC
› AKC-UKC-ASCA CH Rainyday's Hard Habit To Break AKC-ASCA CD AKC RE ASCA RM ASCA REX HSAs STDc OTDd ATDs NA NAJ OAJ RS-E JS-E-SP GS-E-OP GV-E-OP JV-E-SP RV-E
› AKC GCH-ASCA CH Rainyday's For Your Eyes Only CD RE ROM O-I

CONVERSATIONS

Susan Landry Whiticar · What a nice tribute to a wonderful dog! I judged Merlin as a six-month old puppy in Texas. His movement blew me away! I awarded him Reserve Winner's Dog at that show and always admired and will always remember him. I am lucky to own one of his sons, ASCA CH Rondolay's Moonglow Mystique "Tique."

Gail Karamalegos · Merlin was major pointed from the puppy class, and Sheila stopped showing him because he wasn't moving right in his front. It took months for the correct diagnosis to be determined, then they performed surgery. He was such a lovely dog—one of the best I've ever seen in my life.

Ann Fulton · What a beautiful dog!

Lisa Durand · I feel very blessed to have had a breeding to Merlin with our girl Swift in 2015, using frozen semen. Merlin graced our litter with his undeniable presence, and we kept Olde Bay's Pony Up "Pony" who is just starting his show career. I cannot thank Sheila Hall enough for being my mentor and friend for over 10 years now. Pony resembles his grandsire, Wizard, has a strong drive for stock, and a loving personality like his sire. We hope he will be able to continue this gorgeous line of working dogs.

Danielle Dumais · Merlin was an amazing dog!

Anne Heckle · I was so blessed to have my AKC GCH-ASCA CH Peppertree's Presto Chango "Presto." He had gorgeous movement, a goofy personality, and was as smart as they come. That boy was my life. Thanks to Sheila Hall for allowing me to have Presto as part of my family.

Merlin's great-grandson MEX CH JCH Breezy Oaks Riding Solo at Dux "Jax." Born 2016. Photo at four months old. By AKC GCH CH Bayouland's All About Gumbo x AKC GCH Breezy Oaks Talk Of The Town. Photo courtesy of Maria Cardena Criadero. (MEXICO)

Merlin's grandson Multi JCH Jesse's Legacy of Hickory Lake "Ghost." Born 2014. By Opal Aussie Enigma and Back to Charmois x Goodwill by Darling du Chemin de la Lune aux Reves. Photo courtesy of Emily Vignozzi. (ITALY)

Merlin's son AKC GCH-UKC BIS CH-ASCA RTCH CH Mpossible Magic Victory CD RE THD CGCA CGCU ASCA-CD ASCA-REX ASCA-RMX ASCA-REMX TDIA "Jax." Born 2009. By Merlin x AKC CH Everwood's One Honest Heart CD RN ROM X-I ROM O-II. Photo courtesy of Greg and Robin Quintana. Photo credit: Teddy Li.

Celeste Lucero Telles · Merlin was a great dog and great sire! Love what he produced. I believe if he would have not been injured he would have gone far in the show ring! He was a half-brother to my Mystic. They were both sired by the great MBISS AKC-INT-ASCA CH Moonlight's Must Be Magic ROM X-II ASCA HOF "Wizard."

Jennifer Hampton · Loved Merlin and his father Wizard.

Merlin's grandson Mpossible Magic Zoran CGCA CGCU ASCA-RN TDI "Zoran." Born 2013. By AKC GCH-UKC BIS CH-ASCA RTCH CH Mpossible Magic Victory x Broken Arrow G's Sheila. Photo courtesy of Greg and Robin Quintana. Photo credit: Malinda Julien.

Merlin's daughter AKC-ASCA CH Rainyday's Awesome Blossom ROM X-II ROM P-III ROM O-III ASCA HOF "Poppy." Born 2003. By Merlin x AKC-ASCA CH Rainyday's Roses Are Red USASA HOFX-ASCA HOF. Photo courtesy of Kate Johnson. Photo credit: Thornapple.

Allison Plaza · What an amazing boy!

Emily Vignozzi · I'm truly honored to have Merlin's grandson Multi JCH Jesse's Legacy of Hickory Lake "Ghost." I chose to take him because he came from Merlin's bloodline.

Josefine Junge · Truly amazing!

Myrjam Langen · Awww.... I loved Merlin and still love my Merlin son Windypine's CU Later I'm A Gator "Ollie." He's a certified Therapy Dog. His dam was AKC CH Windypine's Autumn Colors.

Greg and Robin Quintana · We have a wonderful Merlin son AKC GCH-UKC BIS CH-ASCA RTCH CH Mpossible Magic Victory CD RE THD CGCA CGCU ASCA-CD ASCA-REX ASCA-RMX ASCA-REMX TDIA "Jax." Our Merlin grandson sired by Jax is AKC pointed Mpossible Magic Zoran CGCA CGCU ASCA-RNTDI "Zoran."

Maria Cardenas Criadero · MEX JCH Breezy Oaks Riding Solo at Dux "Jax" is a great-grandson of Merlin on his mother's side. He's had amazing movement since he was a baby. Jax is such a playful boy, always trying to say "Hi" to new people and loving his toys. I'm proud to have Merlin's bloodline in my kennel.

Adrianne Tullier · I am so honored to share a lovely Merlin x Miss V son with Sheila Hall, bred by Madalay Aussies! He was my favorite from the first pictures I saw and it was purely coincidence that he was Sheila's pick. I could not be happier with him! He is lovely from his structure to his temperament!

Linda Grant · We have two daughters from Merlin and one grandpuppy. I love my Merlin kids. We have one of his ASCA working trial champions WTCH Rainyday's C Ya' at Da' Top CD HSAds HIAs JS-N CGC. Her dam was AKC-

Merlin's son AKC-ASCA CH Rainyday's Perro Rojo ASCA HOF "Perro." Born 2002. By Merlin x AKC-ASCA CH Rainyday's Roses Are Red USASA HOFX-ASCA HOF. Photo courtesy of Kate Johnson.

Merlin's son Windypine's CU Later I'm A Gator, Therapy Dog "Ollie." Born 2010. By Merlin x AKC CH Windypine's Autumn Colors. Photo courtesy of Myrjam Langen. (GERMANY)

Merlin's son SVCH PCH ATCH WTCH AKC-ASCA CH Rainyday's Remember When AKC-ASCA CDX AKC RAE ASCA REM HIAs HSAcd RTDs AX AXJ NF NAP NJP RS-E-OP JS-E-OP GS-E-SP EAC NGC NJC TG-O WV-O TN-N "Jackson." Born 2003. By Merlin x AKC-ASCA CH Rainyday's Violets Are Blue USASA HOFX-ASCA HOF. Photo courtesy of Danielle McJunkins.

ASCA CH Rainyday's Violet are Blue USASA HOFX-ASCA HOF.

Bev Shaw · Love my Merlin kids. All are doing well in shows. Lisa Ussery's Wendy was in the Top 10 for Utility and after the last show is moving to Super Dog. Lexi is now #2 in Top 10 for Nationals. She is doing wonderfully. We can see Merlin in everyone of them. He was a wonderful sire.

Susan Landry Whiticar · My favorite Merlin son is my AKC-ASCA CH Rondolay's Moonglow Mystique "Tique." His dam is MBIS AKC-ASCA CH Windypine's Winter Willow and his breeder is Carolyn Asquith.

Merlin's daughter A-CH Rainyday's Maybe I'm Amazed RV-O JV-E GV-E "Maizie." Born 2007. By Merlin x AKC-ASCA CH Rainyday's Violets Are Blue USASA HOFX-ASCA HOF. Photo courtesy of Danielle McJunkins. Photo credit: Dorinda Pugh.

Merlin's son UKC-ASCA CH Jail House Magic Serenade AKC RN RATI CGCA TKI ASCA RNX RNC "Duke." Born 2014. By Merlin x ASCA CH StarN Jail House Gems Easywind. Photo courtesy of Serena Cohen. Photo credit: Amber Jade Aanensen.

Lauren Wright · Loved Merlin and what he produced!

Gail Karamalegos · UKC GCH BIMBS (Best In Multi Breed Show)-ASCA CH Callisto's Ziggy Stardust ASCA HOF "Ziggy" won an ASCA Top 10 Merit Award. She was by Merlin and out of CH Callisto's Rosie O'Donnell ASCA HOF. She's still going strong at age 15.

AKC Premier CH-UKC GCH BIMBS (Best In Multi Breed Show)-ASCA CH Callisto BadaBingBadaBoom "Bing" was an ASCA Top 10 Merit Award winner for five years running. He was probably the best moving dog I ever bred. He was by Merlin and out of CH Callisto's Rosie O'Donnell ASCA HOF.

Sierra Echo · Absolutely amazing story. What a handsome gentleman!

Cristina Freixes · I loved Merlin! He was one of my favorite dogs.

Kim Eden · I feel very blessed to have a Merlin daughter, my heart dog! UKC-ASCA CH Peppertree's Dream of Me "Dream" is the foundation bitch for my kennel, Keona Aussies. Out of two litters with Dream, Sheila Hall and I have bred three ASCA champions, one AKC champion, one CKC champion, two CGC titled, and two have won Winner's at a USASA Specialty. Words can't begin to express how thankful I am to have Sheila and Dream in my life!

Danielle McJunkins · I also owned "Toby Keith" A-BISS ASCA A-CH Rainyday's Howdoyoulikemenow? AKC-ASCA CD AKC-ASCA RA OA OAJ NAP NJP RS-E JS-E GS-E NAC NGC NJC TG-N WV-N. He was by Merlin and out of AKC-ASCA CH Rainyday's Roses Are Red USASA HOFX-ASCA HOF. Toby Keith was bred by Kate Johnson and Linda Phillips. During his career, he earned 172 A-BOB wins including one A-BISS win at the 2007 ASCA National Specialty and two A-BOB wins at National Pre-shows (2007 and 2010). He earned 38 A-BOS wins including A-BOS at the 2009 ASCA National Specialty.

Merlin's daughter UKC-ASCA CH Callisto's Meet Me at Catera "Ali-cat." Born 2002. By Merlin x ASCA CH Callisto's Rosie O' Donnell ASCA HOF. Photo courtesy of Amy Hiscock.

Merlin's son AKC-ASCA CH Jail House Shot In The Dark "Ruger." Born 2014. By Merlin x AKC-ASCA CH StarN Jail House Gems Easywind. Photo courtesy of Tina Miller.

Merlin's grandson AKC-ASCA CH Keona's Best Part of Wakin' Up By Madalay "Jo." Born 2014. By ASCA CH Northbay Summit Cut The Mustard x UKC-ASCA CH Peppertree's Dream of Me. Photo courtesy of Kim Eden. Photo credit: Kohler.

Merlin's granddaughter ASCA CH Keona's Coffee In Your Cup By Madalay CGC "Brezza." Born 2014. By ASCA CH Northbay Summit Cut The Mustard x UKC-ASCA CH Peppertree's Dream of Me. Photo courtesy of Kim Eden.

Merlin's daughter UKC-ASCA CH Peppertree's Dream of Me "Dream." Born 2006. By Merlin x AKC-ASCA CH Rainyday LifeInTheFastLane CD OA OAJ RS-E JS-O GS-N EAC OJC NGC TN-N TG-N. Photo courtesy of Kim Eden. Photo credit: Luis Sosa.

Merlin's son AKC GCH-UKC-ASCA CH Catalina's Knight of Peppertree CGC "Lance." Born 2011. By Merlin x AKC-ASCA CH Catalina Come Sail Away. Photo courtesy of Sheila Hall. Photo credit: Caviness Photo.

Merlin's son AKC Premier CH-UKC GCH BIMBS- ASCA CH Callisto BadaBingBadaBoom "Bing." Born 2004. ASCA Top 10 Merit Award for five years. By Merlin x ASCA CH Callisto's Rosie O'Donnell ASCA HOF. Photo courtesy of Gail Karamalegos. Photo credit: Heidi Mobley.

Merlin's daughter UKC GCH BIMBS-ASCA CH Callisto's Ziggy Stardust ASCA HOF "Ziggy." Born 2002. ASCA Top 10 Merit Award. By Merlin x ASCA CH Callisto's Rosie O'Donnell ASCA HOF. Photo courtesy of Gail Karamalegos. Photo credit: Heidi Mobley.

Angelyn Scarvaci · What a wonderful dog! He is one of my all-time favorites, a legend, known for his great contribution to the Aussie breed.

Diana Hefti · A beautiful boy with a lovely legacy!

Manu Hoffmann · Love this boy!

Tammy Csicsila · Love!

Tina Miller · I'm the breeder of two exceptional sons by Merlin and out of AKC-ASCA CH StarN Jail House Gems Easywind. One is owned by Serena Cohen, UKC-ASCA CH Jail House Magic Serenade AKC RN CGCA RATI-ASCA RNC RNX "Duke." They are working on herding titles and in AKC conformation. My boy from that litter is AKC-ASCA CH Jail House Shot in the Dark "Ruger."

Lori Acierto · Merlin looks like his daddy Wizard.

Ann Fulton · What a beautiful dog!

Danielle McJunkins · Love my "Jackson" who was by Merlin and out of AKC-ASCA CH Rainyday's Violets Are Blue USASA HOFX-ASCA HOF. He was bred by Kate Johnson and Linda Phillips. Jackson was my first Aussie and is why I fell in love with this breed and their "do anything" attitude. He is still, as far as I know, the only AKC Group winning WTCH in breed history. Jackson is AKC Multiple Group winning SVCH PCH ATCH WTCH AKC-ASCA CH Rainyday's Remember When AKC-ASCA CDX AKC RAE-ASCA REM HIAs HSAcd RTDs AX AXJ NF NAP NJP RS-E- OP JS-E-OP GS-E-SP EAC NGC NJC TG-O WV-O TN-N. He was 14 in October 2017!

Merlin's granddaughter ASCA CH Rainyday's More Than A Memory AKC-ASCA CD AKC RE ASCA RAX HSAd STDs OTDd OA OAJ NF RS-O JS-E GS-O "Birdie." Born 2010. By AKC-ASCA CH Rainyday's Desperado ROM X-III ROM P-II ROM O-I ASCA HOF x AKC-ASCA CH Rainyday's Awesome Blossom ROM X-II ROM P-III ROM O-III ASCA HOF. Photo courtesy of Kate Johnson. Photo credit: KayLeigh Kandids.

Merlin's daughter Olde Bay's Merlin's Folly for Catera "Noni." Born 2015. By Merlin x Olde Bay's Teardrops On My Guitar. Photo courtesy of Amy Hiscock.

Merlin's son Olde Bay's Pony Up "Pony." Born 2015. By Merlin x Olde Bay's Tear Drops On My Guitar. Photo courtesy of Lisa Durand.

Merlin's granddaughter Zestforlife Twilight MH "Kuura." Born 2009. By SRN Eagle Red Hot Masquerade x Callisto's Glittering Willow. Photo courtesy of Sanna Niiranen. (FINLAND)

Merlin's grandson A-CH Rainydays Come to Conquer AKC BN CD RN "Cyrus." Born 2007. By SVCH PCH ATCH WTCH AKC-ASCA CH Rainyday's Remember When x AKC-ASCA CH Rainyday GirlsJus WannaHavFun ROM X-III ROM O-I ROM P-I. Photo courtesy of Ashley Patin. Photo credit: 2MC Design.

Merlin's grandson OpalAussie Jumping With Joy "Jagger." Born 2014. By Moon Shine Blue Just an American Boy x OpalAussie Fade to Black. Photo courtesy of David Baggs. Photo credit: Paula McDermid. (FRANCE)

Merlin's son AKC-ASCA CH Rondolay's Moonglow Mystique "Tique." Born 2009. By Merlin x MBIS AKC-ASCA CH Windypine's Winter Willow. Photo courtesy of Susan Landry Whiticar. Photo credit: K & M Photography.

Merlin's great-grandson BISS AKC GCH-ASCA CH Samwise Never Say Never "Vaughn." Born 2013. By BIS AKC GCH-CKC-ASCA CH Hearthside's Standing Ovation CGC TDI ROM X-I ASCA HOF x AKC-ASCA CH Rainyday's You Took Me By Surprise AKC-ASCA CD RE HIT. Photo courtesy of Star Mathis. Photo credit: Dan Pearson.

Merlin's grandson AKC-ASCA CH Rainyday's I Got My Game On AKC-ASCA CD AKC RE ASCA REM STDs NA NAJ RS-E GS-E JS-E-OP "Trace." Born 2007. By AKC-ASCA CH Calais Carolina Rebel Yell ASCA HOF x AKC-ASCA CH Rainyday's Awesome Blossom USASA ROM X-II ROM P-III ROM O-III ASCA HOF. Photo courtesy of Danielle McJunkins.

Merlin's grandson AKC-ASCA CH Catalina's It's In The Cards "Cards." Born 2014. Award of Merit 2017 USASA National Specialty. By MBIS MBISS AKC Platinum GCH-ASCA CH Catalina's Master of Illusion x AKC-ASCA CH Catalina's Little Miss Millions. Photo courtesy of Joyce Siddall. Photo credit: Amber Jade Aanensen.

A-BISS A-CH Rainyday's Howdoyoulikemenow?

AKC-ASCA CD AKC-ASCA RA OA OAJ NAP NJP RS-E JS-E GS-E NAC NGC NJC TG-N WV-N

"Toby Keith." Born 2003. By Merlin x AKC-ASCA CH Rainyday's Roses Are Red USASA HOFX-ASCA HOF

Photo credit Dorinda Pugh

Toby Keith had an extensive career as an ASCA Altered special with 172 A-BOB wins. His most exciting wins included one A-BISS win at the 2007 ASCA National Specialty and two A-BOB wins at ASCA National Pre-shows (2007 and 2010). He was also successful in the AKC ring as a Veteran. His wins include two Awards of Merit at regional USASA specialties out of the Veterans class and a Best In Show Veteran win at the October 2011 Belton, Texas, AKC show. Thank you to Kate Johnson and Linda Phillips, Rainyday, for sending us this wonderful dog.

- Danielle McJunkins

Amy Hiscock · Merlin blessed Catera Aussies with four of his beautiful offspring. ASCA CH Callisto's Meet Me at Catera "Ali-cat" was our third champion and she had Merlin's stunning gate. We now have Olde Bay's Merlin's Folly For Catera "Noni" who is another stunning moving bitch getting ready for the show ring. My thanks go to Gail Karamalegos for trusting me with my sweet Ali who I miss every day; to Sheila Hall for sharing Merlin with me through his offspring; and to Lisa Durand for my sweet Noodle—may she continue the legacy that Merlin started so many years ago.

Merlin's great-granddaughter AKC-ASCA CH Lastcall's Goodbye My Dear "Fly." Born 2013. By AKC GCH-ASCA CH Highpoint's Sweet William x ASCA CH Lastcall's Lady in Black CD JV-E RV-O GV-O. Photo courtesy of Kim Gorman. Photo credit: Amber Jade Aanensen.

Merlin's grandson CKC-ASCA CH Keona's BluMarlin of Peppertree CGC "Jack." Born 2013. By CKC-ASCA CH Risk 'N Hope's I Rock the World x UKC-ASCA CH Peppertree's Dream of Me. Photo courtesy of Kim Eden.

"I always believed that the key to a good breeding program was a strong bitch line, and Gussie put that belief into practice. Bred to three different stud dogs, Gussie produced exceptionally sound, intelligent offspring each time."

- Kate Johnson

Photo credit: Kate Johnson

Cobbercrest Propwash Obla-De
USASA HOFX Dam #1 - ASCA HOF Dam #151

Call Name: Gussie
Born: 1994
Sire: AKC-ASCA CH Propwash Hey Jude
Dam: Propwash Motion Carried
Breeders: Tim J. Preston, Cobbercrest, and Leslie Frank. Propwash
Owners: Kathrin (Phillips) Johnson and Linda Phillips, Rainyday

"Looking back on acquiring Gussie leaves me without much to say except that it must have been fate. We were not looking for a puppy at the time, and worked out some kind of a cockamamie trade with our friend and mentor, Tim Preston. He joked that even at eight weeks old, she was so much puppy that she needed the focus and attention that my mom, Linda Phillips, put into raising a puppy. We agreed, sight unseen, to raise the little maniac, but not to keep her.

She was a funny little puppy with a sturdy body and helicopter ears. She carried herself with great confidence and seemed to have an agenda already, even though at eight weeks, she wasn't much bigger than a football. She was balanced even then, and trotted everywhere she went with an easy, efficient gait. When she arrived, she was called Gizmo, and she took over the house. Tim pointed out that she had a pedigree full of breed greats, and had potential to be exactly what we were looking for. I remember looking at her, and seeing how she looked at me. I wasn't sure she should stay. None of us liked the name Gizmo, and after I started calling her Gizzard the Lizard, Tim agreed that we could change her name. I guess it was the beginning of reality: she was not leaving. At some point a new deal was made, and it was official, Gussie was ours.

Gussie was indeed a handful. As a young puppy, she lacked a conscience. She was naughty to an extreme, and nonplussed when confronted with her transgressions. Luckily, she was a quick study, and learned whatever was asked. One day when she was about five months old, Mom looked up from weeding the garden to discover that Gussie was following behind her, yanking up the bean plants. Mom showed Gussie how to pull the weeds, and they continued on together, with Mom pointing at the plants she wanted Gus to pull up.

Gussie was shown a few times and earned some good looks, plus reserves to 5-point majors, but she tore an ACL as a youngster and it healed poorly. While she was sound enough to live a full life, she was not able to return to the ring.

Tim was right, Gussie's pedigree read like a dream. She was sired by AKC-ASCA CH Propwash Hey Jude, and on the paternal side of her pedigree she was the great-granddaughter of ASCA CH Arrogance of Heatherhill CDX STDd ASCA HOF, and ASCA CH Sitting Pretty of Sunnybrook ASCA HOF. Her maternal grandsire was WTCH SVCH AKC-ASCA CH Beauwood's Rustlin in the Sun AKC-ASCA UDT CKC CD RDa RV-E NA HTD-2s TT CGC ASCA HOF and her dam was a full sister to AKC-ASCA CH Propwash Flounce and AKC-ASCA CH Propwash St. Elmo's Fire USASA HOFX-ASCA HOF. Both sides of Gussie's pedigree include many beautiful, sound-moving dogs with brains.

Gussie's maternal granddam Bayshore Propwash Fogbow ASCA HOF "Foggy." Born 1987. Photo courtesy of Leslie Frank.

Gussie's paternal granddam AKC CH Bayshore's Lucy In The Sky CD ASCA HOF "Lucy." Born 1984. Photo courtesy of Leslie Frank.

Pedigree

```
                                              CH Arrogance Of Heatherhill CDX STDd HOF
                            CH Topper's Levi Blues
                                              Copper Canyon's Red Flannel
            AKC-ASCA CH Propwash Hey Jude
                                              CH Winchesters Three Cheers
                            CH Bayshore's Lucy In The Sky CD ASCA HOF
                                              CH Sitting Pretty Of Sunnybrook HOF
Cobbercrest Propwash Obla-De USASA HOFX-ASCA HOF
                                              CH Sunspot Of Windermere
                            AKC-CKC-ASCA CH Beauwoods Rustlin' In The Sun HOF
                                              CH Peppers Special K
            Propwash Motion Carried
                                              CH Propwash Sambal
                            Propwash Bayshore Fogbow HOF
                                              CH Propwash Capriole Of Bayshore
```

Gussie's sire AKC-ASCA CH Propwash Hey Jude "Jude." Born 1992. Photo courtesy of Thornapple Aussies.

Gussie's dam Propwash Motion Carried "Mojo." Born 1991. Photo courtesy of Tim Preston.

Gus was full of exuberance. She was known to all who visited our home, because you could not lean forward to greet Gussie without risking a broken nose and black eyes. She was notorious for leaping straight up in the air to say hello, and she would crash into your face if you were reaching down for her. Gussie never jumped over fences, but she jumped straight up in the air to look over them. She passed this trait down to her progeny. A granddaughter, Rose (AKC-ASCA CH Rainyday's Roses Are Red USASA HOFX-ASCA HOF), would easily launch her 18" body through the air to look over our seven foot fence. Rose also perfected a swimmer's turn—on the fence. She would run at the wood fence, leap, bank off it (around three feet off the ground) and land headed back the way she had come.

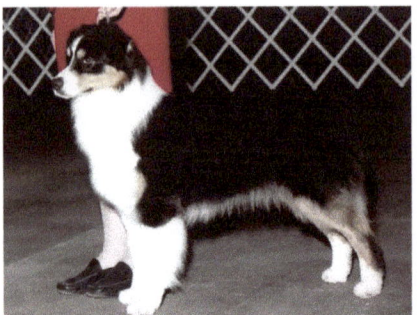

Gussie's granddaughter AKC-ASCA CH Pacific's Sweet Victorie AKC-ASCA CD NA NAJ RS-O JS-N GS-N "Toria." Born 2002. By AKC-ASCA CH Rainyday's I'm On Fire HT ROM X-III ROM C-I ROM P-I ASCA HOF x ASCA CH Friendship's Victoria's Secret STDds ROM X-I. Photo courtesy of Kate Johnson. Photo credit: Luke Allen.

Gussie's great-grandson BIS AKC-ASCA CH Rainyday's Bend It Like Beckham "Beckham." Born 2003. By Peppertree's Magic By Moonlight USASA HOFX-ASCA HOF x AKC-ASCA CH Rainyday's Violet Are Blue USASA HOFX-ASCA HOF. Photo courtesy of Lily Bhalang and Tina Beatty. Photo credit: Mike Johnson.

Gussie's great-granddaughter AKC CH Peppertree's This One's For The Girls RN "Cory." Born 2007. By AKC-ASCA CH Melody's The Beat Goes On x AKC-INT-ASCA CH Rainyday's You Made Me Love U. Photo courtesy of Lisa Durand. Photo credit: Fritz Clark.

Gussie's daughter AKC CH Rainyday's Free As A Bird CGC USASA HOFX-ASCA HOF "Wren." Born 1995. By AKC-ASCA CH Cobbercrest's Shooting Star TDI CGC x Gussie. Dam of two USASA HOFX-ASCA HOF daughters. Photo courtesy of Kate Johnson. Photo credit: Booth.

Gussie once leaped into the air, caught a robin, and delivered it to the other dogs. Everyone stood around, looking at the downed bird, and then reacted with great surprise when it recovered and flew away.

Gussie oozed proper Aussie type. She had her mother's beautiful front—both moving and standing—and she passed it down. Gussie also had proper Aussie temperament. She was not, as the expression goes, a Golden Retriever in an Aussie suit. Gussie was reserved with strangers, would place herself between a family member and a newcomer, and made it abundantly clear, that if needed, she would come to our defense. Once she was sure that a visitor was welcome, she was friendly and affectionate. Gussie was keen witted, quick to learn, and an excellent mother.

I always believed that the key to a good breeding program was a strong bitch line, and Gussie put that belief into practice. Bred to three different stud dogs, Gussie produced exceptionally sound, intelligent offspring each time. The cross that was truly golden was to AKC-INT-ASCA CH Bluestems Man-O-Firethorne USASA HOFX-ASCA HOF "Yukon." This cross produced truly outstanding puppies. Several of these offspring went on to become stellar producers as well and can be found behind some of the top winning and producing dogs in the breed.

For example, Gussie's daughter from her first litter, AKC CH Rainyday's Free As A Bird CGC USASA HOFX-ASCA HOF "Wren," was a typey, sound little black tri bitch with her father's big sidegait and much more of a conscience than Gussie ever had. A kind, rule-follower of a dog, Wren, turned out to be an incredible producer just like her mother. Also, just like her mother, the "golden" cross turned

Gussie's daughter MBIS MBISS AKC-ASCA CH Rainyday's Red Red Wine "Merlot." Born 1998. By AKC-INT CH Firethorne's Intimidator x Gussie. Photo courtesy of Kate Johnson. Photo credit: Thornapple.

Winner of 3 All-Breed BIS; winner of 5 specialty BOB wins (one from Veterans); 45 group ones; 67 group placements; BOS Eukanuaba Classic 2001; BOS Westminster 2002, 2003, 2005; AOM Westminster 2004; AOM USASA Nationals in 2005 from Veterans; Best Veteran in Sweeps USASA Nationals 2005; ranked in the top 4 in AKC 2001, 2002, 2003, 2004; ranked in the top 10 in AKC in 2000; ranked #9 in ASCA 2002; BOS ASCA Nationals preshow 2001, then two Premier Awards (only attended preshows).

out to be with Yukon. Done twice, this cross produced 13 puppies. Both of the bitches from the first cross, Rose and Violet, both went on to become USASA HOFX-ASCA HOF Dams. Violet, in fact, is the mother of the only litter in breed history to produce both an AKC BIS winner (two of them actually) as well as a WTCH (and he's also a group winning AKC-ASCA CH, SVCH, PCH, ATCH). One of the daughters from that litter is not only a BIS winner, but a USASA HOFX Dam as well.

While Gussie was not our first Aussie; she became our foundation bitch and all Rainyday dogs go back to her. She was sound in both mind and body, with true Aussie type and temperament.

Gussie was the first bitch to earn HOFX status in USASA. One of her daughters, two granddaughters and a great-granddaughter followed her, earning five of the seven USASA HOFX awards awarded so far (Oct. 2017). Many BIS, BISS, MACH, ATCH, and WTCH go directly back to Gussie. Gussie produced a MBIS/MBISS daughter, a BISS son, and has a BIS grandson and three BIS great-grandchildren.

Some of the highlight's of Gussie's achievements include: USASA HOFX #1, ASCA HOF #151, and the Pedigree Award for Top Producing Bitch in 2001. Her daughter AKC-ASCA CH Rainyday's The Beat Goes On ROM X-I ROM C-III earned the same Pedigree Award in 2009."

- Kate Johnson

Gussie's great-granddaughter ASCA A-CH Rainyday's Busby Babe AKC-ASCA CD AKC RE ASCA RA NAJ AXP OFP RS-N JS-N GS-O AD CGC "Tessa." Born 2007. By Peppertree's Magic By Moonlight USASA HOFX-ASCA HOF x AKC-ASCA CH Rainyday's Violets Are Blue USASA HOFX-ASCA HOF. Photo courtesy of Kathleen Holt Photo credit: Danielle McJunkins.

Gussie's great-grandson SVCH PCH ATCH WTCH AKC-ASCA CH Rainyday's Remember When AKC-ASCA CDX AKC RAE ASCA REM HIAs HSAcd RTDs AX AXJ NF NAP NJP RS-E-OP JS-E-OP GS-E-SP EAC NGC NJC TG-O WV-O TN-N. "Jackson." Born 2003. By Peppertree's Magic By Moonlight USASA HOFX-ASCA HOF x AKC-ASCA CH Rainyday's Violets Are Blue USASA HOFX-ASCA HOF. Photo courtesy of Danielle McJunkins. Photo credit: Nugent Photography.

Gussie's grandson AKC-ASCA CH Rainyday's Joint Venture RN NA NAJ HIC "Venture." Born 1999. By AKC-INT-ASCA CH Bluestems Man-O-Firethorne USASA HOFX-ASCA HOF x AKC CH Rainyday's Free As A Bird CGC USASA HOFX-ASCA HOF. Photo courtesy of Kim Waller and Beth Rice. Photo credit: Tien Tran.

Gussie's double great-granddaughter ASCA CH Rainyday's More Than A Memory AKC/ASCA CD AKC RE ASCA RAX HSAd STDs OTDd OA OAJ NF RS-O JS-E GS-O "Birdie." Born 2011. Sired by AKC-ASCA CH Rainyday's Desperado ROM X-III ROM P-II ROM O-I ASCA HOF x AKC-ASCA CH Rainyday's Awesome Blossom ROM X-II ROM P-III ROM O-III ASCA HOF. Photo courtesy of Kate Johnson. Photo credit: Kate Johnson.

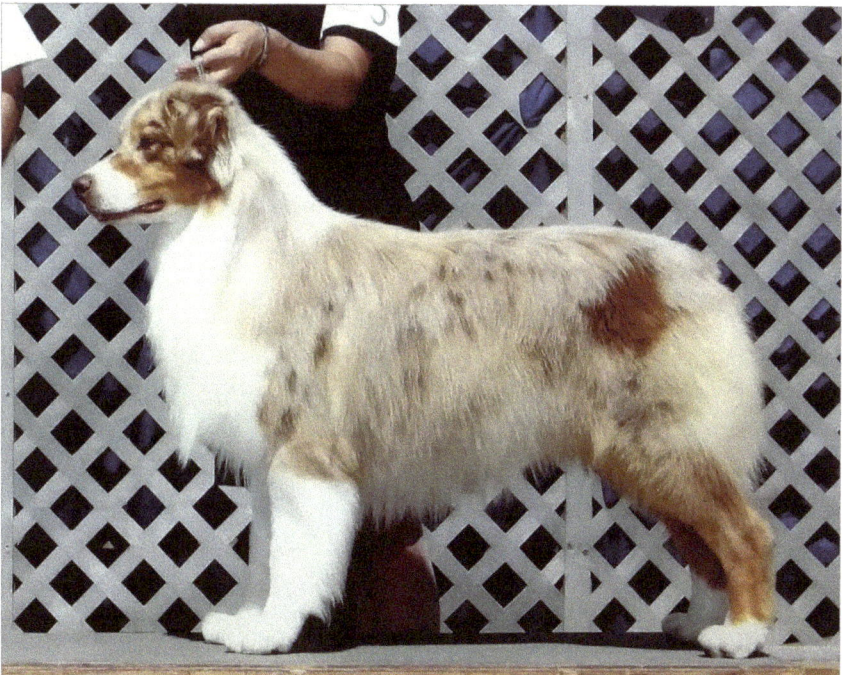

Gussie's son AKC-ASCA CH Rainyday's I'm On Fire HT ROM X-III ROM P-I ROM C-I ASCA HOF "Spark." Born 1999. By AKC-INT-ASCA CH Bluestems Man-O-Firethorne USASA HOFX-ASCA HOF x Gussie. ASCA Hall of Fame Sire #201, sire of three WTCH. Multiple group winner, multiple BOB winner in AKC and ASCA, multiple Premier Award Winner, Best Veteran in Sweeps 2009 USASA National Specialty. Photo courtesy of Kate Johnson. Photo credit: Dan Pearson.

First Place Brood Bitch class 2005 USASA National Specialty. (Left to right)
Dam: Gussie's granddaughter AKC-ASCA CH Rainyday's Roses Are Red USASA HOFX-ASCA HOF
› AKC-ASCA CH Rainyday's Awesome Blossom ROM X-II ROM P-III ROM O-III ASCA HOF
› AKC-ASCA CH Rainyday's Forget-Me-Not ROM X-II
› AKC-ASCA CH Rainyday's Copy Me At Peppertree PT STDs CGC
Photo courtesy of Kate Johnson. Photo credit: Sharon Turner.

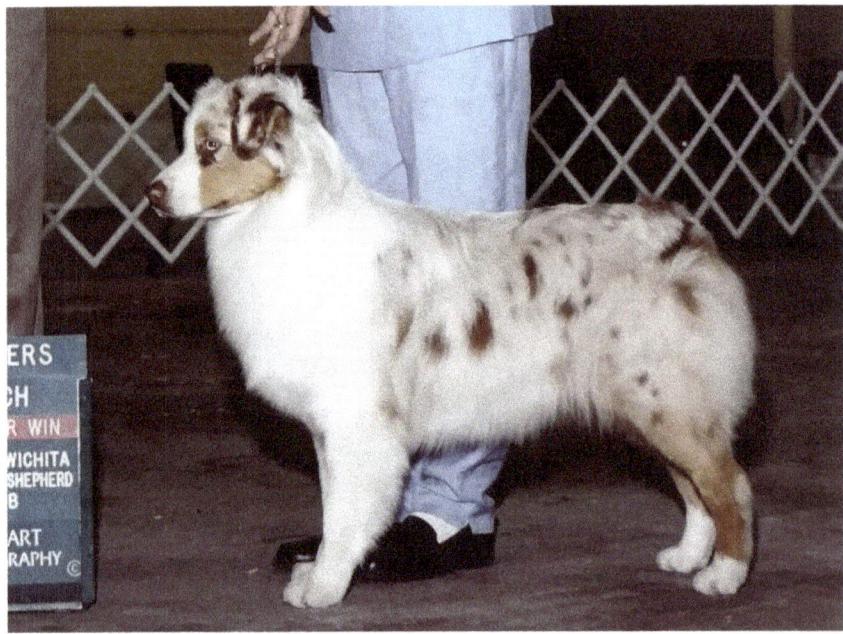

Gussie's granddaughter AKC-ASCA CH Rainyday's Roses Are Red USASA HOFX-ASCA HOF "Rose." Born 1999. By AKC-INT-ASCA CH Bluestem's Man-O-Firethorne USASA HOFX-ASCA HOF x AKC CH Rainyday's Free As A Bird CGC USASA HOFX-ASCA HOF. Photo courtesy of Kate Johnson. Photo credit: Rinehart.

WB from 12-18 at the Greater Wichita Australian Shepherd Club specialty, winner of brood bitch class at USASA nationals the only two years shown, mother of AKC-ASCA CH Rainyday's Awesome Blossom ROM X-II ROM P-III ROM O-III ASCA HOF, AKC-ASCA CH Rainyday's Perro Rojo ROM X-II ASCA HOF , AKC-ASCA CH Rainyday's Forget-Me-Not ROM X-II, AKC-ASCA CH Rainyday's Eleanor Rigby ROM X-II ROM P-I, and A-BISS A-CH Rainyday's Howdoyoulikemenow? AKC-ASCA CD AKC-ASCA RA OA OAJ NAO NJO RS-E JS-E GS-E NAC NGC NJC TG-N WV-N.

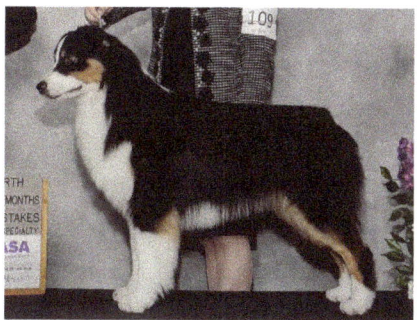

Gussie's daughter AKC-ASCA CH Rainyday's Life in the Fast Lane AKC-ASCA CD OA OAJ RS-E JS-O GS-N EAC OJC TN-N TG-N "Jane." Born 2000. By AKC-INT-ASCA CH Bluestems Man-O-Firethorne USASA HOFX-ASCA HOF x Gussie. Dam of MBIS AKC CH Rainyday's Reason To Believe and AKC-ASCA CH Rainyday's Desperado ROM X-III ROM P-II ROM O-I ASCA HOF. Photo courtesy of Kate Johnson. Photo credit: Rinehart.

Gussie's great-great-grandson Samwise Besame Mucho @ Rainyday AKC-ASCA RN CGC (major pointed ASCA/pointed AKC) "Finn." Born 2014. By AKC GCH-ASCA CH Hearthside Standing Ovation ROM X-I ASCA HOF x AKC-ASCA CH Rainyday's You Took Me By Surprise AKC-ASCA CD RE HIT. Photo courtesy of Kate Johnson. Photo credit: Jeffrey Hanlin.

Gussie's granddaughter AKC-ASCA CH Rainyday's Violets Are Blue USASA HOFX-ASCA HOF "Violet." Born 1999. By AKC-INT-ASCA CH Bluestem's Man-O-Firethorne USASA HOFX-ASCA HOF x AKC CH Rainyday's Free As A Bird CGC USASA HOFX-ASCA HOF. Photo courtesy of Kate Johnson. Photo credit: Rinehart.

Dam of two BIS winners and two WTCH (one is also a SVCH). Third generation USASA ASCA HOF. Violet's first litter is the only litter in breed history to have both an ASCA WTCH and an AKC BIS winner. The litter included two AKC BIS winners, and the WTCH was also an AKC and ASCA CH SVCH ATCH PCH. There were four AKC group winners in that first litter and a second WTCH in her third litter. Littermate to AKC-ASCA CH Rainyday's Roses Are Red USASA-ASCA HOF.

Gussie was crossed with three sires, and the quality in each litter was remarkable.

GUSSIE and AKC-ASCA CH COBBERCREST'S
SHOOTING STAR CGC TDI

> AKC CH Rainyday's Free As A Bird CGC USASA HOFX #2 ASCA HOF #196. Dam of:
  > AKC-ASCA CH Rainyday's Roses Are Red USASA HOFX #3 ASCA HOF #212
  > AKC-ASCA CH Rainyday's Violets Are Blue USASA HOFX #6 ASCA HOF #233. Dam of two AKC BIS winners, two WTCH (one an SVCH as well) and a USASA HOFX
  > AKC-ASCA CH Rainyday's I'm No Angel ROM X-I
  > AKC-ASCA CH Rainyday's Preston Phillips
  > AKC-ASCA CH Rainyday's Tiger Lily AKC-ASCA CD
  > AKC-ASCA CH Rainyday's Joint Venture RN NA NAJ HIC ROM X-I
  > AKC-UKC CH Rainyday's Achy Breaky Heart CGC
  > MACH Rainyday's Fire in the Sky CD RN RS-O GS-N OAC NGC AAD SSA SR AG AJ
  > MACH Rainyday's Walk This Way VCD2 UD RE MXB MJS
> AKC CH Rainyday's Ticket To Ride
> C-ATCH C-ATE Rainyday's Life On Mars MX MXB MXJ MJB AXP AJP RV-O JV-O GV-N OAC OGC OJC-O PI AD CGC
> Rainyday's Mistletoe AKC-ASCA CDX OA OAJ RS-O JS-N GS-N

Gussie's great-great-granddaughter AKC-ASCA CH Rainyday's Playin' With The Boys "Charlie." Born 2007. By AKC-ASCA CH Carolina Calais Rebel Yell ASCA HOF x AKC-ASCA CH Rainyday's Awesome Blossom ROM X-II ROM P-III ROM O-III ASCA HOF. Photo courtesy of Kate Johnson. Photo credit: Jeffrey Hanlin.

Gussie's daughter AKC-ASCA CH Rainyday's The Beat Goes On ROM X-I ROM C-III "Tempo." Born 2000. Pedigree Award Winner 2009 Top Producing Bitch. By AKC-INT-ASCA CH Bluestems Man-O-Firethorne USASA HOFX-ASCA HOF x Gussie. Photo courtesy of Kim Waller and Beth Rice. Photo credit: Don Meyer.

GUSSIE and AKC-INT-ASCA CH BLUESTEMS MAN-O-FIRETHORNE USASA HOFX-ASCA HOF

- AKC-ASCA CH Rainyday's I'm On Fire HT ROM X-III ROM C-I ROM P-I ASCA HOF #201. Sire of three WTCH.
- AKC-ASCA CH Rainyday GirlsJusWannaHavFun ROM X-III ROM O-I ROM P-I
- BISS AKC-INT CH Rainyday's Tinsel Town RN
- AKC-ASCA CH Rainyday's The Beat Goes On ROM X-I ROM C-III. Pedigree Award for Top Producing Bitch 2009.
- AKC-ASCA CH Rainyday's We Have No Secrets
- AKC CH Rainyday's Love Me Do
- ASCA CH Rainyday Dawn's Early Light
- AKC-ASCA CH Rainyday's Life in the Fast Lane AKC-ASCA CD OA OAJ RS-E JS-O GS-N TN-N EAC OJC NJC. Dam of:
    - AKC-ASCA CH Rainyday's Desperado ROM X-III ROM P-II ROM O-I ASCA HOF #272. Sire of multiple MACH, ATCH, and nationally ranked offspring.
    - MBIS AKC CH Rainyday's Reason to Believe
    - Rainyday's Take It To The Limit MX MXB MXJ MJB NJP XF GJ-N

GUSSIE and AKC-INT CH FIRETHORNE'S INTIMIDATOR

- MBIS MBISS AKC-ASCA CH Rainyday's Red Red Wine
- AKC CH Rainyday's Ruby Tuesday AKC-ASCA CD OA OAJ RS-O JS-N OAC OJC HIC ROM X-I

Gussie's double great-granddaughter AKC-ASCA CH Rainyday's Eleanor Rigby ROM X-II ROM P-I "Eleanor." Born 2006. By AKC-ASCA CH Rainyday's Desperado ROM X-III ROM P-II ROM O-I ASCA HOF x AKC-ASCA CH Rainyday's Roses Are Red USASA HOFX-ASCA HOF. Photo courtesy of Kate Johnson. Photo credit: Pix N Pages.

Gussie's great-granddaughter AKC-ASCA CH Rainyday's Forget-Me-Not ROM X-II "Petal." Born 2003. By Peppertree's Magic By Moonlight USASA HOFX-ASCA HOF x AKC-ASCA CH Rainyday's Roses Are Red USASA HOFX-ASCA HOF. Photo courtesy of Jennifer Bernard. Photo credit: Olivia Frost.

CONVERSATIONS

Marsha Settles · How sweet, very pretty dog!

Kim Waller · The intelligence lives on in her descendants. I have Gussie's great-great-granddaughter Spice, who without any training decided it was her job to help me get stainless steel food bowls out of the crates after watching me pick them up. She started helping at just three months old and now at not quite three years old she still helps. I can also send her out into the backyard to retrieve toys the other dogs take out and leave. Her great-grandmother is AKC-ASCA CH Rainyday's The Beat Goes On ROM X-I ROM C-III "Tempo."

Mari Jebens · Gussie's great-granddaughter is KyrokaNShaman Kentucky Rain RA OA OAJ ASCA JS-N RS-N RN "Macy." Her sire is Kyroka's Keepin' the Beat and her dam is Shaman You Know Who.

Ann Fulton · Gussie certainly did her share!

Sharon Sparks · I knew who Gussie was from just seeing her picture. She sure had a stamp. Pretty girl.

Nancy Brooke · AKC GCH-CH ASCA CH Hearthside Nothin' To Lose CD RN CGC AKC ROM-C-II ROM X-III ASCA HOF is a great-grandson of Yukon and Gussie. Reading about them, I can definitely see the family traits. It's a wonderful way to gain insight into their personalities and learn about the qualities they passed down to their kids, grandkids and great-grandkids.

Paula Kardum-Booth · Love those ears!

Gussie's granddaughter Rainyday's Rockin' Robin AKC-ASCA CD RA NAC TN-E NJC WV-O NJC GS-N PS1 PD1 PJ1 CL1-S CL1-R CL2-F CL1-H CGC TDi "Robin." Born 2003. By AKC-CKC-ASCA CH Written and Directed By Timaru x AKC CH Rainyday's Free As A Bird CGC USASA HOFX-ASCA HOF. Photo courtesy of Karyn Jones. Photo credit: Kenneth Reed.

Gussie's great-great-grandson Rainyday's Fire 'N Ice NA NAJ RS-O GS-O-OP JS-O JSA-N GSA-N "Gunner." Born 2013. By AKC-ASCA CH Rainyday's I Got My Game On AKC-ASCA CD AKC RE ASCA REM STDs NA NAJ RS-E GS-E JS-E-OP x AKC-ASCA CH Rainyday's Eleanor Rigby ROM X-II ROM P-I. Photo courtesy of Sydney Munger. Photo credit: Heidi Dahms Foster Photography.

Gussie's grandson AKC-ASCA CH Rainyday's Desperado ROM X-III ROM P-II ROM O-I ASCA HOF "Baker." Born 2002. By AKC-CKC-ASCA CH Written N Directed By Timaru x AKC-ASCA CH Rainyday's Life in the Fast Lane AKC-ASCA CD OA OAJ RS-E JS-O GS-N EAC OJC TN-N TG-N. Baker is the sire of AKC GCH-ASCA CH Hearthside's Nothin' To Lose CD RN ROM X-II ROM C-II ASCA HOF. Photo courtesy of Kate Johnson. Photo credit: Rinehart.

Lisa Durand · AKC CH Peppertree's This One's For The Girls RN "Cory" is Gussie's great-granddaughter. Her sire is AKC-ASCA CH Melody's The Beat Goes On and her dam is AKC-INT-ASCA CH Rainyday's You Made Me Love U.

Claudia Bosselmann · Love her ears. Her great-great-grandson Kanoa has them too.

Lacey Kafer · Gussie's great-granddaughter ASCA Alt Premier A-CH ATCH II Mithril's Kiss Me Kate AKC RA ASCA RNX RM STDc OTDs OA OAJ "Roxie" was the 2016-2017 #1 Altered Conformation Dog as well as the #1 Altered bitch, #2 overall in 2014-2015.

Roxie is an independent thinker with a naughty streak, much like her great-granddam Gussie. She is sassy, serious, and my constant shadow. Some people would describe her as a harder dog, but she was exactly what I needed. I couldn't imagine a more perfect dog to learn with, she forgave me time and time again for terrible handling in agility, incorrect commands in stock, and heightened stress levels in the conformation ring.

Laurie Reeter-Brown · My heartdog is Elliot and Gussie's granddaughter Rainyday's Elliot Can Fly AX AXJ RS-E JS-E GS-O NAC NCC CGC "Elliot." She's sired by SVCH PCH ATCH WTCH AKC-ASCA CH Rainyday's Remember When AKC-ASCA CDX AKC RAE ASCA REM HIAs HSAcd RTDs AX AXJ NF NAP

NJP RS-E-OP JS-E-OP GS-E-SP EAC NGC NJC TG-O WV-O TN-N and out of AKC-ASCA CH Rainyday GirlsJusWannaHavFun ROM X-III ROM O-I ROM P-I.

Kim Waller · Gussie's grandson AKC-ASCA Rainyday's Joint Venture NA NAJ RN HIC ROM X-I "Venture" is sired by AKC-INT-ASCA CH Bluestems Man-O-Firethorne USASA HOFX-ASCA HOF and out of AKC CH Rainyday's Free As A Bird CGC USASA HOFX-ASCA HOF.

Deborah Hanson · My multi-titled Rainyday's Life On Mars "Marley" was from Gussie's second litter with AKC-ASCA CH Cobbercrest's Shooting Star CGC TDi, and she was a singleton. She was my first agility dog and the first of four beloved Rainyday agility dogs that I have had the pleasure of calling my teammates. Marley and I got hooked on agility and competed in six venues. She ended up with these titles before her death Sept. 15, 2007. AKC: MX, MXJ, AXP, AJP, and CGC. ASCA: GV-N, RV-O, JV-O. CPE: C-ATCH, C-ATE. NADAC: OAC, OGC, OJC-O. UKC: U-ACH. USDAA: AD, PD1. I thank Kate and Linda and Marley for the lifestyle that I enjoy today!

Gussie's great-granddaughter ASCA Alt Premier A-CH ATCH II Mithril's Kiss Me Kate AKC RA ASCA RNX RM STDc OTDs OA OAJ "Roxie." Born 2011. #1 Altered Conformation Dog in 2016-2017, #1 Altered bitch, #2 overall in 2014-2015. By AKC-ASCA CH Rainyday's Desperado ROM X-III ROM P-II ROM O-I ASCA HOF x ATCH A-CH Mithril's Meant to be Kissed ASCA HOF. Photo courtesy of Lacey Kafer.

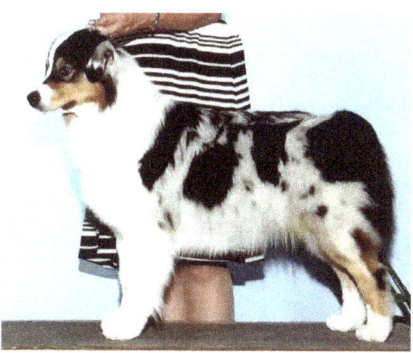

AKC-ASCA CH Rainyday's As You Like It NAP NJP NF JS-N "Arden." Born 2012. She has three lines to Gussie. By AKC GCH-ASCA CH Highpoint's Sweet William x AKC-ASCA CH Rainyday's Time After Time. Photo courtesy of Kate Johnson. Photo credit: Downey.

Gussie's great-great-granddaughter BISS AKC-AKC Bronze GCH Empyrean n CopperRidge's Queen B "Bria." Born 2013. By GCH CopperRidge's Quincy Jones ROM X-II ROM C-I x AKC GCHS CopperRidge's Sugar n Spice ROM C-I. Photo courtesy of Stephen Blanco. Photo credit: Amber Jade Aanensen.

Gussie's great-granddaughter AKC CH Myshara's Homecoming Queen "Haley." Born 2008. By AKC CH Fiann Silver Sabre at Myshara x AKC CH Myshara's Prom Queen. Photo courtesy of Sharon Fontanini. Photo credit: Bill Meyer.

Gussie's grandson AKC GCH Fiann Silver Sabre of Myshara "Lance." Born 2006. By AKC CH Briarbrooks Quicksilver ROM X-II ROM C-II x AKC-ASCA CH Rainyday's The Beat Goes On ROM X-I ROM C-III. Photo courtesy of Sharon Fontanini.

Gussie's granddaughter Rainyday's Elliot Can Fly AX AXJ RS-E JS-E GS-O NAC NCC CGC "Elliot." Born 2007. By SVCH PCH ATCH WTCH AKC ASCA CH Rainyday's Remember When AKC ASCA CDX AKC RE ASCA REM HIAs HSAcd RTDs AX AXJ NF NAP NJP RS-E-OP JS-E-OP GS-E-SP EAC NGC NJC TG-O WV-O TN-N x AKC-ASCA CH Rainyday GirlsJusWannaHavFun ROM X-III ROM O-I ROM P-I. Photo courtesy of Laurie Reeter-Brown.

Gussie's daughter C-ATCH C-ATE Rainyday's Life On Mars MX MXB MXJ MJB AXP AJP RV-O JV-O GV-N OAC OGC OJC-O PI AD CGC "Marley." Born 1996. By AKC-ASCA CH Cobbercrest's Shooting Star CGC TDi x Gussie. Photo courtesy of Deborah Hanson.

Karyn Jones · My girl "Robin," Gussie's granddaughter, Rainyday's Rockin' Robin AKC-ASCA CD RA NAC TN-E NJC WV-O NJC GS-N PS1 PD1 PJ1 CL1-S CL1-R CL2-F CL1-H CGC TDi was born in 2003 Her sire was AKC-CKC-ASCA CH Written and Directed By Timaru and her dam was AKC CH Rainyday's Free As A Bird CGC USASA HOFX-ASCA HOF. Robin was dubbed the "rocket" by our fellow agility competitors. Her drive and willingness to please was over the top and she had a "turn-off" switch no one could believe. I once joked to Kate that she sent me an adult dog in an eight-week-old puppy suit—always so serious, never doing anything wrong. We did so many first things together. She is my once in a lifetime dog!

Stephen Blanco · Gussie's great-great-granddaughter "Bria" is BISS AKC Bronze GCH Empyrean n CopperRidge's Queen B. She was born in 2013. She was sired by AKC GCH CopperRidge's Quincy Jones ROM X-II ROM C-I and her dam is AKC Silver GCH CopperRidge's Sugar n Spice ROM C-I. Bria finished quickly in a few weekends out. She won a large USASA Best in Specialty Show at two years old.

Gussie's great-grandson AKC GCH-ASCA CH Hearthside Nothin' To Lose CD RN CGC ROM-X-III ROM-C-II ASCA HOF "Bodie." Born 2006. BOS Veteran 2016 ASCA National Specialty, BOS 2011 Westminster, #1 ASCA Intact Conformation Dog 2009-10. By AKC-ASCA CH Rainyday's Desperado ROM-X-III ROM-P-II ROM-O-I ASCA HOF x AKC-ASCA CH Hearthside Say Goodnite Gracie. Photo courtesy of Nancy Brooke. Photo credit: Amber Jade Aanensen.

Gussie's granddaughter AKC-ASCA CH Rainyday's Roses Are Red USASA HOFX-ASCA HOF "Rose." Born 1999. By AKC-INT-ASCA CH Bluestems Man-O-Firethorne USASA HOFX-ASCA HOF x AKC CH Rainyday's Free As A Bird CGC USASA HOFX-ASCA HOF. Photo courtesy of Kate Johnson. Photo credit: Thornapple.

Gussie's great-granddaughter AKC-ASCA CH Rainyday's Awesome Blossom ROM X-II ROM P-III ROM O-III ASCA HOF "Poppy." Born 2003. By Peppertree's Magic By Moonlight USASA HOFX-ASCA HOF x Rose (above). Photo courtesy of Kate Johnson. Photo credit: Thornapple.

Gussie's great-great-granddaughter AKC-ASCA CH Rainyday's Playin' With The Boys "Charlie." Born 2007. By AKC-ASCA CH Calais Carolina Rebel Yell ASCA HOF x Poppy (above). Photo courtesy of Kate Johnson. Photo credit: Pix N Pages.

Gussie's great-granddaughter BIS BISS AKC GCH- ASCA CH Myshara's Dancing Queen "Abby." Born 2008. Winner of AKC All-breed Best In Show, Best In Specialty Show, Award of Merit USASA National Specialty. By AKC CH Fiann Silver Sabre at Myshara x AKC CH Myshara's Prom Queen. Photo courtesy of Sharon Fontanini. Photo credit: Turley.

Gussie's granddaughter AOM BISS AKC CH Fiann Windchimes ROM C-I "China." Born 2006. Award of Merit 2009 Westminster Kennel Club show. By AKC CH Briarbrooks Quicksilver ROM X-II ROM C-II x AKC-ASCA CH Rainyday's The Beat Goes On ROM X-I ROM C-III. Photo courtesy of Heather Moyer and Patti Herhold. Photo credit: John Ashbey.

"Yukon's impact on this breed was phenomenal. Yes, his pedigree dictated such a destiny; but all too often, the best of the best on paper doesn't mean the dog will make his mark.

A few are born great; a few achieve greatness; a few produce greatness. Yukon was truly one of the few great dogs!"

— Tim Preston

Photo courtesy of Tim Preston

AKC-INT-ASCA Champion
Bluestem's Man-O-Firethorne
USASA HOFX Sire #8 - ASCA HOF Sire #140

Call name: Yukon
Born: 1996
Sire: Briarbrooks Black Arrogance
Dam: AKC CH Firethorne's Finishing Touch
Breeder: Bruce Isaacson
Owners: Tim J. Preston and Debbie Duffecy and Jenna Duffecy, Cobbercrest

"Yukon was bred by Bruce Isaacson under the guidance of Ken Kimball DVM. I first saw the puppy at seven weeks of age at Ken's veterinary clinic. I attempted to buy him then, but other plans for Yukon had already been made.

The following year, my friend Linda Wilson of Briarbrook mentioned she was showing a blue dog for Ken. She said the dog was quite handsome and thought I'd find him appealing. We had a good laugh because Linda had misunderstood Ken when he told her the dog's name, which was "Utah." The dog didn't seem to know his name anyway and Linda had been calling him Yukon for months! I was surprised to learn this was the puppy I had been unable to buy from Ken the previous year.

At that time I owned "Chevy" who was from Ken's breeding program, and who had proven to be a red producer. Ken was keenly interested in owning a red-producing dog. Chevy had sired a beautiful litter and one of the pups became the lovely MBIS MBISS AKC-ASCA CH Rainyday's Red Red Wine "Merlot."

While I'd been successful in showing Chevy to his AKC and International championships, I was not convinced I wanted to keep him. So I suggested to Ken that we trade. He could have the red-producing dog in exchange for the blue dog that I'd wanted all along—Yukon.

In anticipation of the trade happening, I brought Chevy to the next show with me. After Yukon finished competing (he was Winner's Dog that day), the trade was made. We both felt victorious. Little did we know what a huge impact Yukon was about to make on the Australian Shepherd breed!

When I brought Yukon home, I noticed there was an area in his lower back that didn't look or feel right, and his rear movement (especially one leg) had a hitch in the action. There was the possibility that he just wasn't as clean-moving in the rear as I would have preferred. But there were so many other things about Yukon that I loved that I decided it would only be a concern if he was unable to pass his OFA hip exam. I immediately scheduled his preliminary hip X-ray, which showed some mild misalignment; his first prelim rating was OFA Fair.

After several chiropractic visits over the next few months, Yukon made excellent, rapid improvement. He had a second preliminary exam and received an OFA Good.

In 1999, Yukon, who was three years old, won an Award of Merit at Westminster. He also received an Award of Merit at Westminster the following year. Photo courtesy of Tim Preston. Photo credit: John Ashbey.

```
                                CH Briarbrooks Valedictorian HOFX-HOF
Pedigree            AKC CH Kaleidoscope Case In Point ROM C-III
                                CH Briarbrooks Oh My Oh
        Briarbrooks Black Arrogance
                                CH My Main Man Of Heatherhill HOF
                    AKC CH Heatherhill Make Mine Mink
                                CH Starswepts Made Of Mink
AKC-INT-ASCA Ch Bluestem's Man-O-Firethorne USASA HOFX-ASCA HOF
                                CH My Main Man Of Heatherhill HOF
                    AKC CH Briarbrooks Valedictorian HOFX-HOF
                                CH Briarbrooks Silver Sequence ROM C-III
        AKC CH Firethornes Finishing Touch
                                CH Carolina's Oliver Twist CD
                    Lakespring Sophisticated Twist
                                Sudden Reinbow Of Copper Creek
```

Yukon's paternal grandsire AKC CH Kaleidoscope Case In Point ROM C-III "Casey." Born 1994. Sire of 27 champions. Photo courtesy of Linda Wilson. Photo credit: Downey.

Yukon's dam AKC CH Firethorne's Finishing Touch "Heather." Born 1994. Photo credit: Booth.

Soon, Yukon was old enough for his adult OFA grade and it too came back OFA Good.

I can honestly say I always wished he had a bit cleaner rear movement, but because of the severity of the injury to his back and hip region, his chiropractor believed it had improved as much as it was going to. An interesting note is one of the many desirable traits Yukon stamped on his offspring was beautiful rears. I have no doubt his injury was the only factor affecting his own rear movement.

Yukon was a true ambassador of the breed. His temperament was outstanding! He would fiercely alert us to any sign of disturbance or danger, and when all was well, he was the most comical and fun-loving dog you ever met. His gentle, soft eyes were a window into his soul. While he was my best friend, his true devotion was to his co-owner, my dog partner in Cobbercrest, Debbie Duffecy. I teased her that Yukon was at her place for 95% of the breedings so that's why he liked her best (but I knew differently).

Yukon had a tremendously successful show career that included many Best of Breed awards against tough competition in both AKC and ASCA. He was also honored with the prestigious first Award of Merit at Westminster in both 1999 and 2000.

Yukon's impact on this breed was phenomenal. He stamped a regal look on his offspring, which is apparent many generations down the line. He consistently passed on his classic head, beautiful arch of neck, fit of neck to shoulders, clear richness in color and appealing structure. His progeny display proper balance in angulation, proportion and substance.

Yukon was the sire of 63 champions. He was Pedigree's Top Producing Sire for three years and the # 2 sire for two more years. He continues to be one of the top four producing sires in the history of the breed."

- Tim Preston

Some of Yukon's wonderful offspring include:

› AKC-ASCA CH Rainyday's I'm On Fire HT ROM X-III ROMP-I ROM C-I ASCA HOF. Sire of three WTCH.
› AKC-ASCA CH Rainyday's Violets Are Blue USASA HOFX Dam #6, ASCA HOF #233. Dam of:
  › Two AKC BIS winners, two WTCH (one a SVCH as well), one USASA HOFX Dam

Yukon's son AKC CH Cobbercrest Ring of Saturn "Turner." Born 2000. By Yukon x Cobbercrest Rainyday's Yoko Ono. Photo courtesy of Kelley Curtin Catterson. Photo credit: Downey.

Yukon's son AKC-ASCA CH Rainyday's I'm On Fire HT ROM X-III ROM P-I ROM C-I ASCA HOF "Spark." Born 1999. By Yukon x Cobbercrest Propwash Obla-De USASA HOFX-ASCA HOF. Photo courtesy of Kate Johnson. Photo credit: Dan Pearson.

AKC-INT-ASCA CH Bluestem's Man-O-Firethorne USASA HOFX-ASCA HOF

Yukon's great-grandson AKC CH Snowbelt's Copy That! "Jackson." Born 2010. Winner's Dog 2013 USASA National Specialty. By BIS AKC GCH Briarbrooks Copyright x AKC CH Fiann Windchimes ROM C-I. Photo courtesy of Patti Herhold. Photo credit: Jeffrey Hanlin.

Yukon's son AKC-ASCA CH Rainyday's Preston Phillips "Wally." Born 1999. By Yukon x AKC CH Rainyday's Free As A Bird CGC USASA HOFX-ASCA HOF. Photo courtesy of Cheryl Bradley.

› AKC-ASCA CH Rainyday's The Beat Goes On ROM X-I ROM C-III. Pedigree Award for Top Producing Bitch of 2009. Granddam of:
  › BIS BISS AKC GCH-CKC-ASCA CH Copperridge's Fire N Bayouland USASA HOF #12 ASCA HOF #314

› AKC-ASCA CH Rainyday's Life in the Fast Lane AKC-ASCA CD OA OAJ RS-E JS-O GS-N TN-N EAC OJC NJC. Dam of BIS winner. Granddam of:
  › BISS AKC GCH-ASCA CH Hearthside Nothin' To Lose CD RN ROM X-III ROM C-II ASCA HOF #281

› AKC-ASCA CH Rainyday's Roses Are Red USASA HOFX Dam #3 ASCA HOF #212

› AKC-ASCA CH Rainyday GirlsJusWannaHavFun ROM X-III ROM O-I ROM P-I

› BISS AKC-INT CH Rainyday's Tinsel Town RN

› AKC CH Cobbercrest Ring of Saturn. Multiple champion sire

› AKC-ASCA CH Rainyday's We Have No Secrets

› AKC CH Thornapple Kahlua N Cream. Great-granddam of:
  › MBIS BISS CH Wind Spirit Rod's Amazing Grace

› AKC CH Thornapple Silken Flame. Dam of:
  › VEW 2015, INT-DNK-NOR CH Thornapple Ruby Passion
  › AKC-DNK-GBR-NOR-DEU CH Thornapple Aftershock. Sire of:
    DNK-KLBVE CH Thornapple Up The Ante
    DNK-NOR CH-NORD JW 2012 Chiljas Annie Get Your Gun
    DEU-VDH-CH DNK Illumineer Magnolia Mill
    BALT-EST-LT-LV JCH-LT JW 2012 Leading Angel's The Devils Diamond

- MACH CKC-UKC-ASCA CH After All's Under Cover AKC-ASCA CD AKC RN ASCA RNX STDds MXB MJS MXP MJP RS-E GS-N JV-E-SP SSA AD PJ3 HIT CGCA
- AKC CH Thornapple Bedazzled
- AKC CH Shoreland's Wish Upon a Star
- AKC GCH Alnairs Liberty For All BN RN CGCA
- OTCH Navarro's Runs with Scissors UDX18 OM7
- AKC CH Cobbercrest Razzle Dazzle
- AKC CH Cobbercrest Red Ruffian
- MACH3 Triple T Cooper MXC MJC MXP2 MJP
- MACH Rainyday's Fire In The Sky CD RN MXS MJS
- Cobbercrest Jackpot of T-K CDX RE OA OAJ AXP AJP

Yukon was a great sire whose sons and daughters also became outstanding sires and dams of the next generation. Yukon's name can be found in the pedigrees of many Australian Shepherds in conformation show rings today, both in the United States and abroad.

Yukon's grandson AKC-DNK-GBR-NOR-DEU CH Thornapple Aftershock "Diablo." Born 2003. World Winner 2008, VWW 2012, Crufts Winner 2007, 2008, 2011, 3 x DK Winner 2006, 2007, 2009. By CH Ragtime's Light It Up x AKC CH Thornapple Silken Flame. Photo courtesy of Bitta Wöhliche. (DENMARK)

Yukon's daughter AKC CH Thornapple Bedazzled "Dazzle." Born 2000. By Yukon x Thornapple Godess of The Hunt. Photo courtesy of Thornapple.

Yukon's daughter AKC CH Thornapple Silken Flame "Halle." Born 2000. By Yukon x Thornapple Godess of The Hunt. Photo courtesy of Thornapple.

Yukon's great-grandson DNK-NO-PL-INT-KLB CH KBHV15 Leading Angel's Gaze At The Stars "Brad Pitt." Born 2012. By Multi CH Collinswood House Rules x DNK-NOCH-KLBVE CH KBHVV15 Thornapple Queen of Diamonds. Photo courtesy of Bitta Wöhliche. (DENMARK)

Yukon's double great-grandson DNK-PL CH Leading Angel's Diamond Shockwave "Shahen." Born 2010. By AKC-DNK-GBR-NOR-DEU CH Thornapple Aftershock x DNK-NOCH-KLBVE CH KBHVV15 Thornapple Queen of Diamonds. Photo courtesy of Bitta Wöhliche. (DENMARK)

Yukon's granddaughter DNK-NOCH-KLBVE CH KBHVV15 Thornapple Queen of Diamonds "Sycamore." Born 2006. By AKC CH Thornapple King of Diamonds x AKC CH Thornapple Bedazzled. Photo courtesy of Bitta Wöhliche. (DENMARK)

Yukon's great-great-granddaughter Multi CH Leading Angel's Gondola Courtship "Venice." Born 2010. By Multi CH Thornapple Cuba Blue x CH Thornapple Up The Ante. Photo courtesy of Bitta Wöhliche. (DENMARK)

Yukon's grandpups. (Left to right) Oklahoma Sky of Woolly Rocks "Sky." One Dozen Roses of Woolly Rocks "Doa." Ol' Time Rock and Roll of Woolly Rocks "Rock." Oranje Blossom Special of Woolly Rocks "Hazel." Born 2015. By ASCA CH Carolina Calais Get UR Motor Runnin OTDs ATDd RS-N JS-O RN x Lilac Wine of Woolly Rocks. Photo courtesy of Jill Foreman. (BELGIUM)

CONVERSATIONS

Marlene Deleage · Gorgeous!

Ann Fulton · Beautiful dog!

Tim Preston · There are so many beautiful Yukon descendants! His handsome grandson AKC-DNK-GBR-NOR-DEU CH Thornapple Aftershock "Diablo," who was owned by Bitta Wöhliche in Denmark, was an outstanding sire.

Tan Ja Heit Müller · Yukon was the beautiful great-grandfather of my boy INT CH Leading Angel's Diamond Afterglow "Coffee." He was by Multi CH Thornapple Aftershock x Multi CH Thornapple Queen of Diamonds.

Nevenka Nikolic · Yukon was just a perfect, beautiful and gorgeous Aussie!

Klári Király · Very, very nice.

Karen Rose · My new boy, Gatorheaven's Break the Bank, is Yukon's great-great-grandson.

Sherry Randall Ball · Yukon was the best of the best!

Patti Herhold · Yukon's granddaughter AKC CH Fiann Windchimes ROM C-I "China" was born in 2006. She was awarded an AOM at the 2009 Westminster show and BOS at the 2008 HVASA National Specialty. China was by BIS CH Briarbrooks Quicksilver ROM X-II ROM C-II x AKC-ASCA CH Rainyday's The Beat Goes On ROM X-I ROM C-III. She had a gorgeous long neck, great shoulders and forearm, and she passed those qualities on to many of her offspring. Her son AKC CH Snowbelt's Copy That! was Winner's Dog at the 2013 USASA Nationals.

Yukon's son ASCA CH Carolina Calais Get UR Motor Runnin OTDs ATDd RS-N JS-O RN "Huck." Born 2007. By Yukon x AKC-ASCA CH Calais Carolina Mustang Sally. Photo courtesy of Geneviève Chomé. (BELGIUM)

Yukon's great-great-grandson DJCH-Dutch CH Dailo's Running With My Boots On "Frazer." Born 2014. By CH Dailo's Black Label x Dailo's Pocket Full of Sunshine. Photo courtesy of Renate Agterberg. Photo credit: Michel Agterberg. (NETHERLANDS)

Yukon's great-great-granddaughter CH Clubwinner 2016 Los Perros Locos Cute Flowerpower VT RO-B RO-1 "Kate." Born 2011. By RisingStar Message In A Bottle x Old Kauri Tree Absolutely Cute. Photo courtesy of Josefine Junge. (GERMANY)

Yukon's great-great-great-grandson Soulwind A Touch of Magic "Oscar." Born 2015. By CH JCH Happy Spark All Fired Up NLJCH, BEJW'13 x CH Los Perros Locos Cute Flowerpower RO-B RO-1 VT CLUBSGR'16 Photo courtesy of Josefine Junge. (GERMANY)

Yukon's great-granddaughter Coultrip's Robin La Rouge "Happy." By AKC CH Echolake's Merlin Rouge x Coultrip's Lucille Ball. Photo courtesy of Robin De Villiers. (CANADA)

Yukon's daughter AKC CH Thornapple Kahlua N Cream "Kahlua." Born 2000. By Yukon x Paradox Ponder This. Photo courtesy of Thornapple.

Yukon's great-great-grandson MBISS Multi ASCA Premier ASCA-INT-BE-LUX-NL-DE-Dt.(Club) CH Sunnycreek's Heavenly Happy Hunk RN RS-N JS-O GS-N NLJCH BECW'17, BS'13'16, NLJW'11 "Thunder." Born 2010. By CH Moon Rise Latin Lover x CH Pur Plesurs Soft Rendition. Photo courtesy of Karin Dekker. Photo credit: Amber Jade Aanensen. (NETHERLANDS)

Laura Kirk · Yukon's granddaughter China was a really beautiful girl.

Tim Preston · Yes, China was so beautiful!

Alex Weber · Yukon was a great, great dog!

Renate Agterberg · Ohhh I loved this boy.

Lyn Scanlan · Handsome!

Cedar Hill Aussies · My AKC-ASCA CH Cedar Hill Bel Ami Park Ave Blues "Parker" is a double Yukon granddaughter.

Jenna Duffecy · Parker is beautiful!

Lish Curtis · Yukon's grandson Prestige All Charged Up is by ASCA CH Spring Fever's Got My Game On (Yukon x AKC-ASCA CH Spring Fever's I'll Be True ASCA HOF) and out of BISS AKC-ASCA CH Stone Ridge She's All That (AKC-AUS-ASCA CH Heatherhill Montel Williams ASCA HOF x ASCA CH Stoneridge CR Red Legend ASCA HOF).

Lisa Durand · I have a lovely Yukon great-granddaughter AKC CH Peppertree's This One's For The Girls RN (ASCA major pointed) "Cory." Her sire is ASCA

Yukon's great-great-grandson RBIS MBISS AKC Gold GCH-ASCA CH Shadomoons The Competitive Edge RN CA CGC "Trump." Born 2012. By BIS AKC GCH-ASCA CH Equinox The Edge of Reason RE x UKC CH Shenandoah Diamond In The Ruff. Photo courtesy of Pat Zapf. Photo credit: Jeffrey Hanlin.

CH Melody's The Beat Goes On and her dam is AKC-INT-ASCA CH Rainyday's You Made Me Love U. Cory was bred by Sheila Hall and is a great-granddaughter of Yukon through her dam. She's my heart dog, the love of my life, and a wonderful producer of outstanding Aussies.

Kate Johnson · Cory's dam AKC-INT-ASCA CH Rainyday's You Made Me Love U was a daughter of AKC-ASCA CH Rainyday's I'm On Fire HT ROM X-III ROM C-I ROM P-I ASCA HOF "Spark" out of a bitch who was a sister of AKC-INT-ASCA CH McMatt's EZ Going OA OAJ USASA HOFX-ASCA HOF "Cruiser."

Pat Zapf · My RBIS MBISS Gold GCH ASCA CH Shadomoons The Competitive Edge RN CA is Yukon's great-great-grandson.

Judy Chard · Love, love, love!

Renate Agterberg · Yukon was the great-great-grandsire of my DJCH-Dutch CH Dailo's Running With My Boots On "Frazer."

Kirstie Venton New · Shenkiri Rolling Thunder "Bumble" is Yukon's grandson. He was born in 2006 and is still enjoying life. His sire is AKC-FIN-SWE-EST

CH Thornapple Hot Wheels and his dam is Moortime Magic Of The Moors at Shenkiri ShCM. He's owned by Gemma and Robyn Taylor Jones and Louise Taylor, and I always handle him in the showring. At his only time at Crufts he earned a Very Good 2nd in the Veteran class. Bumble's litter sister Shenkiri Dancing Rainbow Over Mistyisle ShCM "Bea" gained one RCC in the UK.

Josefine Junge · CH Clubwinner '16 Los Perros Locos Cute Flowerpower VT RO-B RO-1 "Kate" is Yukon's great-great-granddaughter. She's by RisingStar Message In A Bottle and out of Old Kauri Tree Absolutely Cute. Her son is linebred to Yukon. He's Yukon's great-great-great-grandson Soulwind A Touch of Magic.

Tracy Thorstenson · AKC GCH Bailiwick Red Hot Chili Pepper "Foster" is by Yukon and out of AKC CH Alnairs Hot Topic. Foster is a goofball, always happy. After reading Tim's comments about Yukon, I now know where Foster gets his personality. I've been told he has some of Yukon's other habits too.

Heather Mee · Lamintone Enchanted Fire is Yukon's granddaughter through her sire AKC-ASCA CH Rainyday's I'm On Fire HT ROM X-III ROM C-I ROM P-I ASCA HOF. She is out of Lamintone It's All About Me and was bred by Jayne Holligan and myself.

Karen H. Wilson · We bred our foundation bitch AKC CH Thornapple's Hope Diamond HSAs to Yukon for her last litter and were blessed with 12 puppies. Two became champions and all the puppies had great temperaments.

Yukon's great-granddaughter AKC-ASCA CH Lastcall's Test for Echo "Echo." Born 2013. By AKC GCH-ASCA CH Highpoint's Sweet William x ASCA CH Lastcall's Lady in Black CD RV-O JV-E GV-O. Photo courtesy of Kim Gorman. Photo credit: Amber Jade Aanensen.

Yukon's great-great-grandson INT CH Narita Farms Will to Win HCT JHD HT "Wally." Born 2007. By CH Peppertree's Irish Crème x Casa Dey's Lace A Mickey Girl. Photo courtesy of Narita Siegel. Photo credit: Cheryl Siler.

Yukon's great-granddaughter CH Rafter Creek's Daddy's Girl "Neyla." Born 2011. By CH Mill Creek's Night Flight x CH Mill Creek's Guidance By The Stars. Photo courtesy of Claudia Bosselmann. Photo credit: Michaela Jüstel. (GERMANY)

Yukon's son MACH CKC-UKC-ASCA CH After All's Under Cover AKC-ASCA CD AKC RN ASCA RNX STDds MXB MJS MXP MJP RS-E GS-N JV-E-SP SSA AD PJ3 HIT CGCA "Spencer." Born 2001. By Yukon x INT-UKC-ASCA CH Dewmoor Work of Art Afterall HIC ASCA HOF. Photo courtesy of Ron Niemzyk. Photo credit: Alex Smith.

Yukon's daughter Thornapple Moon On Fire "Lunar." Born 2004. By Yukon x CH Thornapple Honey I'm Home. Photo courtesy of Kennel Easy. (SWEDEN)

Yukon's great-great-granddaughter BISS NUCH Illumineer Wonderful M "Kiera." Born 2013. By Multi CH Leading Angel's Esteemed Thornapple RN RA HT PT x DKCH DKRLCH Bayshore Stonehaven Vanilla Twilight RN RA LP1. Photo courtesy of Elisabeth Eknes. Photo credit: Simone Lunheim. (NORWAY)

Yukon's great-great-granddaughter RBIS-INT-NL-BE-DE-Dt. CH (Club) CH Skaye's Adoring Shining Sparkle NLJCH, NLJW'10 "Sparkle." Born 2009. By CH Mill Creek's Night Flight x CH Jess's Dancing in the Skaye. Photo courtesy of Karin Dekker. (NETHERLANDS)

Jennifer Hampton · My Yukon daughter ASCA CH Happy Trails Tattoo Tears, my beautiful "Angelina," received a Premier Award at the 2007 ASCA National Specialty. She's given me many beautiful offspring. I also had Mill Creek's Bling It On "Hawk" who was sired by Yukon's son AKC CH Cobbercrest Ring Of Saturn.

Marsha Settles · Yukon was a beautiful dog!

Judy Gassert · Gorgeous!

Tina Lass · He was Aussome!

Kelley Curtin Catterson · Yukon was one of the best in our breed. I loved that dog.

Melanie Magamoll · Handsome dude!

Kate Johnson · One of my all-time favorite dogs.

Nellie Morack · I have a Yukon granddaughter and two of his great-grandkids. All are champions and have wonderful temperaments.

Jayne Holligan · Mine too!

Sandy Cornwell · Yukon was a gorgeous dog.

Michael Mayhew · My Yukon grandson AKC CH Storm Front's Take No Prisoners PT CAT "Thunder" was the first Australian Shepherd in the world

Yukon's great-grandson Multi BIS, Multi CH Risingstar's Billion Dollar Baby "Christoff." Born 2011. By AKC GCH CH-ASCA CH Two By Two's The Pipes Are Piping x CH Risingstar's Sugar 'N Spice. Photo credit: Ximena Barrera. (EL SALVADOR)

Yukon's great-grandson C.I.B DK CH DKV-10, FIV-10, NORDV-11, SEVV-16 Thornapple Mercury All Jacked Up "Jack." Born 2008. By AKC CH Thornapple All Fired Up x AKC CH Thornapple Straight Up. Photo courtesy of Kennel Easy. (SWEDEN)

Yukon's great-grandson AKC Silver GCH-ASCA CH Adore's Double Deuce "Dalton." Born 2010. By AKC GCH-ASCA CH Hearthside's Ready Set Go! RN TD x CH Adore's Hot Shot OAJ. Photo courtesy of Kim Gorman. Photo credit: Amber Jade Aanensen.

Yukon's granddaughter Lamintone Enchanted Fire "Haze." Born 2017. By AKC-ASCA CH Rainyday's I'm On Fire HT ROM X-III ROM C-I ROM P-I ASCA HOF x Lamintone Its All About Me. Photo courtesy of Heather Mee. Photo by Lamintone. (UNITED KINGDOM)

Yukon's great-grandson Multi GCH-Multi CH Hyland's Keylime "Keylime." Born 2007. Caribbean Breed Winner (Guatemala 2011). By CH Sherbil's Hearttrobdesertsky x Hyland's Starlite Starbrite. Photo credit: Ximena Barrera. (EL SALVADOR)

Yukon's great-granddaughter AKC GCH-ASCA CH Rainyday's Wonderful Tonight NAJ RS-N JS-O GS-N "Layla." Born 2016. By AKC-ASCA CH Goldcrest Cameo Captivator x AKC-ASCA CH Rainyday's Eleanor Rigby ROM X-II ROM P-I. Photo courtesy of Jennifer Criswell Bernard. Photo credit: Sarah Kalkes.

Yukon's grandson VDH CH-Dt CH (Club) ObCH -MVA Mill Creek's Night Flight "Kanoa." Born 2004. VDH Bundessieger 2006/2007/2009. By AKC CH Cobbercrest Ring of Saturn x CH Mill Creek's She'll Be A McMatt. Photo courtesy of Claudia Bosselmann. (GERMANY)

to complete his CAT Trial and be awarded the Coursing Ability Test title. This boy did everything ever asked of him and more.

Claudia Bosselmann · My dog Multi CH Mill Creek's Night Flight "Kanoa" was a son of AKC CH Cobbercrest Ring of Saturn. It was a big present to get this dog from Debbie Tapp as he was a truly versatile and beautiful dog. He was a Multiple Champion, Multiple Club Winner, Multiple National Winner, FCI Century Winner and VDH Century Winner. Those titles were won under American breeder judges. On top of that he was an Obedience Champion and a National Champion Rally Obedience at the age of 11 years. He was a wonderful performance dog and he loved Obedience. Kanoa was a successful sire with champions in several countries in Europe. We unfortunately lost him last year, but he will leave his pawprint in his progeny here in Europe.

Kanoa's daughter CH Rafter Creek's Daddy's Girl "Neyla" is linebred on Yukon. She is out of CH Mill Creek's Guidance By The Stars "Jamie" who is Yukon's great-granddaughter. Neyla is a very successful show dog. She's a Multiple Champion, National Winner, Club Winner and a wonderful performance dog. She was Most Versatile Australian Shepherd Female two years in a row in Germany.

Lynn Godbee · I'm proud to have a Yukon grandson as one of my two heart dogs. He is AKC GCH-CKC CH Spotlight's Roll Tide Roll BN CD RA "Saban."

Summer Jewel Fuls · I'm so glad to have Yukon in my pedigrees.

Robin De Villiers · Coultrip's Robin La Rouge "Happy" is Yukon's great-granddaughter. Her name Happy totally defines her spirit. She's balanced, confident, and resourceful. She takes charge in a quiet manner. She's a remarkable girl. I have Happy descendants, and we are all very happy for this.

Yukon's great-grandson INT CH Leading Angel's Diamond Afterglow "Coffee." Born 2010. By Multi CH Thornapple Aftershock x Multi CH Thornapple Queen of Diamonds. Photo courtesy of Tanja Heit Müller. Photo by Jennifer Fiedler. (GERMANY)

Yukon's daughter ASCA CH Rainday Dawn's Early Light "Rori." Born 1999. By Yukon x Cobbercrest Propwash Obla-De USASA HOFX-ASCA HOF. Photo courtesy of Tim Preston. Photo credit: Debbie Duffecy.

Yukon's great-great-granddaughter CKC BIS GCH Starwoods Exclusive Affair RE CD "Ziva." Born 2010. By AKC GCH Briarbrooks All Rights Reserved x CKC CH Starwoods Focus On A Dream RN. Photo courtesy of Phyllis McCullum. Photo credit: Bonnie O'Brien.

Yukon's great-great-granddaughter DJCH-Dutch CH Dailo's Thinking Out of the Box "Candy." Born 2014. By CH Dailo's Black Label x Dailo's Pocket Full of Sunshine. Photo courtesy of Renate Agterberg. Photo credit: Michel Agterberg. (NETHERLANDS)

Petra Mostert · Yukon is in all my pedigrees from Thornapple. He was beautiful!

Becky Hornburg Pugh · Wow!

Phyllis McCullum · CKC BIS GCH Starwoods Exclusive Affair CD RE "Ziva" is Yukon's great-great-granddaughter via the Ricki x Tempo cross. Her sire is AKC GCH Briarbrooks All Rights Reserved and her dam is CKC CH Starwoods Focus On A Dream RN.

Ximena Barrera · Ohhh Yukon! He's hands-down one of my all time favorite Aussies! I'm so lucky and grateful to have two great-grandsons of Yukon in Central America! One boy is my Multi Group Winner, International CH, Latin American CH, Pan American CH, The Americas & The Caribbean Breed Winner (Guatemala 2011), Guatemala CH, Salvadoran GCH, Cuzcatleco GCH Hyland's Keylime "Keylime." And my other handsome boy is Multi BIS, Multi Group Winner, International CH, Central American CH, Pan American CH, Latin American CH, UNCACEN (Union of The Caribbean & Central America) CH, Guatemalan CH, Salvadoran CH, Cuzcatleco CH Risingstar's Billion Dollar Baby "Christoff." Both of them heart dogs and the foundation to my breeding program!

Georgann Weisgerber · Beautiful!

Kimberly Daemers · I have Yukon's great-great-grandson BE-MONT-HR CH Amigo Labakan Slovakia. He was born in 2011 and is by Silver Dreams Aussie Land Rover and out of Chessie Labakan Puella Fera.

Tim Preston · ASCA CH Rainday Dawn's Early Light was owned by Cobbercrest and bred by Rainday. She was by Yukon x Cobbercrest Propwash Obla-De USASA HOFX-ASCA HOF.

Yukon's great-great-grandson Limistars The Winner Takes It All "Dias." Born 2013. By INT-DNK CH Thornapple Mercury All Jacked Up x Dalorogarden Olivia. Photo courtesy of Cassandra Milly Wikgren. Photo credit: Erika Fundberg. (SWEDEN)

Yukon's great-great-granddaughter CKC GCH Thornapple I've Got Everybody Lookin' "Sade." Born 2015. By AKC GCH Thornapple Headout OnThe Hiway x AKC CH Thornapple Lips Unbuttoned. Photo courtesy of Julie Plourde. Photo credit: Angela Slauenwhite and Collin Veinot. (CANADA)

Julie Plourde · CKC GCH Thornapple I've Got Everybody Lookin' "Sade" is out of AKC GCH Thornapple Headout OnThe Hiway "Sturgis" x CH Thornapple Lips Unbuttoned "Kiyana." Yukon is Sade's great-great-grandsire.

Stephen Blanco · AKC GCH Empyrean's Bullseye at CopperRidge "Archer" finished in three weekends, going BOB over the #1 and #2 Aussies in the country. He won the 6-9 class at the USASA National Specialty under respected judge Houston Clark. He is by AKC GCH CopperRidge's Quincy Jones ROM X-II ROM C-I and out of AKC Silver GCH CopperRidge's Sugar n Spice ROM C-I.

Yukon's great-great-grandson AKC GCH Empyrean's Bullseye at CopperRidge "Archer." Born 2013. By AKC GCH CopperRidge's Quincy Jones ROM X-II ROM C-I x AKC Silver GCH CopperRidge's Sugar n Spice ROM C-I. Photo courtesy of Stephen Blanco. Photo credit: Amber Jade Aanensen.

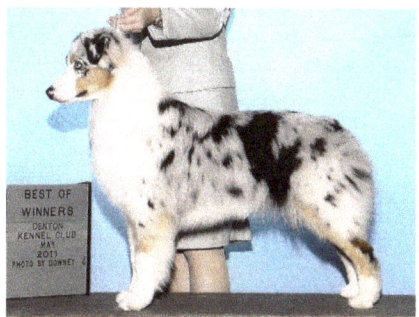

Yukon's granddaughter AKC-ASCA CH Rainyday's Forget-Me-Not ROM X-II "Petal." Born 2003. By Peppertree's Magic By Moonlight USASA HOFX-ASCA HOF x AKC-ASCA CH Rainyday's Roses Are Red USASA HOFX-ASCA HOF. Photo courtesy of Jennifer Criswell Bernard. Photo credit: Jeffrey Hanlin.

Yukon's double granddaughter AKC-ASCA CH Cedar Hill Bel Ami Park Ave Blues "Parker." Born 2009. By AKC CH Cobbercrest Red Ruffian x Cobbercrest Louisiana Hail Mary. Photo courtesy of Cedar Hill Aussies. Photo credit: Downey.

Yukon's grandson Prestige All Charged Up "Kilo." Born 2009. By ASCA CH Spring Fevers Got My Game On x BISS AKC-ASCA CH Stone Ridge She's All That. Photo courtesy of Lish Curtis. Photo credit: Nancy Moe.

Yukon's daughter ASCA CH Happy Trails Tattoo Tears "Angelina." Born 2005. Premier 2007 ASCA National Specialty. By Yukon x Countrywood's Faithful Follower. Photo courtesy of Jennifer Hampton. Photo credit: John Beals.

Yukon's son AKC-ASCA CH Cobbercrest Carpe Diem "Maverick." Yukon x Cobbercrest Rnydays Yoko Ono. Photo courtesy of Douglas Allen. Photo credit: Debbie Duffecy.

Yukon's son AKC CH Cobbercrest Red Ruffian. "Manny." Born 2000. By Yukon x AKC CH Thornapple's What It Takes. Photo courtesy of Tim Preston.

"After Cruiser retired from his conformation career, Becky showed him in agility. While he seemed to enjoy it, sitting on the couch next to me was clearly his Olympic sport.

One of my funny memories of Cruiser was at an agility trial at Purina Farms. Becky was running a course with him, and when he got to the middle of the dog walk, he suddenly stopped. He turned and stared at a cute little black tri bitch who was walking outside the ring with her owner. Becky could not get Cruiser's attention to continue running; he just stared like he had seen a ghost! Everyone laughed, but it surely wasn't funny to Becky or me—very embarrassing, to say the least. Finally, the Aussie girl and her owner passed on by and Cruiser finished the course—way over time. I had to find out why he focused on this girl. I found out it was one of his daughters who he had never met. She was adorable, but I have no idea why she caught his eye while he was going through the course. He just did his own thing.

Most people who are passionate about a breed spend most of their lives working to improve the breed, hoping to have a 'once-in-a-lifetime' dog. I've been very fortunate to have had several, with Cruiser at the top of the list. I was there when he was born and I was there when he passed over the bridge. I love you Cruiser with every bit of my heart."

- Flo McDaniel

Photo courtesy of Flo McDaniel

AKC-INT-ASCA Champion
McMatt's EZ Going OA NAJ
USASA HOFX Sire #13 - ASCA HOF Sire #232

Call name: Cruiser
Born: 1997
Sire: AKC CH McMatt's EZ Victor USASA HOFX-ASCA HOF
Dam: AKC-ASCA CH Castle's Image of McMatt
Breeders: Flo and Matt McDaniel, McMatt
Owners: Flo and Rebecca McDaniel, McMatt

"Cruiser's name was the perfect reflection of his smooth, easy-going movement. He moved correctly because he was built correctly. He had outstanding structure, including a phenomenal shoulder assembly and a perfect rear. Cruiser had balanced angulation, excellent short hocks, beautiful tight feet, and a solid topline that was perfectly level when he gaited.

Along with exceptional soundness, Cruiser had strong bone and gorgeous breed type. He carried a handsome, masculine head with a strong underjaw. Although he measured only 20½" at the shoulder, Cruiser's proud carriage and stocky build made him appear larger.

Cruiser was a prepotent sire who produced excellent offspring, and he was known for producing exceptional bitches. He stamped his lovely front, topline and bone, and put pretty headpieces on his progeny. His litters often contained multiple puppies who became champions. Cruiser sired 55 AKC champions, 10 who achieved Hall of Fame status, and twenty-five performance-titled progeny.

Cruiser was not a dog who would go with just anyone. He was very loyal to his family and particularly to me. We were inseparable. He was definitely 'aloof' with strangers until he got to know them well.

Cruiser would let you know when he was offended. He never liked the 'down' command when Becky worked with him in agility. He gave her a 'look' that made it clear he was not a fan. Even so, he earned his AKC Open Agility title as well as his Novice Jumpers with Weaves title.

Cruiser did not like being away from his home and was not truly happy in the show ring unless he was with my daughter, Becky. She could bring out the best in him.

He loved to play with Becky and she taught him silly pet tricks which eased his stress in the show ring. She taught him to spin, do grapevine weaves, retrieve, roll over, and other games to keep his mind stimulated during conformation showing.

I wanted to campaign Cruiser for a short while, which required sending him out with a handler. He was on the show circuit for about four months. During that time he garnered 16 Group firsts.

After his campaign was over, I picked up Cruiser from the handler, and he was thrilled to come home. I went to visit the handler about a month later and she was excited to see Cruiser. We met up with her and when Cruiser saw her, he jumped

AKC-INT-ASCA CH McMatt's EZ Going OA NAJ USASA HOFX-ASCA HOF "Cruiser" at the 2005 USASA National Specialty. Photo courtesy of Flo McDaniel.

AKC-INT-ASCA CH McMatt's EZ Going OA NAJ USASA HOFX-ASCA HOF "Cruiser" winning an Award of Merit at the 2005 USASA National Specialty. Photo courtesy of Flo McDaniel. Photo credit: Sharon Turner.

Pedigree

```
                                          CH McMatt's Where There's Smoke
                            Castle's Days of Thunder
                            |             CH McMatt's Sarah's Crystle Castle
              AKC CH McMatt's EZ Victor USASA HOFX-ASCA HOF
                            |             CH Showtime's Sir Prize CD ASCA HOF
                            AKC CH McMatt's All That Joy
                                          CH Marquis Sun-Up Sarah McMatt ASCA HOF
AKC-INT-ASCA CH McMatt's EZ Going OA NAJ USASA HOFX-ASCA HOF
                                          CH Jimmee Blue of Adelaide ASCA HOF
                            AKC-ASCA CH Caledonia's Crowd Pleaser HOFX-HOF
                            |             CH Butterfields Silky Suzann
              AKC-ASCA CH Castle's Image of McMatt
                            |             CH Showtime's Sir Prize CD ASCA HOF
                            AKC CH McMatt's Sarah's Crystle Castle
                                          CH Marquis Sun-Up Sarah McMatt ASCA HOF
```

Cruiser's sire AKC CH McMatt's EZ Victor USASA HOFX-ASCA HOF "Victor." Born 1996. Photo courtesy of Tina Beck.

Cruiser's dam AKC CH Castle's Image of McMatt "Emmy." Born 1993. Photo courtesy of Flo McDaniel.

back into my van, turned his back to her, and wouldn't even look at her. He did not want to go on the show circuit again!

Along with his Group wins, Cruiser's accolades also included an impressive trifecta at the 2005 USASA National Specialty where he won an Award of Merit, Best Veteran, and First Place in the Stud Dog Class. He also won the Stud Dog class at the 2003 and 2004 USASA National Specialties, and was First Select in Futurity at the 1999 ASCA National Specialty."

- Flo McDaniel

Cruiser passed away September 6, 2012, just three months shy of his 16th birthday.

Some of Cruiser's wonderful offspring include:

- AKC CH Lil' Creek's Hug Me Tight ROM C-III. Dam of four Best in Show winners (see pages 34-35 for photos):
    - BIS AKC GCH-CKC-ASCA CH Bayouland Creme Brûlée CGC USASA HOFX-ASCA HOF
    - BIS AKC-ASCA CH Bayouland Flamin Glory
    - BIS AKC-ASCA CH Bayouland's Dazzle Me Razz ASCA HOF
    - BIS AKC GCH-ASCA CH Paradigm's Bayouland on Broadway ASCA HOF

- AKC-ASCA CH McMatt's Too Good To Be Blue AKC-ASCA CD NA NAJ CGC ROM X-II ASCA HOF. Dam of three AKC GCH (see page 36 for photos):
    - AKC GCH-CKC-ASCA CH TreeStarr's Northwind Breeze ROM X-I
    - AOM Select AKC GCH-CKC-ASCA CH TreeStarr Rmzcrk's I'm on Fire CGC TDI ROM X-I ROM C-II ASCA HOF
    - MBIS AKC GCH-CKC GCHEx-ASCA CH TreeStarr's Billion Dollar Baby CD HIC ASCA HOF

- AKC-ASCA CH McMatt's EZ To Please. Sire of:
    - AKC-ASCA CH Graffiti's Life Just Got Easier ROM C-I. Sire of:
        - MBIS MBISS AKC Platinum GCH-ASCA CH CopperRidge What's Your Dream
        - BIS AKC Silver GCH CopperRidge's Unforgettable
        - MRBIS MBISS AKC Gold GCH CopperRidge's Debonair CD RA CGC
        - AKC Silver GCH CopperRidge's Sugar n Spice ROM C-I

- AKC-ASCA CH McMatt's Bajas Tiger Lily. Dam of:
    - AKC GCH-BIS CKC GCH-UKC-ASCA CH Valor's King of Blue
    - BISS AKC-ASCA CH Valor Drop of Blue

Cruiser's daughter AKC CH Lil' Creek's Hug Me Tight ROM C-III "Whitney." Born 2000. Dam of 18 CH including four Best in Show winners. By Cruiser x AKC-ASCA CH Lil' Creek's Bushfire Blonde. Photo courtesy of Yvette LeBlanc.

Cruiser's great-granddaughter AKC-ASCA CH CopperRidge's Graffiti Mona McMatt "Mona." Born 2011. By AKC-ASCA CH Graffiti's Life Just Got Easier ROM C-I x AKC-ASCA CH Bayoulands For A Limited Time Only. Photo courtesy of Vicki Wehrle.

Cruiser's granddaughter MBIS MBISS AKC Platinum GCH-ASCA CH McMatt's Autumn Breeze "Breezy." Born 2010. Best of Breed 2015 USASA National Specialty. Winner of five All-Breed Bests in Show. By AKC-ASCA CH Ivory Isle's Meets The Criteria ASCA HOF x McMatt's Cruisin' The Surf. Photo courtesy of Tina Beck and Flo McDaniel. Photo credit: (left) Jeffrey Hanlin, (right) Amber Jade Aanensen.

- BIS BISS AKC Multi CH McMatt's Blue Graffiti. Vice Champion 2011 World Show
- BIS AKC-ASCA CH Crocker's Weekend Warrior. Sire of:
  - AKC CH Mill Creek's Maka Mega Legacy ROM C-III. Dam of 10 champions including:
    - AKC Gold GCH-CKC-ASCA CH Legacy's Power Play USASA HOFX-ASCA HOF
    - AKC GCH-ASCA CH Legacy's Bold Venture
  - AKC-AUST-ASCA CH McMatt's Lovely Lily. Foundation dam in Australia
- Multi CH Propwash Spectacular Bid. Champion Europe 2002, Vice-Champion Europe 2004
- BIS BISS AKC-ASCA CH Halfmoon Embellishment ASCA HOF
- MBIS AKC-DK-CLUB CH CH Halfmoon Full of It. Jub.W'07, Club W'07
- A-CH URO3 Halfmoon Bialy Stella Artois STDcs HT AKC-ASCA CD JV-E RV-O GV-O OA OAJ NF AKC-RE ASCA-REM
- WTCH AKC GCH-ASCA CH Shell Bluffs Renaissance Man HSBd HIAds OFTDm AFTDds RTDs. Select Dog 2016 USASA National Specialty
- AKC CH Bayshore Stonehaven King of Hearts HSAs AX AXJ
- Multi CH Bayshore Stonehaven Meet Joe Black
- AKC-CKC CH Bayshore Stonehaven Heart Breaker, Group Placer and Best In Sweeps at Canadian National Specialty
- VCH WTCH AKC-ASCA CH NiteStar's Mardi Gras Queen JS-E RS-O GS-O
- Premier ASCA A-CH UKC A-CH Bainbridge's Bound to Please AKC-ASCA CD AKC RN-ASCA RNX RM OAP OJP NFP JS-N JV-E GV-O-SP RV-O-SP CL2-R CL1-F CL1-H CGC TDI TKN

Cruiser's dam AKC CH Castle's Image of McMatt (on podium) winning the Brood Bitch class at the 1985 ASCA National Specialty with Cruiser and his litter sister AKC CH McMatt's Megapup of Mill Creek. Photo courtesy of Flo McDaniel.

AKC-INT-ASCA CH McMatt's EZ Going OA NAJ USASA HOFX-ASCA HOF "Cruiser" winning one of many Group placements. Photo courtesy of Flo McDaniel. Photo credit: Halverson.

◆

CONVERSATIONS

Josefine Junge · Proud to have Cruiser in my dogs' pedigrees.

Susan Landry Whiticar · My girl, Graffiti McMatt EZ Million "Millie" has a blaze very similar to Cruiser's only on the other side of her face. She's Cruiser's great-granddaughter and her pedigree has four crosses to him. She's just a year and a half old. She does have a pretty head piece. She was bred by Flo McDaniel (McMatt) and Vicki Wehrle (Graffiti). She's been shown in ASCA and has thirteen points with three majors.

Karen Papadopoulos · Cruiser's daughter AKC-AUST-ASCA CH McMatt's Lovely Lily "Tilley" was imported to Australia from the United States by Amanda and Ben Helps. She was a foundation dam of many Aussies in Australia.

Cruiser's son BIS AKC-ASCA CH Crocker's Weekend Warrior. "Simon." Born 2000. By Cruiser x AKC-ASCA CH Lil' Creeks Bushfire Blonde. Photo courtesy of Flo McDaniel. Photo credit: Downey.

Cruiser's son AKC-ASCA CH McMatt's EZ To Please "Nick." Born 2003. By Cruiser x AKC CH Mill Creek's She'll Be A McMatt. Photo courtesy of Vicki Wehrle. Photo credit: Fred Csontos.

Bára Drahonovská · Love him to pieces!

Lacey Kafer · Cruiser's great-grandson Rainyday's A Twist In My Story STDdsc RS-N GS-N-OP JS-N-OP RAX RE AKC RN NA (ASCA mjr pointed) "Oliver" was bred by Kate Johnson. He was sired by Tina Beck's AKC-ASCA CH Goldcrest Cameo Captivator and is out of AKC-ASCA CH Rainyday's Eleanor Rigby ROM X-II ROM P-I. Oliver is two years old and excelling in all venues!

When I was considering dogs that I wanted a puppy out of, I would sit and watch by the conformation ring. Each time I found a dog I liked, I would pull up their pedigree. Time and again, one dog was consistently in every pedigree of the dogs I liked. That dog was Cruiser.

Oliver is one of the most biddable and loyal dogs I have ever met. When I went to visit his litter, he was the puppy that would watch as the siblings played and then waited for the perfect moment to jump in on the action. He was a thinker from a young age. I recall a time when he was six months old and he corralled all the ducks into an area near the apartments where we lived. Once he gathered

First Place Stud Dog class 2004 USASA Nationals

First Place Stud Dog class 2003 USASA Nationals   First Place Stud Dog class 2005 USASA Nationals

Cruiser and his offspring won First Place in the Stud Dog Class at the 2003, 2004, and 2005 USASA National Specialties. AKC-INT-ASCA CH McMatt's EZ Going OA NAJ USASA HOFX-ASCA HOF "Cruiser" (on podium in upper photo, on the left in lower two photos). Photos courtesy of Flo McDaniel.

them, he looked up at me with such confidence and joy. He's willing to try anything and everything I ask of him. To me, he is the epitome of the Aussie personality.

Esme Grace · Stunning!

Stefano Crippa · I have a Cruiser great-granddaughter BIS Multi CH Blue Crazy Breeze Night Time. Her call name is "Night." At 11 years old she is still in great condition and has a wonderful temperament. She was a very successful conformation show dog who also practiced agility and was a pet therapy dog. She's by IT CH Rosewoods Flame of Freedom, who passed away last year at the age of 16½, and she's out of IT CH Toryak's Milaya, a Cruiser granddaughter. Because Cruiser lived to almost 16 years old, I hope for longevity in my dogs.

Pat Parker · I'm so fortunate to have owned Cruiser's full sister AKC-ASCA CH McMatt's Switchin' To Glide "Tilly." She was the foundation of my kennel and granddam of my first HOF, CH Eaglecrest's Touch of Charm ASCA HOF "Charm." Charm and my other Tilley granddaughter ASCA CH Eaglecrest's Touch of Magic "Magic" have continued the line very successfully for me.

Becky Rowan Androff · My Cruiser daughter was AKC-ASCA CH McMatt's Too Good To Be Blue AKC-ASCA CD NA NAJ CGC ROM X-II ASCA HOF "Carly." I was proud to be entrusted with her. Carly had a sweet temperament and loved everyone. She was well-known at home for her "hula girl wiggle butt." Carly made us proud in the show ring and excelled in the whelping box. Cruiser is the grandsire and great-grandsire of all of my current dogs.

Cruiser's son WTCH AKC GCH-ASCA CH Shell Bluffs Renaissance Man HSBd HIAds OFTDm AFTDds RTDs "Patch." Born 2005. Select Dog 2016 USASA National Specialty. By Cruiser x AKC-ASCA CH Hi 5's Diamonds In The Sky HSAds STDds. Photo courtesy of Terry Dickey. Photo credit: Jeffrey Hanlin.

Cruiser's great-grandson DTCH CH Carolina Calais Keep on Walkin' JW'15 BJW'15 NJK JS-N "Jax." Born 2014. Qualified for Crufts 2017. Brabo W 2017, Amsterdam JW 2015, Benelux JW 2015, Dutch JCH. By AKC-ASCA CH Calais Carolina Unmarked Bills STDS JHDs x AKC GCH Carolina Calais Take It EZ. Photo courtesy of Joanne Boerland. Photo credit: Kristof Melis. (NETHERLANDS)

Cruiser's offspring out of AKC CH Westridge Panache "Envy." (Left to right)
- AKC-ASCA CH Halfmoon It's All Good "Chrome." Co-owned by Anne Heckle & Morgan Higgins.
- BISS AKC-ASCA CH Halfmoon Embellishment ASCA HOF "Belli." Best of Breed ASCA National Specialty Pre-show, Award of Merit ASCA National Specialty, Award of Merit USASA Nationals, Best Veteran in Sweeps, Best in Sweeps 2004 USASA Nationals, BOS Futurity USASA Nationals.
- AKC-DK-CLUB CH CH Halfmoon Full of It "Creed." Jub.W'07, Club W'07, Club Veteran CH, Dog of the Year 2007 #2 (specialty club across breeds), Breed Winner #1 in 2007 (specialty club), multiple Best In Show, Group, and Best of Breed wins. Owned by Britt Siegstad. (DENMARK)
- AKC CH Halfmoons First Mate "Sailor." Photo credit: Pet Personalities by Alissa.

Cruiser x AKC CH Westridge Panache

"In 2003, I planned a litter out of AKC CH Westridge Panache "Envy" sired by Cruiser. I wanted a blue boy. I got five boys and one black tri bitch. It turned out to be an amazing litter. Donna Harding and I co-owned Envy and she mentored me as I made this cross—I'll be forever grateful for the knowledge she shared. It was only my second litter as a breeder. When evaluating the puppies, I had absolutely no clue what I was looking for. Well, maybe a few clues, but not many.

I decided to keep two of the blue boys, Creed and Chrome. Belli, the plainly-marked black tri bitch, was going to a pet home until the last minute, when I decided to hang on to her too. The issues with keeping littermates became apparent, and the boys were placed in fabulous homes. The boys became successful, and Belli turned out to be an incredible show dog and the dam of multi-talented offspring. But most of all, she was my girl and a wonderful ambassador for the breed. I miss her so much."

- Gwen Hayes

"Creed gained all the titles possible in Denmark and Sweden. Along with his stunning looks and movement, he was the brightest and funniest male I've ever owned. He had a very high IQ. He charmed the pants off any visitor, whether two- or four-legged. The first time he saw sheep, he knew precisely what to do and did it amazingly well. I still miss him so badly! He was a really fun and bright Aussie. The good thing is, I have his daughters, granddaughters, grandsons, and his frozen semen."

- Britt Siegstad

Cruiser's great-granddaughter at the age of 11. BIS Multi CH Blue Crazy Breeze Night Time "Night." Born 2006. By ITA CH Rosewoods Flame of Freedom x ITA CH Toryak's Milaya. Photo courtesy of Stefano Crippa. Photo credit: Eleonora Masi. (ITALY)

Cruiser's son AKC-ASCA CH Muddyfeet All Or Nothing CD RA STDs CGC CGN TDI "Alex." Born 2006. By Cruiser x Harmony Hill's Elan Ever After. Photo courtesy of Laura Liebenow. Photo credit: Jeffrey Hanlin.

Cruiser's daughter ASCA CH Bainbridge Tymeless Edition "Targa." Born 2003. By Cruiser x AKC- ASCA CH JnD's Spellbound HIC. Photo courtesy of Beth Lynn. Photo credit: Paula McDermid.

Cruiser's daughter Gemmells Inherit The Wind "Rain." Born 2007. By Cruiser x AKC-ASCA CH Blue Isle's Gone With The Wind. Photo courtesy of Rebecca Millsaps.

Cruiser's great-great-granddaughter McMatt's Graffiti On The Wall "Scribble." Born 2011. By AKC-ASCA CH Graffiti's He's EZ On The Eyes NA NHJ NF x AKC CH McMatt's Claudia Joy Shuttrbug. Photo courtesy of Tracy Lyons Merrill. Photo credit: Caroline Charette.

Cruiser's son UKC GCH Bainbridge Final Verdict CD RNX "Morgan." Born 2003. By Cruiser x AKC-ASCA CH JnD's Spellbound HIC. Photo courtesy of Beth Lynn. Photo credit: Paula McDermid.

Cruiser's daughter AKC-ASCA CH McMatt's Too Good To Be Blue AKC-ASCA CD NA NAJ CGC ROM X-I ROM C-II ASCA HOF "Carly." Born 2000. Dam of ROM C-II, ROM X-I and ASCA HOF offspring. By Cruiser x AKC-ASCA CH Lil' Creek's As Requested ASCA HOF. Photo courtesy of Becky Rowan Androff.

Crusier's granddaughter MBIS AKC CH-ASCA GCH McMatt and Graffiti Rumor Has It "Adele." Born 2012. Winner of 7 BIS and 4 RBIS, Select Bitch 2017 USASA Naional Specialty. By AKC-ASCA CH Ivory Isles Meets The Criteria ASCA HOF x AKC CH McMatt's She's Got Style. Photo courtesy of Michael Halley. Photo credit: Jeffrey Hanlin.

Cruiser's son AKC CH-CKC GCH Bayshore Stonehaven Heart Breaker at HHC "Breaker." Born 2007. By Cruiser x AKC CH Bayshore's Be Still My Heart. Photo courtesy of Brenda-lee Hoskins. Photo credit: Tom Digiacomo.

Cruiser's son AKC CH Bayshore Stonehaven King of Hearts HSAs AX AXJ "Gamble." Born 2007. By Cruiser x AKC CH Bayshore's Be Still My Heart. Photo courtesy of Jeff Margeson. Photo credit: Stonehaven.

Cruiser's daughter McMatt's Cruisin' The Surf "Gidget." Born 2007. By Cruiser x BIS AKC-ASCA CH Bayouland's Dazzle Me Razz ASCA HOF. Photo courtesy of Tina Beck.

Cruiser's daughter AKC-ASCA CH McMatt's Bajas Tiger Lily "Lily." Born 2000. By Cruiser x AKC-ASCA CH Lil' Creek's As Requested ASCA HOF. Photo courtesy of Alyssa Janiszak.

Jeff Margeson · One of the most successful crosses we ever did was Cruiser to our bitch CH Bayshore's Be Still My Heart "Flutter." It produced AKC CH Bayshore Stonehaven King of Hearts HSAs AX AXJ; Multi CH Bayshore Stonehaven Meet Joe Black, who was the #1 Herding Dog in Mexico; AKC CH-CKC GCH Bayshore Stonehaven Heart Breaker, who was a Group Placer and Best In Sweeps at a Canadian National; and Bayshore Stonehaven Truly Scrumptious, who has produced some of our most outstanding dogs.

Terry Dickey · Our Cruiser son WTCH AKC GCH-ASCA CH Shell Bluffs Renaissance Man HSBd HIAds OFTDm AFTDds RTDs "Patch" is still going strong at almost 12 years old. He won Veteran Dog 10+ and went on to garner Select Dog at the 2016 USASA National Specialty. His dam was AKC-ASCA CH Hi 5's Diamonds In The Sky HSAds STDds.

Maureen P Retting · Cruiser is stunning!

Olivier Geneste · There are so many descendants of Cruiser, even in France. His great-great-granddaughter Jazzy Voice Des Bergers d'Enguerrand "Jazzy" was born in 2014. Her sire is AKC GCH-ASCA CH Legacy's Remington Steele and her dam is SR CH Heden du Petit Mont d'Eden.

Lauren D. Wright · What an amazing dog he was! I love the description of his physical traits. And thank you, Flo, for the description of his funny personality. I laughed out loud several times, especially at "Cruiser would let you know when he was offended. He never liked the 'down' command when Becky worked with him in agility. He gave her a 'look' that made it clear he was not a fan."

I think his great-granddaughter must have inherited that from him because she definitely has a "look" when she's not happy about something! But she

Cruiser's great-great-grandson German JCH VDH -Club JCH First Choice Miracle Hearts della Terra del Falco "Jackson." Born 2015. By JCH Apple Fruit Go Ahead x Multi CH Golden Dream. Photo courtesy of Kirsten Bähnk. Photo credit: Michael Twesten Photographie. (GERMANY)

Cruiser's great-grandson Rainyday's A Twist In My Story AKC RN ASCA RAX RE STDdsc NA RS-N GS-N-OP JS-N-OP "Oliver." Born 2015. By AKC-ASCA CH Goldcrest Cameo Captivator x AKC-ASCA CH Rainyday's Eleanor Rigby ROM X-II ROM P-I. Photo courtesy of Lacey Kafer.

Cruiser's great-granddaughter CH Edenisle Leia Organa "Leia." By CH POL JCH POL Gemmel Unexpected at Saussurea x INT CH Saussurea Spellbound. Photo courtesy of Leeandra Mifsud Mizzi. Photo credit: Dennis Mifsud. (MALTA)

Cruiser's half-sister AKC CH Goldcrest Greta Garbo "Greta." Born 2005. By AKC CH McMatt's EZ Victor USASA HOFX-ASCA HOF x Northland's Image Maker. Photo courtesy of Tina Beck. Photo credit: Heidi Erland.

Cruiser's great-granddaughter AKC Silver GCH CopperRidge's Sugar n Spice ROM C-I "Harper." Born 2010. Top 5 bitch and Select at Westminster. By AKC-ASCA CH CH Graffiti's Life Just Got Easier ROM C-I x AKC CH CopperRidge's Leather Britches ROM C-III. Photo courtesy of Stephen Blanco. Photo credit: John Ashbey.

Cruiser's great-granddaughter MBIS MBISS AKC Platinum GCH-ASCA CH CopperRidge What's Your Dream "Vivian." Born 2010. Best of Breed 2014 Westminster show. By AKC-ASCA CH Graffiti's Life Just Got Easier ROM C-I x CopperRidge's No Ordinary Olive ROM C-III. Photo courtesy of Stephan Blanco. Photo credit: Amber Jade Aanensen.

Cruiser's daughter A-CH URO3 Halfmoon Bialy Stella Artois AKC-ASCA CD AKC RE ASCA REM HT STDcs OA OAJ NF RV-O JV-E GV-O "Stella." Born 2005. By Cruiser x AKC CH Westridge Panache. Photo courtesy of Brandy Esch.

Cruiser's daughter ASCA CH TreeStarr's Too Good To Be EZ of Pine Spring "Bunny." Born 2010. Reserve Winner's Bitch 2012 Eukanuba Championship. By Cruiser x AKC-ASCA CH TreeStarr's Too Good To Be Tru. Photo courtesy of Janet Matkins.

Kylie is 14 years old and still going strong. Photo credit: Vavra

Premier ASCA A-CH UKC A-CH
Bainbridge's Bound to Please
AKC-ASCA CD AKC RN-ASCA RNX RM OAP OJP NFP JS-N JV-E GV-O-SP RV-O-SP CL2-R CL1-F CL1-H CGC TDI TKN

"Kylie." Born 2003. By Cruiser x AKC-ASCA CH JnD's Spellbound HIC.

Kylie is my first Australian Shepherd and truly my heart dog. Before bringing Kylie into my life, I knew nothing about conformation or competitive dog sports. It's amazing to me how far we've come.

Kylie is an ASCA Altered Champion and has collected nearly 200 Altered Best of Breed or Best of Opposite wins in her career. She placed five different years in ASCA's Altered Top Ten Conformation Standings and placed five separate times in the Top 10 at the ASCA Nationals Altered Conformation Finals.

Kylie and I learned about agility, obedience, and rally together and we've finished over 40 performance titles to date, including an AKC Trick Dog title.

In her sideline career as a professional model, Kylie has worked for Target, Purina, 3M, Woolrich and other national brands and was featured on their retail products. She appeared in magazine ads in "Martha Stewart Living," starred in a national TV spot for Tuesday Morning, and was chosen for Browntrout's annual "Australian Shepherds" calendar.

Beyond her accomplishments, Kylie means the world to me. She's a wonderful, devoted companion, smart as a whip, constantly makes me laugh and she has a portfolio of tricks she loves to show off to anyone willing to watch.

- Kathy Dukinfield

Photo credit: John Beals

Cruiser's great-granddaughter ASCA CH Gemmells Balance and Charisma AKC-ASCA TD "Stevie." Born 2011. By BIS AKC CH Paradigm's Bayouland on Broadway x Gemmels She Is Like The Wind. Photo courtesy of Melanie Magamoll. Photo credit: Mary Bryant.

Cruiser's grandson and great-grandson AKC GCH- UKC-ASCA CH CopperRidge Easy A RN STDs OA OAJ RS-N JS-O CGC "Skyler." Born 2010. By AKC-ASCA CH Graffiti's Life Just Got Easier ROM C-I x McMatt's Hurricane Force. Photo courtesy of Mari Jebens. Photo credit: Amber Jade Aanensen.

Cruiser's great-great-granddaughter Honshu Fuji Shoji De l'Etang De Pincemaille. Born 2012. By Bayouland's Brees By Goldring x Darkside On The Rainbow De l'Etang De Pincemaille. Photo courtesy of Muriel Clementz. (FRANCE)

Cruiser's great-granddaughter Graffiti McMatt EZ Million "Millie." Born 2016. By AKC GCH-ASCA CH Bayouland's Big EZ x AKC-ASCA CH Graffiti's Livin N Paradise @ McMatt. Photo courtesy of Susan Landry Whiticar. Photo credit: Melinda Griffin.

Cruiser's great-great-grandson Born in Rosebud Evidence of Ideal "Eidos." Born 2009. By Risingstar Ballroom Celebrity x Born In Rosebud Catch Me If U Can. Photo courtesy of Juliette Bercovici. (FRANCE)

Cruiser's great-grandson Born In Rosebud Heaven Is Not Enough "Higé." Born 2012. By Risingstar Ballroom Celebrity x Millcreek's Don't U Cry Tonight. Photo courtesy of Juliette Bercovici. (FRANCE)

Cruiser's grandson AKC-ASCA CH Crofton Kid You Not "Josh." Born 2007. Best in Circuit 2011 WASCUNY Sparkler, Best in Circuit 2011 HONYASC Dawg Daze. By AKC-ASCA CH Kaleidoscope Stone Ravenwynd ASCA HOF x AKC CH Crofton It's My Tern. Photo courtesy of Linda Braun. Photo credit: Laura Reynolds.

Cruiser's son Multi CH Propwash Spectacular Bid "Bid." Born 2000. 1 x CACIB, 1 x BOB, 1 x BIG, Champion AKC (Américain) Champion Italie 2002, Champion Europe 2002, Vice-Champion Europe 2004. By Cruiser x Propwash Ghostchime. Photo courtesy of Elodie Di Tommaso. Photo credit: Kennel Crystal Lake. (FRANCE)

must have also inherited that devotion to "her person" like Cruiser had with Becky. She is the most devoted dog imaginable and will do anything I ask of her. So thank you, Cruiser, for passing down your great disposition.

Billie Anderson · All my dogs except one have Cruiser as great-grandfather or great-great-grandfather.

Sandra Balkow · I have a Cruiser granddaughter Cool-Paws Baby I'm a Star "Reina." She's by MBIS Multi CH McMatt's Blue Graffiti "Garrett" and out of Cool-Paws Amazing Shooting Star "Lara." Reina was born in March of 2017 and is a nice, active young lady. When she went to her first puppy class, she entered the playground and was not a bit concerned about all the other dogs.

Jannette Faust · Cruiser was a great sire!

Mary Olson Quam · My Cruiser grandson Treasure Tyme's Ante Up "Andrew" is a joyful goofball. Love him to pieces!

Cruiser's grandson AKC GCH-ASCA CH NiteStar's Bolt of Lightening "Bolt." Born 2015. BOS 2016 AKC National Championship. By WTCH AKC GCH-ASCA CH Shell Bluff's Renaissance Man HSAds HSBd HIAds OFTDm AFTDds RTDs x AKC-ASCA CH Caitland's Sunday Confession RE RNX REX RAX RMX. Photo courtesy of Trisha Herring. Photo credit: Amber Jade Aanensen.

Cruiser's great-grandson and great-great-grandson AKC CH Lk. Michigan's Red Solo Cup "Tobey." Born 2014. Best of Bred By Exhibitor 2016 Royal Canin AKC Nationals. By AKC GCH-CKC-ASCA CH TreeStarr Rmzcrk's I'm on Fire CGC TDI ROM X-I ROM C-II ASCA HOF x AKC CH Bayouland Don't Stop Believin' RN CGC. Photo courtesy of Teresa Pepper-Marble. Photo credit: Amber Jade Aanensen.

Susie Collyott Gilliam · AKC GCH-UKC-ASCA CH Graffiti McMatt Shook Me @Lookouttrail "Dillon" is a prime example of the McMatt lines, from the beautiful, graceful sidegait to the strong, masculine, handsome head, structure and type. Dillon has sired BIS and group-placing offspring even with limited breedings. My Dillon x Starr pups are winning Best of Breed Puppy, Herding Group firsts and even a Best In Show Puppy. In their spare time, this litter of nine are participating in events all over the country. Their talents include herding, agility, dock diving, and barn hunt. This litter is my dream litter and would not have been possible without Flo allowing me to use Cruiser, and for Flo and Vicki allowing me to have Dillon.

Sara Lowe · We have a collection of Cruiser great-great-grandkids. We have four! CKC CH Veritas From Russia With Love, Veritas It's Just That Way, Veritas Here And Now At Styrka, and CKC pointed Styrka's Dark Magic.

ASCA CH Nitestars Royal Cruise

We were at a friend's house for an ASCA club meeting. Large property, large pond. Dogs were having a blast running and swimming. My daughter's young dog had been hesitant to go too deep into the water. Then, a ball was thrown out into the pond and without thinking, my daughter's dog ran down a fallen tree and dove in. To her shock, the water was now over her head, and we quickly realized she couldn't swim. We stood on the shoreline, clapping and yelling for the young dog to come to us. After she went underwater a second time, I quickly took off my shoes and ran to the water's edge. Out of nowhere a black dog shot past me and dove in. It was Spirit. She swam out to her kennel sister and got behind her. She righted the dog and started pushing her just behind the shoulder until she got her into shallow water. It's one of those things I would never believe if I hadn't seen it for myself. She literally saved her drowning "sister's" life. Spirit is a once-in-a-lifetime dog!

- Shannon Wynne Hoppmann Jackson

Cruiser's daughter ASCA CH Nitestars Royal Cruise "Spirit." Born 2011. By Cruiser x BISS AKC-ASCA CH NiteStar's Queen Bee. Photo courtesy Shannon Wynne Hoppmann Jackson. Photo credit: In Motion Photos.

Cruiser's great-grandson AKC GCH-UKC-ASCA CH Graffiti McMatt Shook Me @Lookouttrail "Dillon." Born 2012. By AKC-ASCA CH Croftons Kid You Not x AKC-ASCA CH Graffiti's Constant Joy. Photo courtesy of Susie Collyott Gilliam. Photo credit: Amber Jade Aanensen.

Cruiser's grandson BISS AKC-ASCA CH Valor Drop of Blue "Silas." Born 2005. By AKC CH McMatt's The Entertainer x AKC-ASCA CH McMatt's Bajas Tiger Lily. Photo courtesy of Alyssa Janiszak. Photo credit: Thornapple.

Cruiser's grandson Timberwood's Who's Your Daddy DN "Odin." Born 2015. By McMatt's Muggle Magic x Timberwood's Angel N Disguise. Photo courtesy of Laura Pearson. Photo credit: Monica Christensen.

Cruiser's granddaughter MBIS MBISS AKC Gold GCH-Multi CH McMatt's Isis of Graffiti "Icy." Born 2012. By AKC-ASCA CH Ivory Isle's Meets The Criteria ASCA HOF x McMatt's She's Got Style. Photo courtesy of Patricia L. Rogers. Photo credit: Jeffrey Hanlin.

Cruiser's daughter AKC-AUST-ASCA McMatt's Lovely Lily (imp USA) "Tilley." Born 2000. By Cruiser x AKC-ASCA CH Lil' Creek's As Requested ASCA HOF. Imported to Australia by Amanda and Ben Helps. Photo courtesy of Karen Papadopoulos. (AUSTRALIA)

Cruiser's grandson CKC GCH Tresrullah's All Tuckered Out CGN HIC "Tucker." Born 2011. By CKC GCH Bayshore Stonehaven Heart Breaker At HHC x Northbay Tryfecta Ice Wine. Photo courtesy of Karen Doughty. Photo credit: Dogs By Design. (CANADA)

Cruiser's sister AKC-ASCA CH McMatt's Switchin' To Glide "Tilly." Born 1998. By AKC CH McMatt's EZ Victor x CH Castle's Image of McMatt. Photo courtesy of Pat Parker, Eaglecrest.

Cruiser's son BIS BISS AKC-Multi CH McMatt's Blue Graffiti "Garrett." Born 2006. Vice Champion 2011 World Show. Sub Campeon Del Mundo - Paris 2011. Best In Show - Multi Best In Show Veteran. By Cruiser x AKC CH Graffiti Garnet Rose. Photo courtesy of Cristina Freixes, Cau Fosca. (SPAIN)

Cruiser's granddaughter AKC GCH-ASCA CH NiteStar's Wishing N' Hoping STDds "Hope." Born 2013. By AKC-ASCA CH Blue Isle The Critics Are Raving STDd ASCA-CKC HOF x VCH WTCH AKC-ASCA CH NiteStar's Mardi Gras Queen RS-O JS-E GS-O. Photo courtesy of Trisha Herring. Photo credit: Amber Jade Aanensen.

Cruiser's great-grandson MRBIS MBISS AKC Gold GCH CopperRidge's Debonair CD RA CGC "Devon." Born 2010. By AKC-ASCA CH Graffiti's Life Just Got Easier x CopperRidge's No Ordinary Olive ROM C-III. Photo courtesy of Stephen Blanco. Photo credit: Olivia Frost.

Cruiser's great-great-granddaughter Jazzy Voice Des Bergers d'Enguerrand "Jazzy." Born 2014. By AKC GCH-ASCA CH Legacy's Remington Steele x SR CH Heden du Petit Mont d'Eden. Photo courtesy of Olivier Geneste. Photo credit: Alexandra Carminati. (FRANCE)

Cruiser's grandson Multi CH McMatt Graffiti's Kiss Me Now "Kiss" (center) with his offspring. Born 2016. (Left to right) Skyron Feel The Beat, Skyron Deep Affection, Kiss, Skyron Easy Rider, and Skyron Devil's Advocate. Photo courtesy of Dori Erdesz. (HUNGARY)

Beth Bertolino Hemmer · My Cruiser daughter is RTCH McMatt's Blue Ambiance CDX GS-O JS-O-SP RS-O RAX REMX REX RMX "Dolce." Those are just her ASCA titles. She was born in 2007. Her dam is BIS AKC-ASCA CH Bayouland's Dazzle Me Razz ASCA HOF. Dolce is my heart dog

Ann Madeo · Beautiful dog!

Stephan Blanco Cruiser's great-granddaughter MBIS MBISS AKC Platinum GCH-ASCA CH CopperRidge What's Your Dream "Vivian" was sired by AKC-ASCA CH Graffiti's Life Just Got Easier ROM C-I and out of CopperRidge's No Ordinary Olive ROM C-III. Vivian was the first Platinum Grand Champion Aussie bitch in history and the second Platinum Grand Champion Aussie of either sex. She was a multiple Best in Show and Best in Specialty Show winner. She was the #1 Aussie in the country All-Systems for 2014. She won Best of Breed at the 2014 Westminster Kennel Club show.

Cruiser's great-granddaughter Multiple Group Winning AKC Silver GCH CopperRidge's Sugar n Spice ROM C-I "Harper" was sired by AKC-ASCA CH Graffiti's Life Just Got Easier ROM C-I and out of AKC CH CopperRidge's Leather Britches ROM C-III. She was a Top 5 bitch and Select at Westminster.

Victor's double great-grandson AKC-ASCA CH Goldcrest Crusin' For A Bruisin' "Beast Mode." Born 2012. By AKC GCH-ASCA CH Goldcrest Cameo Appearance x McMatt's Cruisin' The Surf. Photo courtesy of Tina Beck. Photo credit: Holloway.

Cruiser's granddaughter AKC CH Mill Creek's Maka Mega Legacy ROM C-III "Megan." Born 2003. Dam of 10 champions including one Gold GCH, one Bronze GCH, and four GCH. By BIS AKC-ASCA CH Crocker's Weekend Warrior x AKC-ASCA CH McMatt's Megapup of Mill Creek. Photo courtesy of Sue Ritter.

From three litters she currently has 10 AKC Champion offspring with three more major pointed.

BIS AKC Silver GCH CopperRidge's Unforgettable "Ella" was by AKC-ASCA CH Graffiti's Life Just Got Easier ROM C-I and out of AKC CH CopperRidge's Leather Britches ROM C-III. Ella finished her championship in just three weekends out, taking Winner's Bitch at multiple specialties when she was just 12 months old. She then went out to finish her Grand Championship and quickly ascended to the Top 10. She ended her eight-month run as the #3 Australian Shepherd in the country with eight Group 1 wins and a Best in Show to her credit.

MRBIS MBISS AKC Gold GCH CopperRidge's Debonair CD RA CGC "Devon" was by AKC-ASCA CH Graffiti's Life Just Got Easier ROM C-I and out of CopperRidge's No Ordinary Olive ROM C-III. Devon won multiple specialties and Reserve Bests in Show.

Nicole Solomons · Such a beautiful boy.

Karie McBrian · BIS CKC GCH Valor's King of Blue "Blue" is a grandson of Cruiser.

Heather Jahn · Mosaic's EZ to Love "Monroe" is Cruiser's great-granddaughter. She has the same distinctive marking on the right side of her face.

Cruiser's great-granddaughter BIS AKC Silver GCH CopperRidge's Unforgettable "Ella." Born 2013. By AKC-ASCA CH Graffiti's Life Just Got Easier ROM C-I x AKC CH CopperRidge's Leather Britches ROM C-III. Photo courtesy of Stephen Blanco. Photo credit: K. Booth.

Cruiser's grandson POL CH POL JCH Gemmell Unexpected at Saussurea "Rock." Born 2009. 1 x CACIB, 2 x CAC. By AKC GCH Schaefer Vinelake Impulsive x Gemmell's Inherit The Wind. Photo courtesy of Iwona Musial. (POLAND)

Cruiser's great-granddaughter Skyron Devil's Advocate NJK BJK "Razz." Born 2016. By CH McMatt's Grafitti Kiss Me Now x JCH Tryfecta Game On @ Skyron. Photo courtesy of Querine Wijnhoven. Photo credit: Birgit Kornet. (NETHERLANDS)

Cruiser's grandson CH McMatt Graffiti's Kiss Me Now "Kiss." Born 2012. AKC-ASCA CH Ivory Isles Meets The Criteria ASCA HOF x AKC CH McMatt's She's Got Style. Photo courtesy of Marianna Raneri. (ITALY)

Cruiser's great-grandson ASCA CH Goldcrest Polaris Start Me Up! CGC "Mick." Born 2016. By AKC-ASCA CH Goldcrest Cruisin' For A Bruisin' x AKC-ASCA CH Goldcrest Passion Fruit. Photo courtesy of Kate Johnson and Danielle McJunkins. Photo credit: Derek Johnson

Cruiser's daughter VCH WTCH AKC-ASCA CH NiteStar's Mardi Gras Queen JS-E RS-O GS-O "Mardi." Born 2007. By Cruiser x AKC-ASCA CH- BISS FCI CH NiteStar's Queen Bee. Photo courtesy of Trisha Herring. Photo credit: David Clayton.

Cruiser's great-granddaughter BIS AKC GCH-ES CH Bayouland's Fleur de Lea "Lea." Born 2009. By BIS AKC-ASCA CH Bayouland's Big EZ x AKC CH That's Hot N Bayouland. Photo courtesy of Cristina Friexes. Photo credit: Monica Martinez Doallo. (SPAIN)

Cruiser's granddaughter AKC GCH-ASCA CH NiteStar's Dreams Do Come True "Dream." Born 2013. By AKC-ASCA CH Blue Isle The Critics Are Raving STDd ASCA-CKC HOF x VCH WTCH AKC-ASCA CH NiteStar's Mardi Gras Queen JS-E RS-O GS-O. Photo courtesy of Trisha Herring. Photo credit: Amber Jade Aanensen.

Cruiser's great-great-grandpups in Australia. (Left) Cuebiyar For the Fallen AI "Truce." Born 2014. By DkCH-NuCH Thornapple Ragtime Move Over x BIS Aust CH Dangerous Beauty Carcassonne Tolugo. (Right) Aust NuCH Cuebiyar The Lady of the Lake "Misty." Born 2011. By Brandyark The Pendragon x Aust CH Cuebiyar All That N More. Photo courtesy of Karen Papadopoulos. (AUSTRALIA)

Cruiser's great-grandson AKC Gold GCH-CKC-ASCA CH Legacy's Power Play USASA HOFX-ASCA HOF "Player." Born 2006. By AKC CH Legacy's Fly Right x AKC CH Mill Creek's Maka Mega Legacy. Photo courtesy of Sue Ritter. Photo credit: Tom Digiacomo. Sire of:
› MBIS BISS AKC GCH-ASCA CH Woodstock's Belle Starr, Best of Breed 2013 USASA National Specialty, ranked #1 in AKC in 2013, Winner's Bitch 2011 USASA National Specialty.
› AKC Bronze GCH-BPIS CKC-ASCA CH Ninebark Silver Buttons, Top 10 All Breed standings in 2012, Multi Premier Awards at ASCA National Specialties and Pre-shows 2011 and 2013.
› AKC GCH Barnwoods Expensive Hobby CD RA HSAd MX MXJ NF, Best of Opposite Sex and Best Bred-By Exhibitor 2011 Eukanuba Championship show.

Cruiser's daughter RTCH McMatt's Blue Ambiance CDX GS-O JS-O-SP RS-O RAX REMX REX RMX "Dolce." Born 2007. By Cruiser x BIS AKC-ASCA CH Bayouland's Dazzle Me Razz ASCA HOF. Photo courtesy of Beth Bertolino Hemmer. Photo credit: Great Dane Photos.

Cruiser's great-granddaughter CAN GCH CFC JCH Casselcreek For The Love Of It CGN RN HIT "Jetta." Born 2015. By AKC-ASCA CH Goldcrest Cameo Captivator x AKC CH-CKC GCH-ASCA CH Casselcreek Prim and Proper. Photo courtesy of Dawn Beck. Photo credit: Holli Murphy.

Victor and Alley

"Victor and my girl ASCA CH Goldcrest Addictive Allure 'Alley' were Goldcrest's 'married couple' who really enjoyed each other's company. They invented a funny game and loved to play it even after they both got old (but were still young at heart). They'd be goofing around in the yard, and with one glance at each other, off they'd go as fast as they could run, up the driveway to the gate. They'd bark like mad—but nobody was there. They would come halfway home, look at each other, and jet back up to the gate, barking like mad. Repeat...."

- Tina Beck

Photo courtesy of Tina Beck

AKC Champion
Mcmatt's EZ Victor
USASA HOFX Sire #10 - ASCA HOF Sire #230

Call name: Victor
Born: 1996
Sire: Castle's Days of Thunder
Dam: CH McMatt's All That Joy
Breeders: Flo and Matt McDaniel, McMatt
Owners: Flo McDaniel, McMatt, 1996 to 2001; Tina Beck, Goldcrest, 2001 to 2008

"I was looking for a very special stud dog. I had a good bitch who needed a typey, well-constructed dog to take my breeding program where I wanted it to go. Victor was that dog. Before coming to Goldcrest, he had been standing at stud on the East Coast where he had sired outstanding puppies. His offspring were successfully competing in multiple areas of competition, so Victor already had an established 'fan club.'

I inquired about Victor and was offered the option to lease or purchase him outright. My good friend Jann Grant of Riverbend helped me purchase him. After Victor arrived, I observed him closely and visualized the kind of bitches who would complement him. My goal was to keep his amazing beauty while tweaking this and that, always working toward my ideal.

I began bugging people who owned the beautiful bitches I needed. I loved Patty Wirries' bitch AKC-INT-ASCA CH Windfalls At Long Last CGC ROM X-I ROM O-I "Lexi," who was a daughter of BISS AKC-ASCA CH Heatherhill Black-N-Decker ASCA HOF. Lexi was gorgeous and I knew she would work well with Victor. It took some time, but I finally got a pup from that cross—ASCA CH Goldcrest I Candy For Xanadu "Taffy"—who combined the best qualities of Victor and Lexi.

I then bought a bitch from the Midwest, Northland's Image Maker, and she and Victor produced AKC-ASCA CH Goldcrest Globetrotter. During my dog show travels I found another beautiful bitch, ASCA CH Canyon Oaks Hugs-N-Kisses. I was able to lease her for a litter with Victor, which produced AKC-ASCA CH Goldcrest Eyes On The Prize.

Victor had many traits that were very important to my breeding program. He had excellent substance and angulation, a deep chest, and an outstanding front assembly. His topline was level and he had effortless, sweeping sidegait. His head, ears, and expression were absolutely gorgeous.

His temperament was wonderful. Victor was charming and loved to greet visitors. Everyone thought he was a puppy because he always had a toy in his mouth. His offspring were typically very toy-motivated too. Victor sired versatile offspring

AKC CH McMatt's EZ Victor USASA HOFX-ASCA HOF "Victor." Born 1996. Photos courtesy of Tina Beck.

Pedigree

```
                                            CH Brigadoon's California Dude HOF
                              AKC CH McMatt's Where There's Smoke
                                            CH Showtime's Midnight Serenade
                Castle's Days of Thunder
                                            CH Showtime's Sir Prize HOF
                              AKC CH McMatt's Sarah's Crystle Castle
                                            CH Marquis Sun-Up Sarah McMatt HOF
AKC CH McMatt's EZ Victor USASA HOFX-ASCA HOF
                                            CH Shady Acres Soldier Blue
                              AKC-ASCA CH Showtime's Sir Prize CD HOF
                                            CH Silver Spring of Starcross
                AKC CH McMatt's All That Joy
                                            CH Rising Sun of Windermere CDX HOF
                              ASCA CH Marquis Sun-Up Sarah McMatt HOF
                                            CH Best Regards of Windermere
```

Victor's sire Castle's Days of Thunder "Cole." Born 1991. Photo courtesy of Flo McDaniel.

Victor's dam AKC CH McMatt's All That Joy "Joy." Born 1992. Photo courtesy of Flo McDaniel.

who had great play drive and engaging personalities. I believe those qualities are an important part of our breed.

Victor was a very consistent sire. He stamped his gorgeous type, structure, and movement on his puppies. I always paid close attention to the pups that reminded me of Victor and tried to keep them for my own breeding program.

He had many excellent, top-winning bitches come to him for breeding. I credit them just as much as Victor for the quality of his progeny. Several of his offspring became stellar producers like their sire, and can be found behind some of the top-winning and producing dogs in the breed today."

- Tina Beck

Some of Victor's beautiful offspring were:
- WTCH AKC-ASCA CH Sunfire Brookridge And Away We Go CD RS-N ASCA HOF
- AKC-INT-ASCA CH McMatt's EZ Going OA NAJ USASA HOFX-ASCA HOF
- AKC-INT CH Everlasting's Ima Rude Dude CGC RN HSAs OTDds ROM X-I
- VCH OTCH ALCH A-BIS A-BISS V-BIS A-CH Everlasting's Raindrops on Roses ASCA UDX AKC UD RAE RMX RL-1 VER STDc OTDds RS-E JS-E GS-E AX OAJ EAC OGC EJC TN-N TG-N WV-N CGC
- OTCH ASCA CH Bon Ami's Easy On The Eyes UDX2 ASCA-UDX U-CDX PT RE NAP NJP FDCH CGC TDI TT
- BVIS AKC-ASCA-ESP-INT-GIB-PORT CH Gemmells Ghostking LW08 MW08 SCVW16 MW16 MVW16
- AKC-CKC CH Goldcrest Gotta Getta Gund
- AKC-ASCA CH Moorea's EZ To Be Me
- AKC-ASCA CH Goldcrest I've Got The Giggles
- AKC-ASCA CH Gemmells Waylander NA NAJ NJP
- AKC-ASCA CH Windfalls KatchMeIfYouCan
- AKC-ASCA CH Te Amo's Top Gun-Wild Child
- AKC-ASCA CH Te Amo's Infinite Victory STDs
- AKC-ASCA CH Goldcrest Eyes On The Prize
- AKC CH McMatt's Megapup of Mill Creek
- AKC CH McMatt's Legend of Mill Creek
- AKC CH McMatt's Switchin' to Glide
- ASCA CH Goldcrest I Candy For Xanadu

If you see McMatt's EZ Victor in the pedigrees of your dogs, know you have something to be very proud of.

Victor's son AKC-ASCA CH Goldcrest Eyes On The Prize "Angus." Born 2006. By Victor x ASCA CH Canyon Oaks Hugs N Kisses. Photo courtesy of Tina Beck. Photo credit: Myrjam Walter.

Victor's son WTCH AKC-ASCA CH Brookridge SunFire And Away We Go CD RS-N ASCA HOF "Jet." Born 2001. By Victor x BISS AKC CH SunFire's Up N Away STDdsc ASCA HOF. Photo courtesy of David Clayton. Photo credit: In Motion.

Victor's son AKC-INT-ASCA CH McMatt's EZ Going OA NAJ USASA HOFX-ASCA HOF "Cruiser." Born 1997. By Victor x AKC CH Castle's Image of McMatt. Photo courtesy of Flo McDaniel.

Victor's son AKC CH McMatt's Legend of Mill Creek "Logan." Born 1997. By Victor x AKC CH Castle's Image of McMatt. Photo courtesy of Debra Tapp.

CONVERSATIONS

Kathy Fretz · I have a Victor granddaughter ATCH-IV CH Sunpiper's Tears On A River CDX RMX "Rio." Love her! She was born in 2008 and was sired by WTCH CH Briarcliff Onyx Overboard PT GS-O JS-O RS-N. Her dam is ATCH CH Kylin's Ice Blue Eaglett CDX RNX RA ASCA HOF. Rio's son is Victor's great-grandson ATCH AKC-CKC-ASCA CH Sunpiper's By A Landslide BN CD REMX RTX "Slider." Wow, I love this boy!

Karen Papadopoulos · Cuebiyar The Lady of the Lake "Misty" is Victor's great-great-granddaughter through AKC-AUST-ASCA CH McMatt's Lovely Lily "Tilley." Victor passed his type well down the line.

Lyndy Jacob · My beautiful FreeSpirit Mademoiselle "Elan" is Victor's great-granddaughter. Her grandsire is WTCH AKC-ASCA CH Sunfire Brookridge And Away We Go CD RS-N ASCA HOF. Elan has the nice earset Victor produced!

Victor's great-grandson ASCA CH Soundtracks Bossanova RN CGC "Boss." Born 2013. By RTCH-3 ASCA CH Soundtrack's Wishes Away CDX RTX x Soundtrack's Kisses From Heaven. Photo courtesy of Bethany McClure. Photo credit: Melinda Griffin.

Victor's son AKC-CKC CH Goldcrest Gotta Getta Gund "Gundy." Born 2006. By Victor x AKC-ASCA CH Ragtimes Sabotage. Photo courtesy of Tina Beck. Photo credit: Heather Gould.

Victor's daughter AKC-ASCA CH Goldcrest Greta Garbo "Greta." Born 2005. By Victor x Northland's Image Maker. Photo courtesy of Tina Beck. Photo credit: Callea.

Victor's son AKC CH Goldcrest The Inherent Victor "Darrin." Born 2004. Best of Breed Puppy 2004 ASCA National Specialty. By Victor x Northland's Image Maker. Photo courtesy of Mary Detor. Photo credit: Kit Rodwell.

Kirsten Tardiff · I have two young Victor great-great-great-great granddaughters Echolight Fly By Night "Blaire" and Echolight Smoke and Mirrors "Taiga." They were born in 2016. Their sire is BISS AKC-ASCA CH Northbay Wheel and Deal and their dam is Harts Fire And Ice of Wigglebottom.

Terry Dickey · WTCH AKC GCH-ASCA CH Shell Bluffs Renaissance Man HIAsd HSBd OFTDm AFTDsc RTDs "Patch" is Victor's grandson. His great-granddaughter is AKC-UKC-ASCA CH Shell Bluffs Kiss The Cowgirl STDs.

Dotti Guy · Victor was absolutely gorgeous and classic. A tribute to the breed!

Ray Schafer · I'm working to bring Victor into my lines.

Maureen P Retting · My blue stud dog has Victor's bloodlines in his pedigree including McMatt's Legend of Mill Creek, McMatt's Megapup of Mill Creek and others. My long-time mentor and good friend Debra Tapp, who was the owner of Mill Creek Kennel, will be in my heart forever. All our dogs at Rainbow Aussies have these foundation dogs in their pedigrees. Recently I've been crossing with herding lines with amazing results.

Pat Zapf · I have Victor's granddaughter AKC-UKC-ASCA CH Goldcrest's Too Buzz'd To Concentrate "Corona." She was born in 2009. Her sire is LUX-EUR-ASCA CH Melody's Hard To Concentrate and she's out of ASCA CH Goldcrest I Candy For Xanadu.

BIS AKC GCH-ASCA CH Shadomoons The Obvious Choice "Brazen" is Victor's great-granddaughter. She's by AKC GCH-UKC-ASCA CH Graffiti McMatt Shook Me @ Lookouttrail and out of Corona. AKC GCH Shadomoons I'm All The Buzz HT DN CA "Minx" is also Victor's great-granddaughter. She's by AKC-ASCA CH Impact's Pop Rocks and out of Corona.

Victor's son AKC-ASCA CH Windfalls KatchMeIfYouCan "Tag." Born 2003. By Victor x Windfalls Piece Of The Puzzle. Photo courtesy of J. & R. Timperon & Sally Reeve. (UNITED KINGDOM)

Victor's son AKC-ASCA CH Te Amo's Infinite Victory STDs "Excaliber." Born 2001. By Victor x Timberwood's Secret Tux No Tails. Photo courtesy of Kathryn Ross-Nash. Photo credit: Tom Digiacomo.

Victor's son AKC-ASCA CH Gemmells Waylander AX AXJ "Chase." Born 2004. By Victor x AKC-ASCA CH Blue Isle's Gone With The Wind. Photo courtesy of Rebecca Millsaps. Photo credit: Downey.

Victor's daughter Goldcrest Guilty Pleasure "Guilty." Born 2006. By Victor x AKC-ASCA CH Ragtime's Sabotage. Photo courtesy of Tina Beck. Photo credit: Willie Beck.

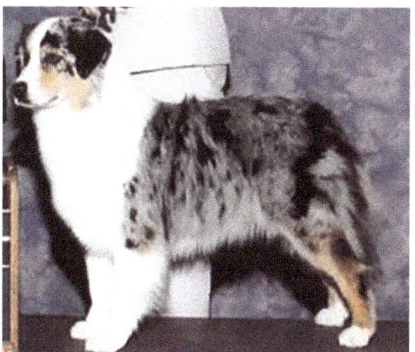

Victor's daughter AKC-ASCA CH Moorea's EZ To Be Me "Cat." Born 2004. By Victor x Moorea's Critics Choice. Photo courtesy of Jacquie Hallenbeck.

Victor's daughter AKC-ASCA CH McMatt's Megapup of Mill Creek "Megan." Born 1997. By Victor x AKC CH Castle's Image of McMatt. Photo courtesy of Flo McDaniel.

Victor's granddaughter SR CH Goldcrest A Friend Story "Fink." Born 2010. By AKC-ASCA CH Stonepine Sirius Black x ASCA CH Goldcrest I Candy for Xanadu. Photo courtesy of Sophie Trotier. Photo credit: Paula McDermid.(FRANCE)

Victor's granddaughter AKC-ASCA CH Freespirit Ready To Go OA OAJ RS-O JS-O GS-O "Lexie." Born 2004. By WTCH AKC-ASCA CH Brookridge Sunfire And Away We Go CD RS-N ASCA HOF x AKC-ASCA CH Broadway's Exotic Jewel.

Victor's great-granddaughter Liskarn Time To Wish At Mistyisle "Mika." Born 2008. By Thornapple Powercore x Shenkiri Princess Lei Zi. Photo courtesy of Kirstie Venton New. (UNITED KINGDOM)

Victor's daughter AKC-ASCA CH Goldcrest I've Got The Giggles "Callie." Born 2006. By Victor x ASCA CH Canyon Oaks Hugs N Kisses. Photo courtesy of Tina Beck. Photo credit: Dart Dogs/Family Tree.

Victor's great-grandson ASCA A-CH Striderite's Exuberance "Zubi." Born 2007. By MACH5 ADCH ATCH AKC-ASCA CH Agile Collinswood Razzmatazz CD MXG2 MJS2 MXF ROM X-I x AKC-ASCA CH Freespirit Ready To Go OA OAJ RS-O JS-O GS-O. Photo credit: Paula McDermid.

Victor's great-grandson DTCH Carolina Calais Keep on Walkin' JS-N JW'15 BJW'15 NJK "Jax." Born 2014. Qualified for Crufts 2018. By AKC-ASCA CH Calais Carolina Unmarked Bills x AKC GCH Carolina Calais Take It EZ. Photo courtesy of Joanne Boerland. Photo credit: Wiard Gorter. (NETHERLANDS)

Tanya M. Nowak · UKC CH Sunchaser T-n-T Kidnap Faith "Isis" is a great-great-granddaughter of Victor. Her sire was Legend's Smok'n Brasados Nitani and her dam was Charmois At'Sunchaser Kathleen. Isis' daughter is INT CH T-n-T's Dreamin Big "Faya" who is by CH Morning Mist Jive Talkin. She is Victor's great-great-great-granddaughter.

Kathy Peloquin · My handsome Cody is Victor's grandson. He's a joy to live with, a great partner and he is the sweetest soul EVER!

Angie Buchanan · AKC CH BriarRidge's Puttin' On The Ritz "Dapper" is Victor's great-great-grandson.

Taylor Gassert · Ryan Creeks Ace of Hearts CGCA "Willow" is Victor's great-great-

Photo credit: MontRose

AKC-ASCA CH Montrose Shadows In The Storm

"Static." Born 2002. By AKC CH Mill Creek's Stonemeadowscotsman x AKC CH Summertime Crimes of the Heart ROM C-I ROM X-I.

Victor's great-granddaughter Static is like a 95-year-old lady that still drives. She says, "I'm not old and I am just as capable as ever!" Static turned 15 in May. Her body and mind both function remarkably well.

This morning I caught her in the basement messing around. I didn't get the door shut perfectly and she used her nose and paw adeptly to open it. That's the second time in a week! She goes up and down stairs just fine, but I don't think she needs to be down in the basement. And, if I don't secure those safety latches on the doggie gates, she somehow gets them open. I thought old dogs were supposed to nap most of the time....

Static has two daughters who are the foundation bitches of two kennels: AKC-CKC CH MontRose Secret Garden SJ-R ROM X-II "Leaf" is the foundation bitch of Ninebark Aussies, and CKC-ASCA CH MontRose Madam de la Grande "Karche" is the foundation bitch of Terwin Aussies. Static's daughters both turned 11 years old in June 2017.

- J Kelsey Jones

granddaughter. She was born in 2013 and is by AKC CH Briarbrooks Johnny Cash and out of Ryan Creeks Crystal Jewel.

Laura Shivers · Victor's lovely daughter ASCA CH Goldcrest I Candy for Xanadu "Taffy" reminds me so much of Victor. She's 13 years old and still going strong!

Teresa Pepper-Marble · Multi Group Placing AKC CH Lk. Michigan's Red Solo Cup CGC "Tobey" is Victor's great-great-grandson. He has two crosses to Victor through AKC-INT-ASCA CH McMatt's EZ Going OA NAJ USASA HOFX-ASCA HOF. Tobey has had limited showing, but will hit the ASCA ring in 2018.

Virginia Hills · My AKC-CKC CH Silverscreen Shoot The Moon "Fannie" was a granddaugher of Victor. She was bred by Sue Leitzan and was sired by BIS AKC-CKC-ASCA CH Silverscreen Mystical Moon OA OAJ and out of Victor's daughter McMatt's Phoebe. Fannie was a great friend and competitor. She was always confident and looking to make friends.

Ana Maldonado · Victor's son BVIS AKC-ASCA-ESP-INT-GIB-PORT CH Gemmells Ghostking LW08 MW08 SCVW16 MW16 MVW16 "Griffen" won the 9-12 Month Dog Class at the 2005 ASCA Nationals. He was #11 All Breeds in Spain in 2010.

Terry Dickey · Select Dog and Select Bitch at the 2016 USASA Nationals were Victor's grandson WTCH AKC GCH-ASCA CH Shell Bluffs Renaissance Man and great-granddaughter AKC GCH-CKC-ASCA CH TreeStarr's Northwind Breeze ROM X-I. Both came out of the Veteran classes. That says a lot!

Kathryn Ross-Nash · My boys AKC-ASCA CH Te Amo's Top Gun-Wild Child CD STDs ROM X-I and AKC-ASCA CH Te Amo's Infinite Victory STDs

Victor's great-great-grandson AKC GCH-CKC-ASCA CH Aliyah's Heartbreak Ridge "Gunny." Born 2008. By MBIS BISS AKC GCH-ASCA CH Aliyah's Semper Fi of Joywalk ROM X-I x Northbay's Bells and Whistles. Photo courtesy of Lynne C. Skinner. Photo credit: Wajoma Smith.

Victor's great-grandson RTCH ATCH AKC-CKC-ASCA CH Sunpipers By A Landslide BN CD REMX RTX RS-E-SP GS-E-SP RS-E-OP "Slider." Born 2012. By AKC GCH-ASCA Premier CH Sazbrat Badlands x ATCH-IV CH Sunpiper's Tears On A River CDX RMX. Photo courtesy of Kathy Fretz. Photo credit: Donna Kelliher.

AKC-CKC-ASCA CH Goldcrest I'm So Vain "Carly." Born 2006. By Victor x ASCA CH Canyon Oaks Hugs-N-Kisses. Photo courtesy of Carol Garzina. Photo credit: Randy Roberts Photography.

Victor's son AKC-ASCA CH Goldcrest Globetrotter "Ponch." Born 2004. By Victor x Northland's Image Maker. Photo courtesy of Tina Beck. Photo credit: Randy Roberts Photography.

Victor's great-great-granddaughter Ryan Creeks Ace of Hearts CGCA "Willow." Born 2013. By AKC CH Briarbrooks Johnny Cash x Ryan Creeks Crystal Jewel. Photo courtesy of Taylor Gassert. Photo credit: Booth.

Victor's granddaughter ATCH-IV CH Sunpiper's Tears On A River CDX RMX "Rio." Born 2008. By WTCH CH Briarcliff Onyx Overboard PT GS-O JS-O RS-N x ATCH CH Kylin's Ice Blue Eaglett CDX RNX RA ASCA HOF. Photo courtesy of Kathy Fretz. Photo credit: Donna Kelliher.

Victor's daughter AKC-AKC CH Merribrook's Roses at Midnight "Ashley." Born 2004. BOB Veteran 2013 ASC Utah Pre-show. BOS Veteran 2012 National Specialty. Premier Champion 2009 ASCA National Specialty. By Victor x ASCA CH Merribrook's Midnight Rose. Photo courtesy of Liz Gibson. Photo credit: Alpensky.

Victor's great-grandson Dream to My Spirit of Shawnee's Home CHR-I CHR-II BH TG "Cooper." Born 2004. CASD Most Versatile Aussie 2007 and 2008. By Breezyoaks Blue By Acura x Todays Her Lucky Day. Photo courtesy of Ralf Onkelbach. (GERMANY)

were Victor's sons. My entire line was based on these talented dogs, and they've earned multiple championships as well as herding and obedience titles. AKC-ASCA CH Sonrisehill Hope of Te Amo STDs is Victor's granddaughter, Te Amo's Wingman STDs is his grandson, and AKC-ASCA CH Te Amo's Siren of Sazbrat and ASCA CH Te Brats Running with Scissors RN are great-grand children.

Karen Papadopoulos · Victor's granddaughters AKC-AUST-ASCA CH McMatt's Lovely Lily "Tilley" and CH McMatt's Bajas Tiger Lily "Lily" were litter sisters. They were by AKC-INT-ASCA CH McMatt's EZ Going OA NAJ USASA HOFX-ASCA HOF and out of AKC-ASCA CH Lil' Creeks As Requested ASCA HOF.

Ros Timperon · Victor was tremendously important in our kennel here in the U.K. His double-granddaughter CH Windfalls Cause I'm Worth It With Triforce "Loreal" gave us everything we could have hoped for and more. We also had her father RBIS AKC-ASCA CH Windfalls Katchmeifyoucan. We are so grateful to Patty Wirries of Windfall for sending us her best. I wish I'd had a chance to see Victor in person.

Judy Flynn Vandersteen · I loved Victor. He had a huge impact on our breed!

Cindy Alison · My Victor grandson AKC-ASCA CH Mandolyn's Fast Break was by WTCH AKC-ASCA CH Brookridge Sunfire And Away We Go CD RS-N ASCA HOF and out of Sunfire's Made to Order ASCA HOF.

Debbie Stuebe Lee · "Rosie" was a daughter of Victor from one of his earliest litters. She was the pup that no one wanted and was the absolute best dog for me. She came into my life at the right time and we did more than I ever dreamed possible. Rosie earned another Altered Premier at the 2011 ASCA Nationals when she was just shy of her 12th birthday. She was OTCH VCH

Victor's daughter ASCA CH Goldcrest I Candy For Xanadu "Taffy." Born 2004. Victor x CH Windfall's At Long Last. Photo courtesy of Laura Shivers.

Victor's son AKC-ASCA CH Te Amo's Top Gun-Wild Child "Maverick." Born 2001. Victor x Timberwood's Secret Tux No Tails. Photo courtesy of Kathryn Ross-Nash. Photo credit: Cedar Glen.

AKC CH McMatt's EZ Victor USASA HOFX-ASCA HOF

Victor's son Everlasting's Simon HSAs OTDds "Simon." Born 1999. By Victor x ASCA CH Everlasting's Ima Slick Chick ROM X-I. Photo credit: Karen Jones.

Victor's son AKC-INT CH Everlasting's Ima Rude Dude RN HSAs OTDds CGC ROM X-I "Rudy." Born 1999. By Victor x ASCA CH Everlasting's Ima Slick Chick ROM X-I. Photo credit: K. Jones.

Victor's granddaughter AKC-CKC CH Silverscreen Shoot The Moon "Fannie." Born 2002. By BIS AKC-CKC-ASCA CH Silverscreen Mystical Moon OA OAJ x McMatt's Phoebe. Photo courtesy of Virginia Hills.

Victor's great-great-granddaughter UKC CH Sunchaser T-n-T Kidnap Faith "Isis." Born 2008. By CH Legends Smok'n Brasandos Nitani x At Sunchaser Kathleen Blue De L'Oree. Photo courtesy of Tanya M. Nowak.

Victor's great-grandson NuCh NV-08 NV-12 Cuebiyar Soul Patrol "Harri." Born 2006. By AUST CH Thornapple Sub Zero (imp USA) x AKC-AUST-ASCA CH McMatt's Lovely Lily (imp USA). Photo courtesy of Tone Pernille Norum. Photo credit: Australian Shepherd Klubb Norge. (NORWAY)

Victor's granddaughter AKC-ASCA CH RaineDance Cruz'n for Mischief "Jolie." Born 2007. By AKC-INT-ASCA CH McMatt's EZ Going OA NAJ USASA HOFX-ASCA HOF x AKC CH RaineDance Merry Mischief PT OA AXJ RS-O JS-E GS-N ROM X-III ASCA HOF. Photo credit: Raine Lutz.

ALCH A-BIS A-BISS V-BIS A-CH Everlasting's Raindrops on Roses ASCA UDX AKC UD VER OTDsd STDc RS-E JS-E GS-E AX OAJ EAC OGC EJC TN-N TG-N WV-N RAE RMX RL-1 CGC. Altered Winners Bitch 2001 ASCA Nationals. 2004 ASCA Champion Utility Obedience Dog. High in Trial, High Combined, Most Promising Started Dog. Numerous Top 10s in agility, conformation, obedience and rally. Agility, conformation and obedience finals competitor. She is always in my heart and I miss her every day.

Flo McDaniel · I always thought Rosie was so well-structured and beautiful to watch move.

Tim Preston · I had no idea Rosie was a Victor daughter! She was an absolutely stunning mover. Always appreciated seeing her in any ring.

Bethany McClure · My Victor grandson is ASCA CH Soundtracks Bossanova RN CGC "Boss." He was born in 2013. His parents are ASCA CH RTCH RTCH-3 Soundtrack's Wishes Away CDX RTX and Soundtrack's Kisses from Heaven. Boss earned his RN in both AKC and ASCA. He's a new ASCA Champion and has a CGC and conformation points in AKC. Boss has one of the best personalities of any dog I've ever known, but I am kind of partial. He's also in training for agility and herding. I'm very excited about his future!

Maureen Retting · My dog Twister is Victor's grandson. He was the most honest dog and he loved to herd.

Victor's granddaughter AKC-UKC-ASCA CH Goldcrest's Too Buzz'd To Concentrate "Corona." Born 2009. By LUX-EUR-ASCA CH Melody's Hard To Concentrate x ASCA CH Goldcrest I Candy For Xanadu. Photo courtesy of Pat Zapf. Photo credit: Shadomoon.

Victor's daughter A-BISS A-BIS V-BIS OTCH V-CH ALCH A-CH Everlasting's Raindrops on Roses (multi performance titles) "Rosie." Born 1999. By Victor x ASCA CH Everlasting's Ima Slick Chick ROM X-I. Photo courtesy of Debbie Stuebe Lee. Photo credit: John Stuebe.

Victor's great-granddaughter BIS AKC GCH-ASCA CH Shadomoons The Obvious Choice "Brazen." Born 2014. By AKC GCH-UKC-ASCA CH Graffiti McMatt Shook Me @ Lookouttrail x AKC-UKC-ASCA CH Goldcrest's Too Buzz'd to Concentrate. Photo courtesy of Pat Zapf. Photo credit: JC Photo.

Karen Jones · The traits I appreciated the most in my Victor kids were their willingness to please and their striking good looks. Everlasting's Simon HSAs OTDds "Simon" had both of these qualities. He was a biddable dog who earned national rankings and year end awards in both ASCA and AKC. "Ewe Must Be Kiddin' Farm" came to be because of Simon's love of herding. I never imagined that one instinct test would lead to a new hobby. His dam was ASCA CH Everlasting's Ima Slick Chick ROM X-I.

Victor's son AKC-INT CH Everlasting's Ima Rude Dude RN HSAs OTDds CGC ROM X-I "Rudy" was a group-placing conformation champion and a talented herding dog rolled into one cute little package. During his show career

Victor's great-great-great-granddaughter INT CH T-n-T's Dreamin Big "Faya." Born 2015. By CH Morning Mist Jive Talkin x UKC CH Sunchaser T-n-T Kidnap Faith. Photo courtesy of Tanya M. Nowak.

Victor's son BVIS AKC-ASCA-ESP-INT-GIB-PORT CH Gemmells Ghostking LW08 MW08 SCVW16 MW16 MVW16 "Griffen." Born 2004. #11 All Breeds in Spain 2010. By Victor x CH Blue Isle's Gone With The Wind. Photo courtesy of Ana Maldonado. (SPAIN)

he earned awards for Most Promising Started Dog, High in Trial and Year End Merit Rankings. Rudy lived a long life of 15+ years and I feel privileged to have been his breeder and owner. He was born on Thanksgiving Day 1999 and every day with him was a true blessing. I could not have asked for a better dog. His dam was ASCA CH Everlasting's Ima Slick Chick ROM X-I.

Victor's daughter AKC-ASCA CH Merribrook's Roses at Midnight "Ashley" (Black tri in the front row between blue merle and red tri). Born 2004. Best of Breed Veteran 2013 ASC Utah Pre-show. Best of Opposite Sex Veteran 2012 ASCA National Specialty. Premier Champion 2009 ASCA National Specialty. By Victor x ASCA CH Merribrook's Midnight Rose. Photo taken in 2016 at the ASCA National Specialty with Ashley and 12 of her kids and grandkids. Photo courtesy of Liz Gibson. Photo credit: Dart Dog.

Victor's great-great-grandson AKC CH BriarRidge's Puttin' On The Ritz "Dapper." Born 2016. By AKC CH Aliyah's Patriot of Mill Creek ROM X-III ROM C-I x AKC GCH Milwin's Enchantment. Photo courtesy of Angie Buchanan. Photo credit: Amber Jade Aanensen.

Victor's great-granddaughter AKC GCH Shadomoons I'm All The Buzz HT DN CA "Minx." Born 2013. By AKC-ASCA CH Impact's Pop Rocks x AKC-UKC-ASCA CH Goldcrest's Too Buzz'd To Concentrate. Photo courtesy of Pat Zapf. Photo credit: Jeffrey Hanlin.

Victor's great-grandson AKC GCH-BIS CKC-UKC-ASCA CH Valor's King of Blue "Blue." Born 2008. Best of Opposite Sex 2013 Westminster. By AKC CH McMatt's The Entertainer x AKC-ASCA CH McMatt's Bajas Tiger Lily. Photo courtesy of Karie McBrian. Photo credit: John Ashbey.

Castlesheps Dear Prudence "Maui." Born 2015. Her pedigree has four crosses to Victor. By CHI CH JCHI Wind Spirit RS Sparks Will Fly x CH JCHI Eva De La Casa Eder. Photo courtesy of Luciana Busso. (ARGENTINA)

Victor's granddaughter AKC-ASCA CH Goldcrest Orange-A-Peel "Smoothie." Born 2009. By AKC-ASCA CH Ivory Isles Meets The Criteria ASCA HOF x Goldcrest Guilty Pleasure. Photo courtesy of Tina Beck. Photo credit: Pat Hutchinson.

Victor's daughter AKC-ASCA CH NiteStar's Color Me If You Can "Doodle." Born 2005. By Victor x A-CH Woodstock's Color Me Rose STDs ASCA HOF. Photo courtesy of Trisha Herring. Photo credit: Bill Meyer.

Victor's great-great-great-grandson MBIS OH-AKC GCH-UKC-ASCA CH Northwind Singin' The Blues "Grizz." Born 2011. By BIS AKC GCH-CKC-ASCA CH Whidbeys Moonlight Frost RA ROM X-I x AKC GCH-CKC-ASCA CH TreeStarr's Northwind Breeze ROM X-I. Photo courtesy of Laurie Thompson and Janet Matkin. Photo credit: Amber Jade Aanensen.

Victor's great-grandson MBIS BISS AKC GCH-ASCA CH Aliyah's Semper Fi of Joywalk ROM X-II ROM C-I "Dallas." Born 2003. BOB Westminster 2007, AOM 2006 & 2008. AOM 2007 Eukanuba. By AKC CH Mill Creek's Stonemeadow Scotsman ROM X-I x MontRose The Golden Harvest. Photo courtesy of Lynne Skinner. Photo credit: John Ashbey.

AKC-ASCA Champion
Briarbrooks Silver Sequence
ROM C-III
holds the AKC record for the all-time leading
Aussie dam with 23 champion offspring.

Photo credit: Petrulis

AKC-ASCA Champion
Briarbrooks Silver Sequence
ROM C-III

Call name: Silver
Born: 1987
Sire: ASCA CH Briarbrooks Coat of Arms
Dam: ASCA CH Shadowmere's Close to Midnite
Breeder: Tina Smith, Shadowmere
Owner: Linda Wilson, Briarbrook

Silver had the enviable traits of being both an outstanding show dog and a phenomenal producer. During her conformation career, she was ranked #1 Aussie in the ASCA standings for 1989 and 1990, and for twelve years she held the ASCA record for defeating the most dogs in a single year. She was Best of Opposite Sex at the 1992 USASA National Specialty and received multiple group placements. When Silver stepped out of the show ring and into the whelping box, she proved herself again. She consistently produced top-quality offspring and holds the AKC record for the all-time leading Aussie dam with 23 champions.

It's no accident that Silver was such an influential brood bitch. Her pedigree includes ASCA CH Fieldmaster's Three Ring Circus ASCA HOF "Bonzo" on both the top and bottom sides. He was the sire of 53 champions, which was a remarkable achievement in the 1980s. His progeny included four National Specialty Best of Breed titleholders and nine Hall of Fame sons and daughters. Silver inherited his prepotency for producing top-quality offspring.

Her dam and maternal granddam also contributed to Silver's genetic prowess. They were beautiful moving bitches with pedigrees that included two of the top sires of the 1970s and 1980s, ASCA CH Windermere's Sunshine of Bonnie-Blu CDX ASCA HOF and ASCA CH Fieldmaster of Flintridge ASCA HOF.

With a powerful pedigree and lovely conformation, Silver's owner wanted to find a sire that would be her equal. She chose BIS BISS AKC-ASCA CH My Main Man of Heatherhill ROM X-I ROM C-III ROM O-I ASCA HOF "Paddy" and the results were outstanding. The quality of the entire litter was so uniformly excellent that the cross was repeated multiple times. Following in the footsteps of their sire and dam, the offspring of Silver and Paddy were outstanding conformation dogs and top producers themselves. Many of them went on to create their own legends.

Silver's most notable offspring were:
› AKC CH Briarbrooks Valedictorian USASA HOFX-ASCA HOF. Sire of 103 champions, ranked #1 Aussie sire in AKC 1996, 1998, 1999, 2000, 2001. Sire of:
   › AKC CH Kaleidoscope Case in Point ROM C-III. Ranked #2 Aussie (right behind his sire) in AKC 1996, 1997, 1998 and #6 in 1999. Sire of 27 champions including the 1998 Westminster Best of Breed winner.
   › MBIS BISS AKC CH Dreamstreet's Season Ticket ROM X-II ROM C-II. Winner of three AKC All-breed Bests In Show, Best of Breed at Eukanuba, Award of Merit at Westminster, Award of Merit at USASA National Specialty. Sire of multiple AKC and ASCA champions, obedience, and agility titled dogs.
   › MBIS AKC CH Briarbrooks Turning Point. Winner of three AKC All-breed Bests In Show, Best Veteran and Award of Merit 2004 USASA National Specialty.
› AKC CH Briarbrooks Silver Medallion USASA HOFX. Sire of 33 champions including the 2009 Westminster Best of Breed winner:
   › BIS BISS AKC Bronze GCH Briarbrooks Copyright ROM C-III. Best of Breed 2009 Westminster. Sire of 76 champions.
› AKC CH Briarbrooks Quicksilver ROM X-II ROM C-II. Best of Breed 2003 Westminster, ranked #1 in Breed and #2 in Group for 2000, winner of 22 Group 1st and 215 Best of Breed awards.
› AKC CH Briarbrooks Full Speed Ahead. Best of Breed 1997 Westminster, Top 10 dog 1995 and 1997.
› AKC CH Briarbrooks Bringin In The Silver. #1 Bitch in the Breed 1994, 1995.
› AKC CH Briarbrooks Checkmate ROM C-I.

Silver contributed her genetic strength to generations of Aussies, and her name can be seen in pedigrees of many of today's conformation show dogs.

```
Pedigree
                                    CH Fieldmaster of Flintridge HOF
                          ASCA CH Fieldmaster's Three Ring Circus HOF
                          Whispering Pines of Flintridge
              ASCA CH Briarbrooks Coat of Arms
                          CH Buck Fever of Blue Mist
                          Fieldmaster's Lodi
                          CH Fieldmaster's Kandee Kisses
  AKC-ASCA CH Briarbrooks Silver Sequence ROM C-III
                                    CH Fieldmaster's Three Ring Circus HOF
                          ASCA CH Briarbrooks Midnight Express
                          Glacier Crest Naughty Pine
              ASCA CH Shadowmere's Close To Midnite
                          CH Sun's Mark of Windermere CD HOF
                          Briarbrooks Marque of Patchwork ROM C-II HOF
                          Three Pines Carbine
```

Silver's sire ASCA CH Briarbrooks Coat of Arms "Cody." Born 1984. Photo courtesy of Linda Wilson.

Silver's dam ASCA CH Shadowmere's Close To Midnite "Connie." Born 1984. Photo courtesy of Linda Wilson.

Silver's paternal grandsire ASCA CH Fieldmaster's Three Ring Circus ASCA HOF "Bonzo." Born 1977. Photo courtesy of Linda Wilson.

Silver's maternal granddam Briarbrooks Marque of Patchwork ROM C-II ASCA HOF "Marque." Born 1982. Photo courtesy of Linda Wilson.

CONVERSATIONS

Kimber Shields · Silver's son AKC CH Briarbrooks Valedictorian USASA HOFX-ASCA HOF "Victor" was, and has always been, one of my most favorite dogs. He was such a great dog. He was just a sweet dog who never got into trouble.

Patti Herhold · Silver's granddaughter AKC-ASCA CH Inverness Sweet Victory "Tori" won Best of Breed at the 2006 National Specialty from the 7-10 year old Veteran's Class! She was by AKC CH Briarbrooks Valedictorian USASA HOFX-ASCA HOF out of AKC CH Snowbelt's Rhapsody In Blue ROM C-I. Her dam finished with a BOB and Group win from the classes. Tori had the same sweet personality as her sire.

Virginia Hills · Loved Tori! So pretty and so sweet.

Jayne Holligan · Tori was an amazing, stunning girl.

Celeste Lucero Telles · Silver was the grandmother of my dogs AKC-ASCA CH La Plata's Taos Legends and ASCA CH La Plata Reina de Las Flores. They were by Silver's son AKC CH Briarbrooks Valedictorian USASA HOFX-ASCA HOF and out of my ASCA CH Cielito Lindo de La Plata. She was a daughter of ASCA CH Agua Dulce Final Option ASCA HOF and granddaughter of ASCA CH Rising Sun of Windermere CDX STDds ASCA HOF. I loved these dogs and miss them today.

Silver's great-granddaughter AKC GCH Briarbrook's Zenyatta "Zenyatta." Born 2010. Winner's Bitch and Best of Winners 2013 USASA National Specialty. By BIS BISS AKC Bronze GCH Briarbrooks Copyright ROM C-III x AKC CH Briarbrook's Always Decked Out. Photo courtesy of Linda Wilson.

Silver's son AKC CH Briarbrooks Valedictorian USASA HOFX-ASCA HOF "Victor." Born 1992. Sire of 103 champions. Ranked #1 sire in AKC 1996, 1998, 1999, 2000, 2001. By BIS BISS AKC ASCA CH My Main Man of Heatherhill ROM X-I ROM C-III ROM O-I ASCA HOF x Silver. Photo courtesy of Linda Wilson.

Silver's daughter AKC CH Briarbrooks Silver Anniversary ROM C-III "Annie." Born 1992. Dam of 14 champions. By BIS BISS AKC ASCA CH My Main Man of Heatherhill ROM X-I ROM C-III ROM O-I ASCA HOF x Silver. Photo courtesy of Linda Wilson. Photo credit: Booth.

Silver's grandson MBIS BISS VBIS AKC GCH- UKC GCH-INT-ASCA CH Skyecove's Color Me Awesome RA URO2 CGC "Griffin." Born 2006. By AKC CH Briarbrooks Silver Medallion USASA HOFX x Briarbrooks Meritage ROM C-I. Photo courtesy of Terri Rein. Photo credit: Lake Michigan.

Silver's son AKC CH Briarbrooks Quicksilver USASA HOFX-ASCA HOF "Ricki." Born 1996. Best of Breed 2003 Westminster, Ranked #1 Breed and #2 Group 2000. By BIS BISS AKC ASCA CH My Main Man of Heatherhill ROM X-I ROM C-III ROM O-I ASCA HOF x Silver. Photo courtesy of Linda Wilson.

Silver's son AKC-INT-ASCA CH Briarbrooks Silver Strike "Striker." Born 1996. By BIS BISS AKC ASCA CH My Main Man of Heatherhill ROM X-I ROM C-III ROM O-I ASCA HOF x Silver. Photo courtesy of Linda Wilson and Tina Smith. Photo credit: Perulis.

Silver's son AKC CH Briarbrooks Full Speed Ahead "Razz." Born 1992. Best of Breed 1996 Westminster, Ranked Top 10 dog 1997 and 1995. By BIS BISS AKC ASCA CH My Main Man of Heatherhill ROM X-I ROM C-III ROM O-I ASCA HOF x Silver. Photo courtesy of Linda Wilson.

Silver's son AKC CH Briarbrooks Silver Certificate "Kato." Born 1996. By BIS BISS AKC ASCA CH My Main Man of Heatherhill ROM X-I ROM C-III ROM O-I ASCA HOF x Silver. Photo courtesy of Linda Wilson.

Juli May Wiseman · AKC CH Briarbrooks Thistledown Fire "KC" was a son of AKC CH Kaleidoscope's Case in Point ROM C-III and a great-grandson of Silver. KC was born in 1999. AKC GCH Skyecove's Bonfire "Bailey" was Casey's great-granddaughter and she was born in 2013. She won a Select Award at Westminster in 2016 and was Best of Opposite Sex at that show in 2017.

Silver's granddaughter Briarbrooks Meritage ROM C-I "Tajie" had four champion offspring when she was bred to AKC CH Briarbrooks Thistledown Fire. She had several more champion offspring from subsequent litters.

Terri Rein · MBIS BISS VBIS AKC GCH-UKC GCH-INT-ASCA CH Skyecove's Color Me Awesome RA URO2 CGC "Griffin" was a Silver grandson. He was sired by AKC CH Briarbrooks Silver Medallion USASA HOFX and was out of Briarbrooks Meritage ROM C-I. I have had three offspring of "Tajie." She was one of my favorite dogs of all time!

AKC-UKC MBIMBS GRCH-INT-ASCA CH Skyecove's Smoke and Mirrors RE BN NJP NAP A-RA URO2 UAG1 CGC "Suzee" is a Silver great-granddaughter on both the sire's and dam's sides of her pedigree. Her sire was MBIS AKC CH Dreamstreet's Season Ticket ROM X-II ROM C-II who was by AKC CH Briarbrooks Valedictorian USASA HOFX-ASCA HOF "Victor." Her dam was Briarbrooks Meritage ROM C-I. Her breeder was Juli Wiseman. I am privileged to own her!

Renate Agterberg · Silver is behind a lot of the dogs in my kennel through CH Alnairs Mailman and CH Alnairs Platinum Edition. I love these lines and type.

Silver's son AKC CH Briarbrook's Silverware "Warren." Born 1996. Award of Merit 1999 USASA National Specialty. By BISS AKC-ASCA CH My Main Man of Heatherhill ROM X-I ROM C-III ROM O-I ASCA HOF x Silver. Photo courtesy of Linda Wilson. Photo credit: Glazbrook.

Silver's daughter AKC-INT-ASCA CH Briarbrooks Silver Bells "Bobbi Sue." Born 1994. Winner's Bitch and Best of Winners 1996 USASA National Specialty, Award of Merit 2001 Westminster. By BIS BISS AKC ASCA CH My Main Man of Heatherhill ROM X-I ROM C-III ROM O-I ASCA HOF x Silver. Photo courtesy of Linda Wilson. Photo credit: Photos by Kat.

Silver's grandson BIS BISS AKC Bronze GCH Briarbrooks Copyright ROM C-III "Copyright." Born 2002. Sire of 76 champions. Best of Breed 2009 Westminster. By AKC CH Briarbrooks Silver Medallion USASA HOFX x CH Briarbrooks Photo Credit. Photo courtesy of Linda Wilson. Photo credit: Garden Studio.

Sunnyrain Aussies · Silver is the ground beneath my kennel. I was honored to own one of Silver's sons AKC-ASCA CH Briarbrooks Silversmith ROM C-II "Smitty." AKC-ASCA CH Sunnyrains Summer Solstice "Celeste" was a Silver granddaughter on the top side and a great-granddaughter on the bottom side of her pedigree.

Silver's grandson AKC CH Kaleidoscope Case in Point ROM C-III "Casey." Born 1994. Ranked #2 Aussie in AKC 1996, 1997, 19989. Sire of 27 champions including the 1998 Westminster Best of Breed winner. By AKC CH Briarbrooks Valedictorian USASA HOFX- ASCA HOF x CH Briarbrooks Oh My Oh. Photo courtesy of Linda Wilson. Photo credit: Downey.

Silver's son AKC CH Briarbrooks Silver Medallion USASA HOFX "Dillon." Born 1996. Sire of 33 champions including the 2009 Westminster Best of Breed winner. By BIS BISS AKC ASCA CH My Main Man of Heatherhill ROM X-I ROM C-III ROM O-I ASCA HOF x Silver. Photo courtesy of Linda Wilson. Photo credit: Kohler.

Cheryl Shick · Silver was a stunning girl!

Erin Holley · Gorgeous! Love, love, love!

Lisa Durand · AKC GCH-CKC-ASCA CH Star's Take A Hint "Clue" is Silver's great-great-great-grandson. He's keeping the dream alive here at Olde Bay Australian Shepherds.

Francine Guerra · Silver's double great-great-granddaughter BIS AKC CH Buff Cap Creslane Arcticmist "Swizzle" was Best In Show at the Annual 2007 National Dog Show, which is held at Thanksgiving. She was by AKC CH

Silver's granddaughter AKC-ASCA CH Inverness Sweet Victory "Tori." Born 1997. Best of Breed 2006 USASA National Specialty from the 7-10 Veteran's Class. By AKC CH Briarbrooks Valedictorian USASA HOFX-ASCA HOF x AKC CH Snowbelt's Rhapsody In Blue ROM C-I. Photo courtesy of Patti Herhold. Photo credit: Maria DeBello.

Silver's grandson AKC MBIS CH Dreamstreet's Season Ticket ROM X-II ROM C-II "Sid." Born 2002. Winner of three AKC All-breed Bests In Show, Best of Breed at Eukanuba, Award of Merit at Westminster, Award of Merit at USASA National Specialty. By AKC CH Briarbrooks Valedictorian USASA HOFX-ASCA HOF x CH Myshara's Shameless. Photo courtesy of Sharon Fontanini.

Silver's granddaughter Briarbrooks Meritage ROM C-I "Tajie." Born 2001. By AKC CH Briarbrooks Valedictorian USASA HOFX-ASCA HOF x Briarbrooks Debutante. Photo courtesy of Juli May Wiseman.

Silver's double great-great-grandson AKC-ASCA CH Buff Cap Bayou City @ Alias "Houston." Born 2010. By BISS AKC GCH-UKC-ASCA CH Copper Hills City Limits x BIS AKC CH-ASCA CH Buff Cap Creslane Arcticmist. Photo courtesy of Francine Guerra.

Kaleidoscope Stone Ravenwynd CD RE HT x AKC CH Gothams Sea Nymph. Swizzle was owned by Nancy Gagnon.

Tina Smith-Lass · I had the privilege of co-owning Silver's son AKC CH-BIS INT CH-ASCA CH Briarbrooks Silver Strike "Striker." He had a beautiful head, clean movement and always had a happy personality. He won Best in Show at an International Show over some top AKC Best in Show Specials. He also earned many group wins, National Specialty Premiers and Awards of Merit.

ASCA CH Shadowmere's Close To Midnite "Connie" was Silver's dam. She had extraordinary side gait and presence. Always fun to show and share life with. She will forever be my heart dog and the reason I love Aussies.

Tim Preston · Connie was absolutely beautiful to watch moving or just standing around. Loved her to pieces.

Susan Landry Whiticar · Who was the blue bitch that I awarded Best In Sweeps at Nationals in Florida, back in the nineties? She was so correct, so undeniable!

Kimber Shields · She was Silver's granddaughter CH Los Pinos Porshe Carrera. She was sired by AKC CH Briarbrooks Valedictorian USASA HOFX-ASCA HOF. Silver's daughter CH Briarbrooks Silver Bells was WB and BOW at that Nationals.

At the 1997 USASA Nationals, Silver's son CH Briarbrooks Dealin In Silver was BOB Sweeps and her daughter CH Briarbrooks Silver Berry was BOS Sweeps.

Phyllis McCullum · Silver's great-granddaughter MBIS BISS CKC CH Clearfires Dreaming In Colour CD TD RN "Harper" was awarded Best of Breed at the 2012 USASA National Specialty from the Veteran's Class. She was by AKC-CKC CH Briarbrooks Turnin' Heads CD TT CGC x Cobbercrest Ain't I Cool CD.

Silver's great-great-great-grandson AKC GCH-CKC-ASCA CH Star's Take A Hint "Clue." Born 2009. By ASCA CH Happy Trails Pork Chop Dupre x AKC CH Briarbrooks Mademoiselle. Photo courtesy of Lisa Durand. Photo credit: Booth.

Silver's son AKC-ASCA CH Briarbrooks Silversmith ROM C-II "Smitty." Born 1994. By BIS BISS AKC ASCA CH My Main Man of Heatherhill ROM X-I ROM C-III ROM O-I ASCA HOF x Silver. Photo courtesy of Sunnyrain Aussies.

Silver's great-granddaughter MBIS MBISS AKC GCH Myshara's Dream Girl "Beyonce." Born 2007. Winner of 16 AKC All-breed Bests In Show, Best of Breed at two National Specialties, Best of Breed Westminster, Best of Breed Eukanuba World Championship Show, Best of Breed The National Dog Show, Number 1 Australian Shepherd 2008, 2009, 2010. 108 Group Firsts. By AKC-ASCA CH Starswept's HiFlyin' At Hisaw x MBIS BISS AKC Briarbrooks I'm Too Sexy. Photo courtesy of Sharon Fontanini. Photo credit: DogAds.

Tim Preston · I loved Harper!

Phyllis McCullum · Harper's daughter Brenna was Silver's granddaughter. Brenna was MBIS CKC GCHEx-AKC CH Starwoods Awake In A Dream CD RE AGN AGNJ. She was by AKC CH Briarbrook Silver Certificate x Harper.

Silver's great-great-great-granddaughter AKC GCH Skyecove's Bonfire "Bailey." Born 2013. Select Award 2016 Westminster, Best Opposite Sex 2017 Westminster. By AKC GCH TK Rocks Running Against the Wind x AKC CH Skyecoves Inferno. Photo courtesy of Juli May Wiseman. Photo credit: John Ashbey.

Silver's double great-great-granddaughter BIS AKC CH Buff Cap Creslane Arcticmist "Swizzle." Born 2002. Best In Show 2007 National Dog Show. By AKC CH Kaleidoscope Stone Ravenwynd CD RE HT x AKC CH Gothams Sea Nymph. Photo courtesy of Nancy Gagnon. Photo credit: John Ashbey.

Silver's great-granddaughter MBIS BISS CKC CH Clearfires Dreaming In Colour CD TD RN "Harper." Born 2001. BOB 2012 USASA National Specialty from Veteran's Class. By AKC-CKC CH Briarbrooks Turnin' Heads CD TT CGC x Cobbercrest Ain't I Cool CD. Photo courtesy of Phyllis McCullum. Photo credit: Pix n Pages.

Silver's grandson AKC-ASCA CH La Plata's Taos Legends "Taos." Born 1994. By AKC CH Briarbrooks Valedictorian USASA HOFX-ASCA HOF x ASCA CH Cielito Lindo de La Plata. Photo courtesy of Celeste Lucero Telles. Photo credit: Kohler.

Silver's double great-granddaughter AKC CH-UKC MBIMBS GRCH-INT-ASCA CH Skyecove's Smoke and Mirrors RE BN NJP NAP A-RA URO2 UAG1 CGC "Suzee." Born 2008. By MBIS AKC CH Dreamstreet's Season Ticket ROM X-II ROM C-II x Briarbrooks Meritage ROM C-I. Photo courtesy of Terri Rein. Photo credit: Cary Manaton.

Silver's great-grandson AKC CH Briarbrooks Thistledown Fire "KC." Born 1999. Best Opposite Sex Veteran Sweeps 2007 USASA National Specialty. By AKC CH Kaleidoscope Case in Point ROM C-III x AKC CH Briarbrooks Silver Anniversary ROM C-III. Photo courtesy of Juli May Wiseman. Photo credit: Tom McNulty.

Silver's granddaughter AKC CH-MBIS CKC GCHEx Starwoods Awake In A Dream CD RE AGN AGNJ "Brenna." Born 2004. By AKC CH Briarbrook Silver Certificate x MBIS BISS CKC CH Clearfires Dreaming In Colour CD TD RN. Photo courtesy of Phyllis McCullum. Photo credit: Jeffrey Hanlin.

Silver's granddaughter AKC-ASCA CH Sunnyrains Summer Solstice "Celeste." Born 1999. By AKC CH Briarbrooks Valedictorian USASA HOFX-ASCA HOF x AKC CH Briarbrooks Calamity Jane. Photo courtesy of Sunnyrain Aussies.

Auggie was a remarkable producer.

She was the dam of 22 champion offspring in six litters; 12 were both AKC and ASCA champions, and five earned ASCA HOF status.

Through her progeny, Auggie's influence continues to be seen across the United States, in Europe, and in Australia.

Photo courtesy of Heatherhill

AKC-ASCA Champion
Oprah Winfree of Heatherhill
ASCA HOF Dam #85

Call name: Auggie
Born: 1988
Sire: AKC-ASCA CH Agua Dulce Final Option ASCA HOF
Dam: Moonspinner of Brigadoon ASCA HOF
Breeders: Alan and Kathy McCorkle, Heatherhill
Owners: Alan and Kathy McCorkle, Heatherhill; Sandy and Jody Cummings

Auggie was an absolutely stunning bitch. She had a beautiful profile, gorgeous head and expression, and breathtaking movement. Her temperament was easy-going and she was a dream to show. Auggie was a tremendous producer who consistently passed her lovely type and movement to her offspring. She was also a beloved pet who lived with her co-owners, Sandy and Jody Cummings, when she wasn't being shown or raising litters at Heatherhill.

Auggie was the dam of 22 champion offspring in six litters; 12 were both AKC and ASCA champions, and five earned ASCA HOF status.

AUGGIE and
ASCA CH BRIGADOON'S ONE ARROGANT DUDE USASA HOFX-ASCA HOF
› AKC-ASCA CH Heatherhill You Talk Too Much ASCA HOF
› AKC-ASCA CH Heatherhill Sweet Talkin Dude CD HS STDs OA OAJ ASCA HOF
› AKC-ASCA CH Heatherhill Montel Williams ASCA HOF
› AKC-ASCA CH Heatherhill Sally Jessie
› AKC-ASCA CH Heatherhill Jenny Jones
› AKC-ASCA CH Heatherhill Joan Rivers
› ASCA CH Heatherhill Regis Philbin

AUGGIE and
ASCA CH BRIGADOON'S CALIFORNIA DUDE CD HS STDS ASCA HOF
› BISS AKC-ASCA CH Heatherhill Black-N-Decker ASCA HOF
› ASCA CH Heatherhill On Line
› ASCA CH Heatherhill Cinderella
› ASCA CH Heatherhill High Caliber
› AKC-ASCA CH Heatherhill Bipity Bopity Boo

AUGGIE and AKC-ASCA CH HEATHERHILL GRAND MARSHAL
› ASCA CH Heatherhill Take A Chance OnMe
› AKC-ASCA CH Heatherhill Whoopie Goldberg
› AKC-ASCA CH Heatherhill My Waterloo ASCA HOF
› ASCA CH Heatherhill Head Over Heels

AUGGIE and AKC-ASCA CH SUERTES ARROGANT WEE WILLIE
› ASCA CH Heatherhill Ricki Lake
› AKC-ASCA CH Heatherhill Overdraft
› AKC CH Heatherhill Over The Edge

AUGGIE and AKC-ASCA CH HEATHERHILL CRUSHED ICE
› AKC CH Heatherhill Rosie O'Donnell
› AKC-ASCA CH Heatherhill Tyra Banks

AUGGIE and AKC-ASCA CH TAYCIN'S STONE WASHED BLUES ASCA HOF
› ASCA CH Heatherhill Oprah's Last Pleasure

Pedigree

```
                                                    CH Winchester's Hotline HOF
                                       ASCA CH Winchester's Rollin Rapids HOF
                                             CH Sundown's Midnight Serenade
                      AKC-ASCA CH Agua Dulce Final Option ASCA HOF
                                             CH Winchester's Hotline HOF
                                       ASCA CH Country Hotline of Agua Dulce CDX HOF
                                             Taycin's Country Girl CD
AKC-ASCA CH Oprah Winfree of Heatherhill ASCA HOF
                                             CH Arrogance of Heatherhill CD STDd HOF
                                       ASCA CH Brigadoon's Moonraker
                                             Patch-Work Thumbelina
                      Moonspinner of Brigadoon ASCA HOF
                                             CH Sunshine of Bonnie-Blu CDX HOF
                                       ASCA CH Windswept of Windermere CD HOF
                                             Blue Heather of Windermere HOF
```

Auggie's sire ASCA CH Agua Dulce Final Option ASCA HOF "Paddington." Born 1986. Photo courtesy of Pam Levin.

Auggie's dam Moonspinner of Brigadoon ASCA HOF "Spinny." Born 1981. Photo courtesy of Heatherhill.

Auggie had an enormous influence on many of the major bloodlines across the United States, in Europe, and in Australia. Some of those include Absoloot, Accra, After All, Agua Dulce, Aristocrat, Bayouland, Bayshore, Broadway, Buff Cap, Catori, Copper Hills, Crazy Heart, Dreamstreet, Eaglecrest, Firethorne, Halfmoon, Heatherhill, Kinetic, Lil' Creek, Limelite, Manape, Meadowlawn, Melody, Merribrook, MontRose, Myshara, Northbay, Paradigm, Paragon, Paradox, PennYCaerau, Prestige, Propwash, Reverie, Rosemere, Shoreland, Stone Ridge, Stonehaven, Stonepine, Thornapple, Threepines, TreeStarr, Vinelake, Windfall, Windrift, Windypine, Woodstock, Wyndcrest, and Wyndstar.

1993 - AUGGIE and
ASCA CH BRIGADOON'S ONE ARROGANT DUDE USASA HOFX-ASCA HOF

The Auggie x Dude litter (The Talk Show Litter) was her most outstanding. Out of eight puppies born, seven became champions, six were both AKC and ASCA champions, and three became ASCA Hall of Fame sires.

AKC-ASCA CH Heatherhill Sally Jessie "Sally."
Photo courtesy of Heatherhill. Photo credit: Kit Rodwell.

AKC-ASCA CH Heatherhill You Talk Too Much ASCA HOF "Rush." Photo credit: B.W. Kernan.

First Place Brood Bitch class 1995 USASA Nationals with three of the Talk Show litter. (Left to right)
› AKC-ASCA CH Oprah Winfree of Heatherhill ASCA HOF with Alan McCorkle
› AKC-ASCA CH Heatherhill You Talk Too Much ASCA HOF with Laura Kirk
› AKC-ASCA CH Heatherhill Montel Williams ASCA HOF with Summer Jewel Fuhls
› AKC-ASCA CH Heatherhill Sally Jessie with Stevens Parr
Photo courtesy of Heatherhill. Photo credit: Callea Photos.

1993 - AUGGIE and
ASCA CH BRIGADOON'S ONE ARROGANT DUDE USASA HOFX-ASCA HOF

AKC-ASCA CH Heatherhill Joan Rivers "Chelsea." USASA Nationals Select. Multiple Best Veteran and group wins. Photo courtesy of Nancy Gagnon. Photo credit: John Ashbey.

AKC-ASCA CH Heatherhill Jenny Jones "Misty." Photo courtesy of Heatherhill. Photo credit: Kit Rodwell.

AKC-ASCA CH Heatherhill Sweet Talkin Dude CD HS STDs OA OAJ ASCA HOF "Shooter." Photo courtesy of Leida Jones.

AKC-ASCA CH Heatherhill Montel Williams ASCA HOF "Montel." Photo credit: Richard Bergman.

ASCA CH Heatherhill Regis Philbin "Regis." Photo courtesy of Heatherhill.

First Place Brood Bitch class 1996 USASA Nationals. (Left to right) Auggie with Kathy McCorkle, Montel Williams with Alan McCorkle, Sweet Talkin Dude with Leida Jones, You Talk Too Much with Jim Polk, Sally Jessie with Virgil Pellegrino, Jenny Jones with Pamela Levin. Photo courtesy of Heatherhill. Photo credit: Cary C. Manaton.

1995 - AUGGIE and
ASCA CH BRIGADOON'S CALIFORNIA DUDE CD HS STDS ASCA HOF

AKC-ASCA CH Heatherhill Bipity Bopity Boo "Boo." Photo courtesy of Heatherhill. Photo credit: Richard Bergman.

BISS AKC-ASCA CH Heatherhill Black-N-Decker ASCA HOF "Buzz." Photo courtesy of Heatherhill. Photo credit: Kohler.

1996 - AUGGIE and
AKC-ASCA CH HEATHERHILL GRAND MARSHAL

AKC-ASCA CH Heatherhill My Waterloo ASCA HOF "Loo." Photo courtesy of Heatherhill. Photo credit: Kohler.

AKC-ASCA CH Heatherhill Whoopie Goldberg "Raven." Photo courtesy of Heatherhill.

ASCA CH Heatherhill Take A Chance OnMe "Abby." Photo courtesy of Heatherhill. Photo credit: Kohler.

ASCA CH Heatherhill Head Over Heels "Heddy." Photo courtesy of Heatherhill.

1997 - AUGGIE and
AKC-ASCA CH SUERTES ARROGANT WEE WILLIE

ASCA CH Heatherhill Ricki Lake "Ricki." Photo courtesy of Heatherhill.

ASCA-AKC CH Heatherhill Overdraft "Zinc." Photo courtesy of Nannette Newbury.

1998 - AUGGIE and
AKC-ASCA CH HEATHERHILL CRUSHED ICE

AKC CH Heatherhill Rosie O'Donnell. Photo courtesy of Heatherhill.

AKC-ASCA CH Heatherhill Tyra Banks "Tyra." Photo courtesy of Nannette Newbury.

1999 - AUGGIE and
AKC-ASCA CH TAYCIN'S STONE WASHED BLUES ASCA HOF

ASCA CH Heatherhill Oprah's Last Pleasure "Millie." Photo courtesy of Heatherhill.

CONVERSATIONS

Tammy Csicsila · Auggie was gorgeous! I remember the first time I saw her at Nationals. She was still in the age classes. She was breathtaking and had beautiful movement!

Celeste Lucero Telles · One of the all-time greats! Loved her!

Raine Lutz · Auggie's grandson AKC-INT-ASCA CH Melody's Park It In First PT ROM X-I ASCA HOF "Parker" was a foundation sire for RaineDance. He was always serious for the camera, but goofy the rest of the time. He loved everyone! He was an incredible althlete and very smart. He was by AKC-ASCA CH Heatherhill You Talk Too Much ASCA HOF and out of ASCA CH Melody's Court'n the Blues.

Kim O'Donovan · Love, love, love! Auggie was stunning!

Terry Dickey · Beautiful!

Laurie Shuren · Loved Auggie. Beautiful dog.

Jennifer Landis Sawyer · I remember Oprah. She was a beauty!

Julie Holligan · Auggie is the great-grandmother of IR CH Armatan Bad Moon Rising ShCM CW'07 CW'10 "Dash." He's by AKC CH Heatherhill Creedence and out of AKC CH Firethorne's C'est La Vive.

Cathryn Jennings · Auggie is my Barbie's grandmother. I can see the resemblance. Miss my girl so much.

Rhonda Rainwater Silveira · I loved Auggie and her brother BIS BISS AKC-ASCA CH My Main Man of Heatherhill ROM X-I ROM C-III ROM O-I ASCA HOF

Ann Fulton · Beautiful!

Tim Preston · Such a beauty!

Julie Plourde · CKC GCH Casa Blanca's First Lady CGN "Ella" is a great-granddaughter of BISS AKC-ASCA CH Heatherhill Black-N-Decker ASCA HOF.

Clare Feler Cox · Auggie is twice great-great-grandmother of Group Winning AKC CH Stonepine Serendipity and great-great-grandmother of AKC CH Heatherhill Rollin' in the Deep.

Megs Da Silva · Stunning! Loved her and her brother!

Trista Hidalgo · She was so cute! I just realized Auggie was a half-sister to my first Aussie and grandmother to my third Aussie.

Auggie's granddaughter AKC-ASCA CH Stonepine Silk "Silk." Born 2004. Best Opposite Sex in Futurity 2005 USASA National Specialty. By AKC CH Heatherhill Rebel Justice x AKC-ASCA CH Heatherhill Tyra Banks. Photo courtesy of Nannette Newbury.

Auggie's grandson ASCA CH Heatherhill Creedence "Jeep." Born 1998. By AKC CH Bayshore Propwash Balderdash USASA HOFX-ASCA HOF x AKC- ASCA CH Heatherhill Sally Jessie. Photo courtesy of Heatherhill. Photo credit: Kit Rodwell.

Auggie's great-grandson Heatherhill Dazzle Revival Man "Deacon." Born 2007. By AKC-ASCA CH Heatherhill Creedence x CH Barking Frog's C'est La Vie. Photo courtesy of Heatherhill. Photo credit: Turley.

Auggie's grandson ASCA CH Heatherhill Macho Man "Macho." Born 2005. By BIS AKC-ASCA CH Heatherhill Black N Decker ASCA HOF x Barking Frog's Wreak N Havoc. Photo courtesy of Heatherhill. Photo credit: Bergman.

Auggie's grandson AKC-INT-ASCA CH Melody's Park It In First PT ROM X-I ASCA HOF "Parker." Born 2001. By AKC-ASCA CH Heatherhill You Talk Too Much ASCA HOF x AKC CH Melody's Court'n the Blues. Photo courtesy of Raine Lutz. Photo credit: Callea.

Auggie's grandson BIS BISS AKC GCH ASCA CH Heatherhill Dazzle Me Montana "Tanner." Born 2006. By BIS CH Heatherhill Black-N-Decker x CH Barking Frog's C'est La Vie. Photo courtesy of Mary Arnold. Photo credit: Cook.

Auggie's double granddaughter AKC-ASCA CH Heatherhill Jada Da Ville "Jade." Born 2003. By AKC-ASCA CH Heatherhill Black N Decker ASCA HOF x ASCA CH Heatherhill Take A Chance OnMe. Photo courtesy of Heatherhill. Photo credit: Kit Rodwell.

Auggie's great-grandson AKC GCH-ASCA CH Heatherhill Park Central "Parker." Born 2011. By AKC CH Heatherhill Black Velvet Thriller x AKC GCH-ASCA CH Heatherhill Dazzle Park Laine. Photo courtesy of Gary and Susan Waag.

Auggie's granddaughter Heatherhill Taboo "Fallon." Born 2002. By AKC-ASCA CH Taycin's Stone Washed Blues ASCA HOF x AKC-ASCA CH Heatherhill Bipity Bopity Boo. Photo courtesy of Heatherhill.

Auggie's great-grandson AKC-ASCA CH Stonepine Stone Temple "Pilot." Born 2010. By AKC-ASCA CH Heatherhill No Stone Unturned x AKC-ASCA CH Stonepine Silk. Photo courtesy of Nannette Newbury.

Auggie's grandson AKC-ASCA CH Heatherhill Linkin Park "Linkin." Born 2011. RWD and 1st Place Stud Dog 2017 USASA National Specialty. By ASCA CH Black Velvet Thriller x BISS AKC GCH-ASCA CH Heatherhill Park Laine. Photo courtesy of Heatherhill. Photo credit: Jeffrey Hanlin.

Auggie's granddaughter BISS AKC-ASCA CH Heatherhill Celine Dion"Celine." Born 1998. By AKC CH Bayshore's Propwash Balderdash USASA HOFX-ASCA HOF x AKC-ASCA CH Heatherhill Sally Jessie. Photo courtesy of Heatherhill. Photo credit: Kit Rodwell.

AKC-ASCA CH Heatherhill Tyra Banks

"Tyra." Born 1998. By AKC-ASCA CH Heatherhill Crushed Ice x Auggie.

I was at the McCorkles for a BBQ when I first saw Tyra and her littermates. A blue merle bitch grabbed the attention of most people at the party, but a plainer black bitch, Tyra, caught my eye. I noticed how sound and correct she was. However, she was already promised to Virgil and Sandy Pellegrino, who owned the litter's sire.

A week later, I visited McCorkles again and told Alan and Kathy how much I liked the black tri female, even though I knew she was promised elsewhere. As I drove away, I couldn't stop thinking about her. I made it about 20 minutes down the road, turned around and headed right back to the McCorkles. I needed to make sure Alan knew I was serious. As Alan, Kathy, and I stood outside the puppy pen I said, "If anything changes and Virgil and Sandy can't take Tyra, could I please have a chance with her?"

Alan said, "Well, you better take her now before I change my mind!" I was stunned. The Pellegrinos had decided they wanted to keep only males at their house and had turned down their option on Tyra. I was ecstatic as I took her home that day.

The Pellegrinos remained Tyra's honorary "Godparents" and were great supporters of her career. Many thanks to Alan and Kathy for entrusting me with this very special Auggie daughter. I'll never forget Tyra and the opportunities she gave me in the breed. I worked with Alan for over 10 years showing great dogs and learning from him. I never planned to have a breeding program. Although Tyra was an integral part of the start of Stonepine, I still consider my breeding program merely an offshoot and continuation of Alan's and Kathy's Heatherhill vision. I treasure our long-term friendship and their mentorship.

My favorite show picture was taken at the 2002 USASA Nationals. Leon Goetz, with Auggie's granddaughter MBIS MBISS CH Bayshore Russian Roulette "Judy," and Auggie's daughter Tyra and I finished our go-arounds. Leon and I were moved to a corner in the ring. The other major contenders were in an opposite corner of the ring. Leon and I were panicked and were convinced we were in the "dump pile!" We couldn't figure out why or what we had done wrong. It turned out that Tyra and Judy were in a battle for Best of Breed and we didn't know it. When we figured that out, we were even more panicked. Judy went on to win the day as Best of Breed and Tyra was the First Award of Merit. Great showmanship and sportsmanship with two great friends and two great dogs!

- Nannette Newbury

Photo credit top right: Family Tree.

Auggie's great-granddaughter AKC-Hungarian-ASCA CH Stonepine Jaded "E.D." Born 2009. Reserve Winners 2013 World Dog Show, Budapest, Hungary. By AKC-ASCA CH Heatherhill No Stone Unturned x AKC-ASCA CH Heatherhill Jada Da Ville. Photo courtesy of Nannette Newbury.

Auggie's granddaughter BISS AKC GCH-ASCA CH Heatherhill Dazzle Park Laine "Laine." Born 2005. Best of Breed 2009 ASCA Nationals. By AKC-ASCA CH Heatherhill My Waterloo ASCA HOF x Passion Fruit of Breezeway. Photo courtesy of Heatherhill. Photo credit: M Fine.

Auggie's great-grandson and Paddy's grandson AKC-ASCA CH Heatherhill Without A Trace "Trace." Born 2006. By ASCA CH Heatherhill Rebel Justice x AKC-ASCA CH Heatherhill Star Jones. Photo courtesy of Heatherhill. Photo credit: Bergman.

Auggie's quadruple great-great-great-granddaughter Stonepine Absolutely "Abby." Born 2016. By AKC-ASCA CH Heatherhill Linkin Park x ASCA CH Stonepine Salute. Photo courtesy of Nannette Newbury. Photo credit: Jeffrey Hanlin.

Auggie's grandson AKC-ASCA CH Heatherhill Mitey Fine Man "Mitey." Born 2008. By AKC-ASCA CH Heatherhill My Waterloo ASCA HOF x ASCA CH Windfalls Makita Made. Photo courtesy of Heatherhill. Photo credit: Ken O'Brien.

Auggie's grandson AKC-ASCA Heatherhill Double-O Heaven "Cazz." Born 2000. Best Opposite Sex in Futurity 2001 USASA Nationals. Reserve Winner's Dog 2001 ASCA Nationals. By AKC-ASCA CH Heatherhill You Talk Too Much ASCA HOF x ASCA CH Heatherhill Cut Out. Photo courtesy of Heatherhill.

Auggie's great-great-granddaughter AKC-ASCA CH Stonepine Sheer Silk "Sash." Born 2005. Finished her AKC CH with three 5-point major wins all at specialty shows. By AKC-ASCA CH Heatherhill Double-O Heaven x AKC-ASCA CH Stonepine Silk. Photo courtesy of Nannette Newbury.

Auggie's great-great-granddaughter AKC CH Stonepine Serendipity. Born 2012. By ASCA CH Heatherhill No Stone Unturned x AKC-ASCA CH Stonepine Shiraz. Photo courtesy of Clare Feler Cox. Photo credit: K. Booth.

Auggie's great-great-grandson AKC-ASCA CH Taycin's Triple Threat "Peyton." Born 2007. By AKC-ASCA CH Taycin's Just A Stones Throw x Heatherhill Taboo. Photo courtesy of Heatherhill. Photo credit: Jeffrey Hanlin.

Auggie's great-great-granddaughter Stonepine Silken "Tulle." Born 2013. By AKC-ASCA CH Heatherhill No Stone Unturned x AKC-ASCA CH Stonepine Sheer Silk. Photo courtesy of Nannette Newbury.

Auggie's and Paddy's great-great-grandson AKC-ASCA CH Heatherhill Point Taken "Preston." Born 2009. By AKC-ASCA CH Heatherhill Without A Trace x Saddle Ridge Latest Craze. Photo courtesy of Heatherhill. Photo credit: Kohler.

Auggie's grandson HOF AKC-ASCA CH Crazyheart's Talk To Me. Born 1997. By AUST-ASCA CH Heatherhill Montel Williams x AKC CH Heatherhill Pagent. Photo courtesy of Stephanie LeBarron.

Auggie's great-granddaughter AKC-ASCA CH Heatherhill Show No Mercy "Mercy." Born 2012. By AKC-ASCA CH Heatherhill Mitey Fine Man x Heatherhill Coral. Photo courtesy of Heatherhill. Photo credit: Callea.

Auggie's great-granddaughter AKC-ASCA CH Stonepine Shiraz "Rozz." Born 2003. By AKC-ASCA CH Heatherhill Double-O Heaven x ASCA CH Heatherhill That's the Ticket. Photo courtesy of Nannette Newbury. Photo credit: Kenneth Reid.

Auggie's great-great-granddaughter AKC GCH-ASCA CH Heatherhill Monet For Madelyn "Monet." Born 2010. By AKC-ASCA CH Heatherhill Without A Trace x BISS AKC GCH-ASCA CH Heatherhill Dazzle Park Laine. Photo courtesy of Heatherhill. Photo credit: Image by Kit.

Auggie's great-granddaughter ASCA CH Heatherhill Thrill A Minute "Minute." Born 2012. Reserve Winner's Bitch 2015 USASA National Specialty. By ASCA CH Heatherhill Black Velvet Thriller x ASCA CH Black Velvet's Vanity Fair. Photo courtesy of Heatherhill. Photo credit: Cook.

Auggie's double great-great-grandson AKC-ASCA CH Stonepine Fuel Injected "Enzo." Born 2010. By AKC-ASCA CH Heatherhill Dazzle Revival Man x AKC-ASCA CH Stonepine Sheer Silk. Photo courtesy of Nannette Newbury. Photo credit: Cook.

Auggie's great-great-grandson ASCA CH Heatherhill Black Velvet Thriller "Michael." Born 2009. By AKC-ASCA CH Heatherhill No Stone Unturned x Heatherhill Coral. Photo courtesy of Heatherhill. Photo credit: Dynamic Dog.

Auggie's great-great-grandson AKC-ASCA CH Heatherhill No Stone Unturned "Turner." Born 2007. By AKC-ASCA CH Taycin's Just A Stones Throw x Heatherhill Taboo. Photo courtesy of Heatherhill. Photo credit: Ken O'Brien.

First Place Brood Bitch class 1998 ASCA Nationals (Left to right)
› AKC-ASCA CH Oprah Winfree of Heatherhill ASCA HOF with Vergil Pellegrino.
› BISS AKC-ASCA CH Heatherhill's Black-N-Decker ASCA HOF with Jim Wirries.
› AKC-ASCA CH Heatherhill Montel Williams ASCA HOF with Erica Peters-Pruitt.
› AKC-ASCA CH Heatherhill My Waterloo ASCA HOF with Sandy Penn.
› ASCA CH Head Over Heels of Heatherhill with Steve Sorensen.

Photo courtesy of Heatherhill. Photo credit: Kohler.

Auggie Osh Kosh: Auggie and child featured in an early Osh Kosh advertisement.

Auggie's great-great-granddaughter ASCA CH Stonepine Salute "Lute." Born 2011. By AKC-ASCA CH Heatherhill Dazzle Revival Man x Dazzle's Pretty Fancy Schmancy. Photo courtesy of Nannette Newbury.

Auggie's great-great-great-grandson Heatherhill Stonepine Fuel the Fire "Fire." Born 2014. England: 2014 Top 7 finalist for Dog World Pup of the Year. 2015: Top Ten finalist for Crufts Junior Warrant. By AKC-ASCA CH Stonepine Fuel Injected x AKC-Hungarian-ASCA CH Stonepine Jaded. Photo courtesy of Nannette Newbury.

Auggie's grandson AKC-CKC-ASCA CH Paradox Propaganda ROM C-II ROM X-II ASCA HOF "Nash." Born 1996. Select Dog 2000 USASA National Specialty. By AKC-ASCA CH Heatherhill You Talk Too Much ASCA HOF x AKC-ASCA CH Paradox Propwash Then Again. Photo courtesy of Alison Smith. Photo credit: Family Tree.

"Paddy came to visit us at Hisaw to sire some litters in the 1990s. He was one of the most laid-back, easy-going dogs I've ever met. He was very sweet-natured and easy on the eyes. We took him on the road a few times in his earlier show career and he was always an absolute gentleman. I truly believe he was a once-in-a-lifetime dog and thank Heatherhill for sharing him with the fancy."

- Regi Bryant

Photo credit: Photos Today

BIS BISS AKC-ASCA Champion
My Main Main of Heatherhill
ROM X-I ROM C-III ROM O-I   ASCA HOF Sire #52

Call name: Paddy
Born: 1988
Sire: ASCA CH Agua Dulce Final Option ASCA HOF
Dam: Moonspinner of Brigadoon ASCA HOF
Breeders: Alan and Kathy McCorkle, Heatherhill
Owners: Alan and Kathy McCorkle, Heatherhill

On October 9, 1988, Moonspinner of Brigadoon "Spinny" whelped her first litter sired by ASCA CH Agua Dulce Final Option ASCA HOF. It was a litter to remember, producing My Main Man of Heatherhill "Paddy" and Oprah Winfree of Heatherhill "Auggie." Both had tremendous influence on the breed.

Paddy became a landmark sire in the breed with over 100 champion progeny, many who achieved ROM and HOF status.

Paddy was not only a great sire, he was also an outstanding conformation dog. He was awarded Best of Breed at both the 1994 USASA National Specialty and the 1994 ASCA National Specialty. He also won a coveted AKC Best in Show.

Paddy had a powerful influence on many bloodlines including Alnair, Agua Dulce, Aristocrat, Bailiwick, Bayshore, Blue Isle, Briarbrook, Catori, Copperridge, Dreamstreet, Ebbtide, Fiann, Firethorne, Gingerbred, Gotham, Heartfire, Hisaw, Inverness, Jazztime, Kaleidoscope, Limelite, Myshara, Ragtime, Starswept, Saddleridge, Snowbelt, Stonepine, Sunnyrain, Taycin, Thornapple, Three Oaks, Tri-Ivory, Westridge, Windhill, Windrift, and a myriad of smaller kennels. Some of his most notable offspring are featured in the following pages.

CONVERSATIONS

Ann Fulton · Paddy was a beautiful dog!

Patrick Fett · A true foundation dog to our wonderful Aussie breed! I own a Paddy great-granddaughter who is a Grand Champion.

Karen Roesner · Paddy left quite a mark in the Aussie world!

Rhonda Rainwater Silveira · Paddy was the best moving dog I have ever had the pleasure to show. He was one in a million. Paddy and ASCA CH Starswepts Couldn't Resist produced 10 champions for Hisaw. Paddy and MBISS AKC-ASCA CH Chambray River Cats Pajamas CGC produced four champions.

First Place Stud Dog class 1995 USASA Nationals. (Left to right)
› BIS BISS AKC-ASCA CH My Main Man of Heatherhill ROM X-I ROM C-III ROM O-I ASCA HOF with Alan McCorkle
› ASCA CH Hisaw's Justin Roper with Rhonda Silveira
› AKC-ASCA CH Starswept's Paris Blues with Carol Earnest
› BISS AKC-ASCA CH Starswept's Untouchable at Hisaw ASCA HOF with Regi Bryant
› AKC-ASCA CH Gotta Be Blue of Heatherhill with Stevens Parr
Award presenter USASA President Georjean Hertzwig
Photo courtesy of Heatherhill. Photo credit: Callea.

Pedigree

```
                                                        CH Winchester's Hotline HOF
                                    ASCA CH Winchester's Rollin Rapids HOF
                                    │                   CH Sundown's Midnight Serenade
                    AKC-ASCA CH Agua Dulce Final Option ASCA HOF
                                    │                   CH Winchester's Hotline HOF
                                    ASCA CH Country Hotline of Agua Dulce CDX HOF
                                                        Taycin's Country Girl CD
BIS BISS AKC-ASCA CH My Main Man of Heatherhill ROM X-I ROM C-III ASCA HOF
                                                        CH Arrogance of Heatherhill CD STDs HOF
                                    ASCA CH Brigadoon's Moonraker
                                    │                   Patch-Work Thumbelina
                    Moonspinner of Brigadoon ASCA HOF
                                    │                   CH Sunshine of Bonnie-Blu CDX HOF
                                    ASCA CH Windswept of Windermere CD HOF
                                                        Blue Heather of Windermere HOF
```

Paddy's sire ASCA CH Agua Dulce Final Option ASCA HOF "Paddington." Born 1986. Photo courtesy of Pam Levin.

Paddy's dam Moonspinner of Brigadoon ASCA HOF "Spinny." Born 1981. Photo courtesy of Heatherhill.

Paddy's great-grandsire ASCA CH Windermere's Sunshine of Bonnie-Blu CDX ASCA HOF "Sunny." Born 1972. Photo courtesy of Judy Williams.

Paddy's great-grandsire ASCA CH Arrogance of Heatherhill CDX STDd ASCA HOF "Ara." Born 1977. Photo courtesy of Heatherhill.

PADDY and ASCA CH STARSWEPTS COULDN'T RESIST

This cross was made three times with outstanding results. Eight offspring are pictured on these two pages.

> BISS AKC-ASCA CH Starswept Untouchable at Hisaw ASCA HOF
> ASCA CH Hisaw's Justin Roper
> ASCA CH Hisaw's Irresistible O'Starswept
> ASCA CH Hisaw's My Girl at Starswept
> AKC-CKC-ASCA CH Hisaw's Resist This of Starswept
> ASCA CH Hisaw's New Man at Starswept
> ASCA CH Starswept Tryd to Resist Hisaw
> AKC-ASCA CH Hisaw's My Starswept Sky CD
> ASCA CH Starswept Make My Day at Hisaw (not pictured)
> ASCA CH Starswept Pretty Woman at Hisaw (not pictured)

ASCA CH Hisaw's Tryd to Resist Starswept "Mickey." Born 1994. Photo courtesy of Regi Bryant. Photo credit: Carol Earnest.

ASCA CH Hisaw's My Girl at Starswept "Vada." Born 1993. Photo courtesy of Regi Bryant. Photo credit: Julie Brown.

ASCA CH Hisaw's Irresistible O'Starswept "Ricky." Born 1993. #11 ASCA Standings. Photo courtesy of Julie Brown-Marron. Photo credit: Callea.

ASCA CH Hisaw's Justin Roper "Roper." Born 1993. Premier Dog 1996 ASCA National Pre-shows. Top 10 ASCA Standings multiple years. Photo courtesy of Lisa Renville. Photo credit: G. Norris.

Paddy's offspring out of ASCA CH Starswepts Couldn't Resist "Ashley" won Second Place in the Brood Bitch class at the 1995 USASA National Specialty. Left to right: Ashley, Ricky, Roper, Vada, and Elliott. Photo courtesy of Heatherhill.

AKC-CKC-ASCA CH Hisaw's Resist This of Starswept "Hope." Born 1994. Best Opposite Sex 1996 ASCA National Pre-show. Photo courtesy of Laura Iwan. Photo credit: Photos Today.

AKC-ASCA CH Hisaw's My Starswept Sky CD "Skyler." Born 1994. Premier Dog 1997 ASCA National Specialty. Premier Dog 1996 ASCA National Pre-shows. Photo credit: G. Norris.

BISS AKC-ASCA CH Starswept Untouchable at Hisaw "Elliott." Born 1994. Premier Dog 1998 ASCA National Specialty & Pre-shows. Premier Dog 1996 ASCA Pre-shows. Photo courtesy of Regi Bryant.

ASCA CH Hisaw's New Man of Starswept "Jiggs." Born 1995. Reserve Winner's Dog 1996 ASCA National Specialty. Photo courtesy of Ronnette Nielsen. Photo credit: Frantic Foto.

There were four Hisaw champions from Paddy and ASCA CH Parkhills Hug Me in the Fog CD ASCA HOF. Paddy and ASCA CH Starswepts Hifalutin of Hisaw ASCA HOF produced two champions. Several dogs in those litters are both AKC and ASCA champions. Paddy's influence can be seen in his Hisaw grandkids and great-grandkids.

Natasha Baxter · Paddy is in so many of my dogs pedigrees. He made a huge contribution to the breed!

Marcia Stiger · My beloved Razz was a Paddy son and the greatest dog ever! Since Razz was my foundation sire, all my kids have descended from Paddy.

Tricia Greenwood Clements · I've had many descendants of Paddy and AKC-ASCA CH Briarbrooks Silver Sequence ROM C-III—grandkids, great-grandkids and great-great-grandkids.

Danielle Dumais · My Paddy son ASCA CH Jazztime's A Shade Above The Rest RS-O JS-O GS-O "Bailey" was Winner's Dog at the 2001 ASCA Nationals. I bred to Paddy twice and had five champions and multiple titled offspring. CH Jazztime's Music Man RS-E JS-E GS-O was also a Paddy son.

Paddy's offspring won First Place in the Brood Bitch class, 2001 ASCA National Specialty. (Left to right) Dam: BISS ASCA CH Shadowrun's Pebbles in the Sand CD STDc ASCA HOF with Donna Wright. Four litter sisters born 1998 (Left to right)
› AKC-ASCA CH Shadowrun's Sand Sandals RS-N RJ-N RG-N NAC NJC NGC CGC with Kristin Rush
› AKC-ASCA CH Shadowrun's Sandpiper RS-O RJ-O RG-O OAC OJC OGC CGC with Claire Thomas
› BISS AKC-ASCA CH Shadowrun's Amazing Grace with Clarissa Shank
› A-BISS AKC-ASCA CH Shadowrun's Barefoot in the Sand CD STDdsc with Kris Churchill
Photo courtesy of Kristin Rush. Photo credit: Kohler.

PADDY and
ASCA CH PARKHILLS HUG ME IN THE FOG CD ASCA HOF
› AKC-ASCA CH Hisaw's Whisper My Name
› AKC CH My Oh My of Hisaw
› ASCA CH Hisaw's My Kind of Girl
› ASCA-AUST CH Hisaw's Man in the Fog

AKC-ASCA CH Hisaw's Whisper My Name "Randi." Born 1994. Photo courtesy of Pat Cook.

AKC CH My Oh My of Hisaw "Cricket." Born 1994. Photo courtesy of Lisa Hart. Photo credit: J. Kay Photo.

ASCA CH Hisaw's My Kind of Girl "McKay." Born 1994. Photo courtesy of Regi Bryant. Photo credit: Ken Silveira.

ASCA CH Hisaw's Man in the Fog "Kix." Born 1994. Photo courtesy of Regi Bryant.

Nellie Morack · My Paddy grandson AKC GCH-UKC GRCH-CKC-ASCA CH Wyndcrest Imagine That! AKC-ASCA RN CGC "Zane" turned 11 years old in June. I also have a Paddy great-granddaughter and great-grandson who are both AKC Grand Champions.

Elizabeth McIntosh · My Paddy granddaughter is by CH Heatherhill Shaquille O'Neal and out of Heatherhill Bookay. She just turned eight years old and is beautiful inside and out.

Donna Harding · Paddy's daughter AKC CH Westridge Poetic Justice was Best of Opposite Sex at the 1997 USASA National Specialty. Her litter brother was AKC-ASCA CH Westridge Man of My Dreams. AKC-ASCA CH Briarbrooks Silversmith ROM C-II was from the amazing cross of Paddy and AKC-ASCA CH Briarbrooks Silver Sequence ROM C-III.

Tina Lass · Paddy's daughter AKC-INT-ASCA CH Briarbrooks Silver Bells "Bobbi Sue" was Winners Bitch and Best of Winners at the 1996 USASA National Specialty in Florida. She received an Award of Merit at the 2001 Westminster show and was a multiple group winner. She had extraordinary sidegait and a special personality. Bobbi Sue was definitely one of my heart dogs!

Celeste Lucero Telles · Paddy was one of my favorites!

MBISS AKC-ASCA CH Chambray River Cats Pajamas (on Regi Bryant's lap) with (left to right) AKC-ASCA CH Hisaw My BVDs of Heatherhill, ASCA CH The Jazz Man of Hisaw, Paddy's niece Jammies sired by AKC-ASCA CH Heatherhill My Waterloo ASCA HOF, ASCA CH Hisaw's Cowboy Cut CD, Paddy's grandson Teddy sired by BISS AKC-ASCA CH Starswept Untouchable at Hisaw. Photo courtesy of Regi Bryant. Photo credit: Family Tree.

PADDY and
MBISS AKC-ASCA CH CHAMBRAY RIVER CATS PAJAMAS CGC

› AKC-ASCA CH Hisaw My BVDs of Heatherhill
› ASCA CH Jazz Man of Hisaw
› ASCA CH Hisaw's Cowboy Cut CD
› C-ATCH Heatherhill Sadie Sue CD NA NAJ RS-O JS-E GS-N AD NAC

ASCA CH Hisaw's Cowboy Cut CD "Wrangler." Born 2000. Photo courtesy of Suzette Pendo. Photo credit: Winsome Imaging.

C-ATCH Heatherhill Sadie Sue CD NA NAJ RS-O JS-E GS-N AD NAC "Sadie." Born 2000. Photo courtesy of Bonnie Badertscher. Photo credit: Bruce Badertscher.

AKC-ASCA CH Hisaw My BVDs of Heatherhill "Sydney." Born 2000. Photo courtesy of Regi Bryant. Photo credit: Curtis Van Leur.

ASCA CH The Jazz Man of Hisaw "Jazz." Born 2000. Photo courtesy of Melissa Williams. Photo credit: Victoria Howard.

Jim Charrette · I'm so happy to have Paddy in our foundation bitch.

Cathy Franklin · Paddy sired my AKC CH Alibi's Flirtation in Elegance HT PT "Flirt," the heart of all heart dogs. She came to live with us when she was seven and lived to be 15½ years old. To say I adored her is an understatement. She was perfect in every way with the gentlest of gentle spirits. I miss her every day.

PADDY and
LAND'S END COUNTDOWN TO ECSTACY CD
› ATCH AKC-ASCA CH Land's End Man About Town CDX
› AKC-ASCA CH Fooling Around at Land's End
› ASCA CH Land's End Clothing Optional (not pictured)

Paddy's son ATCH AKC-ASCA CH Land's End Man About Town CDX "Mr." Born 1997. Reserve Winner's Dog 1999 ASCA Nationals Pre-show. Photo courtesy of Diana Land. Photo credit: Betty Hogan, Family Tree Portraits.

Paddy's son AKC-ASCA CH Fooling Around at Land's End "Travis." Born 1994. Premier Award 1997 ASCA National Specialty. Photo courtesy of Diana Land. Photo credit: Photos Today.

Heatherhill sisters. By Paddy x BISS AKC-ASCA CH Celine Dion of Heatherhill ASCA HOF. Born 2001. (Front row left to right) AKC-CKC-ASCA CH Aristocrat's Zeta Jones, AKC-ASCA CH Aristocrat's Intuition, AKC CH Aristocrat's Vivica Fox. (Back row left to right) AKC-ASCA CH Heatherhill Carmella Soprano, AKC CH Heatherhill Lana Turner. Photo courtesy of Heatherhill. Photo credit: Family Tree.

PADDY and
ASCA CH STARSWEPTS HIFALUTIN OF HISAW ASCA HOF
› MBISS AKC-ASCA CH Starswept's Hi Flyin' of Hisaw HOF
› ASCA CH Starswept Hi Voltage of Hisaw

MBISS AKC-ASCA CH Starswept's Hi Flyin' of Hisaw ASCA HOF "Riley." Born 1998. Winner's Dog 1999 ASCA National Pre-show. Best of Breed Veteran 2005 ASCA National Specialty. Best Opposite Sex at 2005 ASCA National Pre-shows. Photo courtesy of Carol Earnest. Photo credit: Nugent.

ASCA CH Starswept Hi Voltage of Hisaw "Misty." Born 1998. Photo courtesy of Lisa Renville. Photo credit: Kit Rodwell.

PADDY and
AKC-ASCA CH BRIARBROOKS SILVER SEQUENCE ROM C-III

This cross produced 21 champions, a few which are listed below. For photos, see chapter on Briarbrooks Silver Sequence, page 154.

› AKC CH Briarbrooks Valedictorian USASA HOFX-ASCA HOF. Sire of 103 champions, ranked #1 Aussie sire in AKC 1996, 1998, 1999, 2000, 2001.
› AKC CH Briarbrooks Silver Medallion USASA HOFX. Sire of 33 champions including the 2009 Westminster Best of Breed winner.
› AKC CH Briarbrooks Quicksilver ROM X-II ROM C-II. Best of Breed 2003 Westminster, ranked #1 in Breed and #2 in Group for 2000, winner of 22 Group 1st and 215 Best of Breed awards.
› AKC CH Briarbrooks Full Speed Ahead. Best of Breed 1997 Westminster, Top 10 dog 1995 and 1997.
› AKC CH Briarbrooks Bringin In The Silver. #1 Bitch in the Breed 1994, 1995.
› AKC CH Briarbrooks Checkmate ROM C-I.
› AKC CH Briarbrooks Silversmith ROM X-II
› AKC CH Briarbrooks Silver Anniversary ROM C-III. Dam of 14 champions.
› AKC Briarbrooks Sharp Dressed Man ROM X-II

PADDY and
ASCA CH EBBTIDE A BEE IN YOUR BONNET CD

› AKC-ASCA CH Ebbtide I'll Remain CD
› AKC-AUS-ASCA CH Ebbtide Foreign Affair
› AKC-AUS CH Ebbtide Main Squeeze
› AKC-ASCA CH Ebbtide I Saw The Surprise
› AKC CH Ebbtide Garden Party (not pictured)
› CKC CH Ebbtide I Showed Up In Boots (not pictured)

AKC-ASCA CH Ebbtide I'll Remain CD "Remy." Born 1991. Award of Merit 1995 USASA National Specialty. Photo courtesy of Ann Atkinson. Photo credit: Callea Photo by Meg.

AKC-AUS-ASCA CH Ebbtide Foreign Affair "Whitney." Born 1993. Photo courtesy of Ann Atkinson.

AKC-AUS CH Ebbtide Main Squeeze "Squeeze." Born 1991. Photo courtesy of Ann Atkinson. Photo credit: Cabal.

AKC-ASCA CH Ebbtide I Saw The Surprise "Whoopi." Born 1992. Photo courtesy of Ann Atkinson.

Laurie Rubin · I loved, loved, loved Ann Atkinson's Paddy son AKC-ASCA CH Ebbtide I'll Remain CD "Remy." He won an Award of Merit at the 1995 USASA National Specialty. My beautiful A-CH Ebbtide Fennel Hill UD RM "Fennel" is a Paddy great-grandson.

Paddy's son MBIS MBISS AKC-ASCA CH Silverwood's Texas Justice HOF "TJ." Born 1994. By Paddy x Four Storeys On Silverwood Lane ROM C-II ASCA HOF.
Ranked #1 Australian Shepherd AKC All-Breed 2000
Ranked#7 AKC Herding Dog 2000
Ranked#1 in USASA 2001
First Australian Shepherd to win a group placement at a Westminster KC Show
Eight All-breed Best In Show wins
Best of Breed 2001 USASA National Specialty
Best Opposite Sex 1998 USASA National Specialty
Photo credit: WinterChurchill.

Paddy's son BIS AKC-ASCA CH Tri-Ivory Make A Big Wish ASCA HOF "Big E." Born 1997. By Paddy x AKC CH Tri-Ivory I've Gotta Alibi. Photo courtesy of Sheila Farrington Polk. Photo credit: Callea.

"Thank you for stories about all of these wonderful dogs. I feel so proud that my Aussies have all of them in their pedigrees. What a treasure!"

- Lisa Durand

BIS BISS AKC GCH-CKC-ASCA CH CopperRidge's Fire N Bayouland ASCA HOF "Rowan." Born 2006. Best of Breed 2008 Eukanuba show. By BIS AKC GCH-CKC-ASCA CH Bayouland Creme Brûlée CGC USASA HOFX- ASCA HOF x AKC CH Fiann's Silver Sweet Sound. His pedigree includes Bear, Lucy, Blaze, Gussie, Yukon, Cruiser, Silver, Auggie & Paddy. Photo courtesy of Yvette LeBlanc. Photo credit: Tells.

Blended Bloodlines

Many current-day Aussie pedigrees combine the excellent bloodlines of more than one of the foundation sires and dams in this book.

◆

CONVERSATIONS

Karyne Gagné · The pedigree of CAN GHC Oxalis Taïka Black Pearl CD HIT RN CGN has a lot of great foundation dogs in it.

Julie Plourde · CKC GCH Thornapple I've Got Everybody Lookin' "Sade" has so many great dogs in her pedigree!

Karron Jordan · T&S GCH Silvanwood And Loving It HSAs "Loki" descends from Paddy through AKC-AUS CH Ebbtide Main Squeeze.

Kirstie Venton New · Little Red-Cap Du Chemin Des Korrigans "Ember" is a full-on crazy nutter, but has bags of character! She was bred in France from U.S. imports and lives in the U.K., so she's truly an international girl. She descended from Lucy, Blaze, Gussie, Yukon, Cruiser, Silver, and Paddy!

Mary-Lou Trone · My AKC-UKC-ASCA CH Kaleidoscope Stone Ravenwynd CD RE HT has Paddy and Silver in his pedigree. I currently have his grandson RTCH-2 Ravenwynd Dealers Choice RTX, who is #2 in Rally finals.

Sabrina Fogliazza · My CH Melodys Blue Star is 11 years old now, but still a puppy inside! He lives with me in Italy. He has two crosses to Paddy.

Celeste Lucero Telles · AKC-ASCA CH La Plata's Taos Legends "Taos" was sired by AKC CH Briarbrooks Valedictorian USASA HOFX-ASCA HOF. Taos was a grandson of Paddy and Silver and also a great-great-grandson of ASCA CH Rising Sun of Windermere CDX STDds ASCA HOF. Taos was my heart dog. I still miss his sweet disposition and his devotion to me.

Phyllis McCullum · AKC CH-CKC GCHEx Starwood's Awake In A Dream CD RE AGN AGNJ "Brenna" was by AKC CH Briarbrooks Silver Certificate and out of my MBISS MBIS CKC GCHEx SPCH Clearfires Dreaming In Colour TDX CDX RAE AGIS AGIJS MADC CKC HOF. Her pedigree goes back to Auggie and Paddy several times. Brenna was #1 Aussie in Canada in 2008 and Best of Opposite Sex at the 2008 CNASA National Specialty. She was the sweetest dog! She never met a stranger.

Cathy Franklin · Paddy sired my AKC CH Alibi's Flirtation in Elegance HT PT "Flirt," the heart of all heart dogs. She came to live with us when she was seven and lived to be 15½ years old. To say I adored her is an understatement. She was perfect in every way with the gentlest of gentle spirits. I miss her every day.

AKC-ASCA CH Meadowlawn's One More Night ASCA CDX-AKC CD NA NAJ NF RS-E JS-E GS-O "Porter." Born 2006. Award of Merit 2010 Westminster show. By BISS AKC-ASCA CH Firethornes Night Moves ASCA HOF x AKC-ASCA CH Meadowlawn's Standing Ovation AKC CD ASCA CDX NA NAJ NF RS-E JS-E GS-O ASCA HOF. Photo courtesy of Sarah Kalkes. Photo credit: Jeffrey Hanlin.

AKC GCH-ASCA CH Sonkist Evening At The Emmys AKC-ASCA CD "Lena." Born 2009. Best Opposite Sex 2013 ASCA National Specialty. Best of Breed 2013 ASCA National Pre-show, ASCA #2 Conformation Dog 2013-2014. By AKC-ASCA CH Calais Carolina Call Me Classic x AKC-ASCA CH Carolina Calais On The Fly. Photo courtesy of Sarah Kalkes. Photo credit: Brandy Dirksen.

Auggie's grandson AKC-ASCA CH Show Stopper of Stone Ridge CGC ASCA HOF "Dougei." Born 2001. By AKC-AUST-ASCA CH Heatherhill Montel Williams ASCA HOF x ASCA CH C.R. Red Legend of Stone Ridge ASCA HOF. Photo courtesy of Stone Ridge. Photo credit: Kohler.

Sire of: ASCA #1 Conformation Dog 2010-2011, Best of Breed 2010 ASCA National Specialty, Best of Breed 2010 ASCA National Specialty Pre-Show, Premier Bitch 2009 ASCA National Specialty, Best Opposite Sex and Premier 2009 ASCA National Specialty Pre-show, Best In Show 2006 Royal Canin KUSA National (South Africa's Westminster).

BISS AKC-ASCA CH Stone Ridge Devils N Angels STDs "Bliss." Born 2006. Best of Breed 2010 ASCA Nationals and Pre-show. ASCA #1 Conformation Dog 2010-2011. ASCA #5 Conformation Dog 2009-2010. First Award of Merit 2010 USASA National Specialty. Best Opposite Sex 2009 ASCA Nationals Pre-show. Award of Excellence 2008 Eukanuba show. By AKC-ASCA CH Show Stopper of Stone Ridge CGC ASCA HOF x AKC-ASCA CH Bayshore Fast and Furious. Photo courtesy of Stone Ridge. Photo credit: Kohler.

BBX-BIS AKC-ASCA CH Stone Ridge Simply Irresistible ASCA HOF "Bobbei." Born 1997. Premier Award & Best Opposite Sex Veteran 2009 ASCA National Specialty. Best of Breed Veteran 2009 Pre-show. Multiple Specialty Premier Awards. Winner's Bitch and Best of Winners 2005 ASCA National Specialty Pre-show. By AKC-ASCA CH Show Stopper of Stone Ridge CGC ASCA HOF x AKC-ASCA CH Windfall's At Long Last CGC ROM O-I ASCA HOF. Photo courtesy of Stone Ridge. Photo credit: Jennifer Cannon.

Georgianne Balcas Doyle · My first Aussie, Lucky, was Paddy's grandson. I didn't know what an Australian Shepherd was when I agreed to take him. I didn't learn where he was from until months later. His best work was as a therapy dog with hospice clients.

Tanya M. Nowak · My beloved CH T-n-T's New Beginnings CGC "Denali" was by CH Heatherhill Without A Trace and out of CH Sunchaser T-n-T Kidnap Faith. He descends from Bear, Lucy, Paddy, and Auggie.

Ellen Leinoff · AKC Gold GCH Sunwren PennYCaerau PlayNGames "Clue" was awarded Best of Breed at the 2015 Eukanuba National Championship show. Clue is my "dog of a lifetime" and he's currently working in obedience, rally, and preparing for certification as a Therapy dog. His pedigree includes Bear, Lucy, and Auggie.

Kate Dourley · TRI CH (T&H) TS GCH HGCH VHCH Rozate Jackhammer ET RN HXAc HXBd "Thor" was by Windfalls Craftsman and out of Rozate Ironhorse Princess. He has Auggie in his pedigree.

Francine Guerra · My BISS CH Copper Hills City Limits "Austin" is a Paddy great-grandson. He was by CH Buff Cap Schooner and out of ASCA CH Copper Hills Aurora Borealis ASCA HOF. He descended from Bear, Auggie, and Paddy.

AKC Gold GCH Sunwren PennYCaerau PlayNGames "Clue." Born 2009. Best of Breed 2013 Eukanuba Championship show. By CH PennYCaerau's Playin The Field HSAs STDc OTDd ATDs x CH Darwin's Eloquence After All CD. His pedigree includes Bear, Lucy & Auggie. Photo courtesy of Ellen Leinoff. Photo credit: Amber Jade Aanensen.

Blended Bloodlines

INT-ASCA CH T-n-T's New Beginnings CGC "Denali." Born 2013. By AKC-ASCA CH Heatherhill Without A Trace x UKC CH Sunchaser T-n-T Kidnap Faith. Photo courtesy of Tanya Nowak. Photo credit: AJ Tavares.

Ryan Creeks Ace of Hearts CGCA "Willow." Born 2013. By AKC CH Briarbrooks Johnny Cash x Ryan Creeks Crystal Jewel. Photo courtesy of Taylor Gassert. Photo credit: Booth.

Tri Ch (T&H) TS GCH HGCH VHCH Rozate Jackhammer ET RN HXAc HXBd "Thor." Born 2006. By Windfalls Craftsman x Rozate Ironhorse Princess. Photo courtesy of Kate Dourley. Photo credit: Michelle Doe. (AUSTRALIA)

AKC-ASCA CH Stone Ridge Lets Talk About Me "Toby." Born 2002. By AKC-ASCA CH Heatherhill Montel Williams ASCA HOF x ASCA CH C.R. Red Legend of Stone Ridge ASCA HOF. Photo courtesy of Alisha Curtis. Photo credit: Bergman.

BISS AKC GCH-ASCA Multi Premier CH Copper Hill's City Limits "Austin." Born 2006. By AKC-ASCA CH Buff Cap Schooner x ASCA CH Copper Hill's Aurora Borealis ASCA HOF. Photo courtesy of Francine Guerra. Photo credit: Amber Jade Aanensen.

Dutch-Lux CH Stone Ridge Legend of The West "Theo." Born 2002. By AKC-ASCA CH Show Stopper of Stone Ridge CGC ASCA HOF x AKC-INT-ASCA CH Windfalls at Long Last ROM O-I ROM X-I CGC ASCA HOF. Photo courtesy of Geneviève Chomé. (BELGIUM)

Geneviève Chomé · Dutch-Lux CH Stone Ridge Legend of The West "Theo" is by AKC GCH-ASCA CH Show Stopper of Stone Ridge ASCA HOF and out of AKC-INT-ASCA CH Windfalls at Long Last ROM O-I ROM X-I CGC ASCA HOF. His pedigree has two crosses to Auggie.

Helen Detta Johnstone · Zorro, my foundation sire at Blacknblue Aussies, was a grandson of Paddy. I can never envision myself without this incredible breed to share my life with.

Wendy Waggoner · AKC-ASCA CH Windfalls At Long Last ROM O-I ROM X-I CGC ASCA HOF "Lexi" was the sweetest girl ever! She was a granddaughter of AKC-ASCA CH Oprah Winfree of Heatherhill ASCA HOF. Her sire was BISS AKC-ASCA CH Heatherhill Black-N-Decker ASCA HOF and she was out of ASCA CH Tri-Ivory Caress.

Ashley McClure · My RBIS BISS Multiple Group Winning AKC GCH-ASCA CH Ashbers Sugar Daddy "Hef" has Paddy and Silver several times in his pedigree. I'm so grateful to have these legends behind my boy! He is by BISS AKC GCH-ASCA CH Halo Black is Back @ Lil' Creek and out of Limelite's Taste The Rainbow.

Carole Devos · My boy Mangry's Dark Knight is active in herding, agility, and is a certified Visitors Therapy Assistance Dog. His pedigree includes Bear, Lucy, and Yukon.

AKC CH-Multiple Premier ASCA CH Milwin's Silver Ribbon at Inkwell ROM X-I "Ribbon." Born 2004. Reserve Winner's Bitch 2005 ASCA Nationals. Multiple Premier Awards at ASCA Nationals and Pre-shows. By AKC-ASCA CH Bayshore's Sittin' on a Goldmine x AKC-ASCA CH Davlin Milwin Double Trouble. Her pedigree includes Bear, Lucy, Auggie & Paddy. Photo courtesy of Paula Waterman. Photo credit: Inkwell Studio.

MBIS AKC GCH Oakhurst Crusin' In Chrome "Bentley." Born 2006. First male Aussie to receive the AKC GCH title. Award of Excellence 2011 Eukanuba show. Best Opposite Sex Westminster. Best of Breed 2011 Morris & Essex KC. By AKC-ASCA CH Harmony Hills Pay Per View x Bayshore's So Be It. His pedigree includes Bear, Lucy, Auggie & Paddy. Photo courtesy of Belinda Rhoads. Photo credit: Stonehaven.

AKC GCH-CKC-ASCA CH Star's Take A Hint "Clue." Born 2009. By ASCA CH Happytrail's Pork Chop Dupree x AKC CH Briarbrook's Mademoiselle. His pedigree includes Silver & Paddy. Photo courtesy of Lisa Durand. Photo credit: Perry Philips.

AUS CH Sutter Spellbound (AI) RN (Imp NZ) "Merlin." Born 2014. By AKC GCH Melody Hit The Jackpot CD RN PT CGC x NZ CH Sutter No Worries. His pedigree includes Bear, Lucy, Auggie & Paddy. Photo courtesy of Helen Simpson. Photo credit: Mark & Josie Haseldine. (AUSTRALIA)

UK CH Allmark Indecent Proposal JW "Sunny." Born 2010. By Brazilian BIS CH Dazzle's Bill-A-Bing Bill-A-Bong x UK CH Allmark Careless Whisper JW. His pedigree includes Lucy & Auggie. Photo courtesy of Neil and Angie Allan. Photo credit: Lisa Croft Elliot. (UNITED KINGDOM)

Tina Lass · My UKC CH-UAGX-PACH Shadowmere Strikes Black Gold CD RA RAX PAX2 DN CGC "ElleMae" is Paddy's great-granddaughter on both sides of her pedigree. She has group placements in UKC and Total Dog, won a Best In Match, and qualified for both the Agility and Rally National Championships. She's been a TDI Therapy dog. ElleMae is my Best Friend Forever.

My Shadowmere Wicked Blue Moon TKN CGC "Wicked" is a beautiful, smart girl with a promising future. She earned her TKN title at four months old. She loves dock diving, agility, and herding. She's by RBIS INT-UKC-ASCA CH CopperRidge East of a Blue Moon NA NAJ DS and out of UKC CH-UAGX-PACH Shadowmere Strikes Black Gold CD RA RAX PAX2 DN CGC. Her pedigree goes back to Blaze, Silver, Cruiser, and Paddy.

IR CH Allmark Naughty But Nice "Luna." Born 2013. By UK CH Allmark Indecent Proposal Sh cm. JW x AKC CH Bayshore's Cover Girl. Photo courtesy of Tracey Douglas. (UNITED KINGDOM)

BE-MONT-HR CH Amigo Labakan Sloviakia "Yogi." Born 2011. By J. EUW09 Multi CH Silver Dreams Aussie Lands Rover x Chessie Labakan Puella Fera. Photo courtesy of Kimberly Daemers. Photo credit: Nymeria's. (BELGIUM)

UKC CH-UAGX-PACH Shadowmere Strikes Black Gold CD RA RAX PAX 2 CGC DN "ElleMae." Born 2010. By Shadowmere Strikes Again x Shadowmere Stonehart Matilda. Photo courtesy of Tina Lass. Photo credit: Thomas Photo.

ASCA CH Jazztime's A Shade Above The Rest RS-N GS-N JS-O "Bailey." Born 2000. Winner's Dog 2001 ASCA Nationals. By BIS BISS AKC-ASCA CH My Main Man of Heatherhill ROM X-I ROM C-III ROM O-I ASCA HOF x ATCH AKC-ASCA CH Moonlight's Made In The Shade OA OAJ JS-E-SP ASCA HOF. Photo courtesy of Danielle Dumais. Photo credit: Kohler.

BIS BeJCH Midnight At The Oasis of Woolly Rocks. Born 2013. By AKC-NED CH Alnairs Mailman x Talisman Kick Your Heels. Photo courtesy of Jill Foreman. (BELGIUM)

AKC CH Heatherhill Rollin' in the Deep. By ASCA CH Heatherhill No Stone Unturned x Heartfire's Mighty Mouse. Photo courtesy of Clare Feler Cox.

CKC GCH Casa Blanca's First Lady CGN "Ella." Born 2014. By AKC GCH-ASCA CH Stonepine Fuel Injected x ASCA CH Casa Blanca's I've Got A Secret Photo courtesy of Julie Plourde. (CANADA)

AKC-ASCA CH Tesa's First Impression ROM X-I "Paige." Born 2004. By AKC CH Bofelli Smooth x Bayshore Bubblicious. Photo courtesy of Terri Hirsh. Photo credit: Ashbey.

Shadowmere Wicked Blue Moon TKN CGC "Wicked." Born 2016. By RBIS INT-UKC-ASCA CH CopperRidges East of a Blue Moon NA NAJ DS x UKC CH-UAGX-PACH Shadowmere Strikes Black Gold CD RA RAX PAX2 DN CGC. Photo courtesy of Tina Lass. Photo credit: Beal Photo.

AKC CH Alibi's Flirtation in Elegance HT PT "Flirt." Born 1998. By BIS BISS AKC-ASCA CH My Main Man of Heatherhill ROM X-I ROM C-III ROM O-I ASCA HOF x Alibi Keep The Dream Eaglerun. Photo courtesy of Cathy Franklin.

AKC-ASCA CH Windfalls At Long Last CGC ROM O-I ROM X-I ASCA HOF "Lexi." Born 1997. By AKC-ASCA CH Heatherhill Black-N-Decker ASCA HOF x ASCA CH Tri-Ivory Caress. Photo courtesy of Wendy Waggoner.

CH 1st Wind Sunny Colorfull of Blue Rimrock "Riley." Born 2013. By Demon Black Report Du Bois de Chantalouette x First Keeper Lady Blue Du Mazet De La Petite Cigale. Photo courtesy of Patricia Rimrock. (FRANCE)

AKC-CKC CH Shadow Fox's Capt'n Morgan CD RAE "Capt'n." Born 2001. By AKC CH Bayshore's Ralph Lauren x AKC CH Bayshore Shadow Fox. Photo courtesy of Clara Grover.

AKC-INT-UK-LUX-IR CH Bayshore Stonehaven Cat Burglar "Prowler." Born 2007. By AKC CH Rosemere Dragonfly at Bayshore x AKC CH Bayshore's On The Catwalk. Photo courtesy of Jeff Margeson.

RBIS BISS AKC GCH-ASCA CH Ashbers Sugar Daddy "Hef." Born 2011. By BISS AKC GCH- ASCA CH Halo Black is Back @ Lil' Creek x Limelite's Taste The Rainbow. Photo courtesy of Ashley McClure.

Mangry's Dark Knight, Certified Therapy Assistance Dog "Zami." Born 2014. By Silver Dreams Aussies Land Rover x Mangry's She's A Black Snowflake. Photo courtesy of Carole Devos. Photo credit: Jil Roderes. (LUXEMBOURG)

No Woman No Cry Du Val d'Aury "Xangô" (pronounced Chango). Born 2017. By Jazzy's Groove Des Kitchou' Pitchou x First Edition Du Val d'Aury. His pedigree includes Bear, Lucy, Cruiser, Victor & Auggie. Photo credit: Paula McDermid.

I met Xangô when he was four hours old and immediately felt he was my dog. He was different from his brothers and sisters—bigger, furry and really, really cool! At the beginning I thought I would call him Bouddha, because he used to stay apart from the other five puppies. He'd sit under a big tree as if he was meditating. He was and still is a Zen puppy.

I wanted to give him a name that meant something important for me, so I spent a lot of time looking for the right name. I decided to look for it in the Brasilian culture, which is a big part of my life. When I found "Xangô" I felt it was the right name.

For the African, Brasilian and Cuban cultures, Xangô is an Orisha (a god). He's the Orisha of fire and justice. I have a little story about that. As soon as I found his name, my fire alarm rang for thirty minutes without any reason. It made me smile. My Brasilian friends would have probably said, "You called Xango, he answered you!" The spirit of Xangô is protecting me.

- Camille-Charlotte Richard (FRANCE)

(Left) Jump To The Chance Du Val D'Aury "Chance" and (right) Jumpin' Jack Flash Du Val D'Aury "Jack." Littermates born 2014. By SR-INT CH Meadowlawn Boreal Night x SR CH Easy Way Out of Des Minis Toons. Their pedigree includes Bear, Lucy, Cruiser, Victor, Auggie & Paddy. Photos courtesy of Isabelle Guillot. (FRANCE)

Jen Scott Smail · My beloved AKC-UKC CH Halfmoon Supernova Flash CD AKC RE ASCA RA BN HT PT HSAs STDs OA OAJ NF NAP AJP JV-E GS-O RV-O CL2-R CL2-S CL2-F CL2-H CGC "Flash" is an intensely beautiful dog inside and out. He has the most incredible temperament!

Lyndy Jacob · Broken Trees Unchained Melody AKC CDX ASCA CD OA OAJ AD CGC "Melody" was the smartest dog I'd ever seen. She usually learned the first time you showed her something! She performed 57 tricks, did print and TV work, did demos and was a super fast and drivey dog. She was my heart dog and my one-in-a-million Aussie.

Diana Hefti · CKC-ASCA CH Topgun's Black Magic AKC RE ASCA RN AX OAJ NAP NJP NFP RV-E JV-E-SP GS-E EAC O-EJC OCC TN-E TG-E O-WV-N HP-N HIC NADAC Novice Versatility Award "Magic" was by CH Patriot Games of Ironhorse and out of CH Topgun Cruzin' in the Fast Lane. Magic was a wonderful boy and I miss him every day.

Nathalie Kalman · Paddy's grandson Gotham's Leading Man "Sean" arrived in France in 2000 from Sharon and Stevens Parr's Gotham Kennel. He was sired by Auggie's son AKC-ASCA CH Heatherhill You Talk Too Much ASCA HOF and out of Paddy's daughter CH Gotham's Main Event. He was a good producer and has champion kids in Europe. He was everything an Aussie should be.

Trudy Gallavin · Some of the first imports to New Zealand were from Firethorne Kennel in the U.S.A. My CH Rimrock Oz Oklahoma QT "Dallas" was awarded Best of Breed at 11 years of age under Breeder Judge Nancy Pelletier.

AKC-INT-ASCA CH Lakehills Millenni'Em' Mischief PT AX AXJ RS-O JS-O GS-O NAC NJC NGC ROM X-II ASCA HOF "Emma." Born 1999. By AKC-ASCA CH Starswept Just Rope It of Hisaw x ASCA CH Lakehills Oh Whata Nite at Hisaw. Photo courtesy of Raine Lutz. Photo credit: Mark Valente.

CH Jazztime's Music Man RS-E JS-E GS-O "Jingles." Born 2000. By BIS BISS AKC-ASCA CH My Main Man of Heatherhill ROM X-I ROM C-III ROM O-I ASCA HOF x ATCH AKC-ASCA CH Moonlight's Made In The Shade OA OAJ JS-E-SP ASCA HOF. Photo courtesy of Danielle Dumais.

AKC GCH-ASCA CH Meadowlawn's Night To Remember CD "Ethan." Born 2007. By BISS AKC-ASCA CH Firethornes Night Moves ASCA HOF x AKC-ASCA CH Meadowlawn's Standing Ovation CD MX MXJ NF RS-E JS-E-OP GS-N ASCA HOF. His pedigree includes Auggie & Paddy. Photo courtesy of Sarah Kalkes. Photo credit: Sam Litin.

AKC-UKC CH Halfmoon Supernova Flash CD AKC RE ASCA RA BN HT PT HSAs STDs OA OAJ NF NAP AJP JV-E GS-O RV-O CL2-R CL2-S CL2-F CL2-H CGC "Flash." Born 2006. By AKC CH Chambray MasterHand x AKC CH Westridge Panache. Photo courtesy of Jen Scott Smail. Photo credit: Pix n Pages.

Broken Trees Unchained Melody AKC CDX ASCA CD OA OAJ AD CGC "Melody" Born 2000. By Backdrafts Can't Touch This x Hillsides A'del of Willowood. Photo courtesy of Lyndy Jacob. Photo credit: Pix n Pages.

MBIS-World Winner-Multi CH Allmark Fifth Avenue "Tiffany." Born 2010. Top-winning Aussie in UK and Europe. Group winner at Crufts, Group winner at World Show in Finland. By Brazilian BIS CH Dazzle's Bill-A-Bing Bill-A-Bong x UK CH Allmark Careless Whisper JW. Photo courtesy of Neil and Angie Allan. (UNITED KINGDOM)

CKC-ASCA CH Topgun Black Magic AKC RE ASCA RN AX OAJ NAP NJP NFP RV-E JV-E-SP GS-E EAC O-EJC OCC TN-E TG-E O-WV-N HP-N HIC NADAC Novice Versatility Award "Magic." Born 2002. By AKC CH Patriot Games of Ironhorse x CH Topgun Cruzin' in the Fastlane. Photo courtesy of Diana Hefti. Photo credit: Bergman.

Lollypop's No Speed Limit "Regis." Born 2003. First European dog with a tail to win Reserve Winner's Dog at an ASCA National Specialty, which he did in 2006. By Black Velvet's Harley Davidson x Sunnyrain's Book of Etiquette. Photo courtesy of Nadia Schlapp.

INT-Multi CH Rosemere Twinklefly RN RE JHD-s HT "Pippi." Born 2008. By AKC CH Bayshore National Enquirer x AKC CH Rosemere Tidal Wave. Photo courtesy of Naja Baaring. (DENMARK)

Gotham's Leading Man "Sean." Born 2002. By AKC-ASCA CH Heatherhill You Talk Too Much ASCA HOF x CH Gotham's Main Event. Photo courtesy of Nathalie Kalman. (FRANCE)

Dailo's Special Delivery By Mailman "Mercedes." Born 2012. By AKC-NED CH Alnairs Mailman x Dailo's Pocket Full Of Sunshine. Photo courtesy of Renate Agterberg. (NETHERLANDS)

AKC Bronze GCH Oakhurst-Arborview Kick It Up A Notch CD RE "Bubba." Born 2010. By BISS AKC ASCA CH Stormridge's He's All That CD TDI ROM X-III ROM C-II x CH Bayshore's So Be It. Photo courtesy of Ben Swanson. Photo credit: Amber Jade Aanensen.

AKC GCH-CKC CH-UKC GCH-ASCA CH Wyndcrest Imagine That! RN CGC "Zane." Born 2006. By AKC CH Thornapple Code Red x AKC-ASCA CH Aristocrats Intuition. Photo courtesy of Nellie Morack. Photo credit: Thornapple.

INT CH MMM's Perfect Picture "Patric." Born 2014. By AKC-ASCA CH MMM's Picture Perfect x Starswept High on a Feeling. Photo courtesy of Dotti Guy. Photo credit: Vicki Holloway Photo.

IR CH Armatan Bad Moon Rising ShCM CW'07 CW'10 "Dash." Born 2005. By AKC CH Heatherhill Creedence x AKC CH Firethorne's C'est La Vive (Imp USA). Photo courtesy of Julie Holligan. Photo credit: Wally Holligan. (UNITED KINGDOM)

UKC-ASCA CH Boondocks Breakfast at Tiffany's AKC RN ASCA RNX URO1 CGC "Audrey." Born 2009. By AKC CH Briarbrooks Mark the Deck x AKC CH Crystal Winds Kickin Bootie. Photo courtesy of Sara Nicole. Photo credit: Kathleen Riley.

NZ CH Rimrock Oz Oklahoma QT "Dallas." Born 2002. Platinum Certificate of Merit. By AUS-NZ CH Lombardy Lumbee x NZ CH Rimrock Oz Eclipse O Time. Photo courtesy of Trudy Gallavin. (NEW ZEALAND)

Dogs come into our lives to teach us about love and loyalty. They depart to teach us about loss. We try to replace them but never quite succeed. A new dog never replaces an old dog, it just expands our hearts. If you have loved many old dogs, your heart is very big.

AKC-ASCA CH
Shadowrun's Sand Sandals
CGC RS-N RJ-N RG-N NAC NJC NGC

"Teva." Born 1998. By BIS BISS AKC-ASCA CH My Main Man of Heatherhill ROM X-I ROM C-III ROM O-I ASCA HOF x BISS ASCA CH Shadowrun's Pebbles in the Sand CD STDsc ASCA HOF

Teva was six years old when my daughter was born and eight when my son came along. She never really liked kids, so I worried how she'd respond when I brought my babies home from the hospital. But she accepted them amazingly well and they developed wonderful relationships. She and my son were especially close. He told me that she would talk to him and tell him things, and I often caught him whispering in her ear.

Teva passed away in 2014. She lived a good long life, but it still broke my heart when we had to say goodbye. It never gets any easier.

This photo was her last trip to the beach with my son. I still miss her every day.

- Kristin Rush

Abbreviations of Titles
This is not a comprehensive listing

Conformation Titles

Championships earned during the 1970s and 1980s were awarded by ASCA (Australian Shepherd Club of America).

In 1991 Australian Shepherds were recognized by AKC (American Kennel Club) and that club began awarding championships.

Championships are also awarded by other kennel clubs including CKC (Canadian Kennel Club), INT (International Kennel Club), UKC (United Kennel Club), SKC (States Kennel Club), IABKC (International All Breed Kennel Club), CACIB (Mexican Kennel Club), and other countries.

CH	Champion of Record
A-CH	Altered Champion (ASCA)
GCH	Grand Champion. Levels are Silver, Bronze, Gold, Platinum
BIS	Best in Show (MBIS is Multiple Best in Show)
BISS	Best in Specialty Show (MBISS is Multiple Best in Specialty Show)
BOB	Best of Breed
BOS	Best of Opposite Sex
BOW	Best of Winners
WD/WB	Winners Dog/Winners Bitch

Sire and Dam Merit Awards

Title awarded by ASCA
HOF   Hall of Fame sire or dam

Titles awarded by USASA
ROM   Record of Merit. Levels I, II, III. Divisions: Conformation, Obedience, Performance
ROMX   Record of Merit Excellent. Levels I, II, III
HOFX   Hall of Fame Excellent

Obedience, Tracking, and Special Performance Titles

ASCA and AKC have the same designations for obedience titles. Other organizations offer similar titles.

CD	Companion Dog	OTCH	Obedience Trial Champion
CDX	Companion Dog Excellent	TD	Tracking Dog
ODX	Open Dog Excellent	TDX	Tracking Dog Excellent
UD	Utility Dog	VST	Variable Surface Tracking
UDX	Utility Dog Excellent	VCH	Versatility Champion
UDT	Utility Dog Tracking	SVCH	Supreme Versatility Champion

Livestock Herding Titles

The lower case letters following herding titles indicate the type of livestock.

Titles awarded by ASCA
STD   Started Trial Dog - cattle, sheep, ducks
OTD   Open Trial Dog - cattle, sheep, ducks
ATD   Advanced Trial Dog - cattle, sheep, ducks
WTCH   Working Trial Champion
PATD   Post Advanced Trial Dog
RTD   Ranch Trial Dog
OFTD   Open Farm Trial Dog

Herding titles awarded by AKC
HT   Herding Tested
HS   Herding Started, Course A, B, or C - cattle, sheep, ducks
HI   Herding Intermediate, Course A, B, or C - cattle, sheep, ducks
HX   Herding Excellent, Course A, B, or C - cattle, sheep, ducks
HCH   Herding Champion

Agility Titles

Agility titles may be earned from AKC, ASCA, UKC, NADAC, CPE, and other organizations.

Titles awarded by ASCA		Titles awarded by AKC	
RS	Regular Standard-Novice, Open, Elite	NA	Novice
RV	Regular Veteran-Novice, Open, Elite	NAJ	Novice Jumper with weaves
RJ	Regular Junior-Novice, Open, Elite	OA	Open
JS	Jumpers Standard-Novice, Open, Elite	OAJ	Open Jumper with weaves
JV	Jumpers Veteran-Novice, Open, Elite	AX	Excellent
JJ	Jumpers Junior-Novice, Open, Elite	AXJ	Excellent Jumper with weaves
GS	Gamblers Standard-Novice, Open, Elite	MX	Master Excellent
GV	Gamblers Veteran	MXJ	Master Excellent Jumper with weaves
GJ	Gamblers Junior	MACH	Master Agility Champion

Rally Titles

Rally titles may be earned from ASCA, AKC, and other organizations.

Titles awarded by ASCA			
RN	Rally Novice	REMX	Rally Excellent Masters X
RNX	Rally Novice X	RTX	Rally Trial X
RA	Rally Advanced	RTCH	Rally Trial Championship
RAX	Rally Advanced X		
RE	Rally Excellent	**Titles awarded by AKC**	
REX	Rally Excellent X	RN	Rally Novice
RM	Rally Master	RA	Rally Advanced
RMX	Rally Master X	RE	Rally Excellent
REM	Rally Excellent Masters	RAE	Rally Advanced Excellent

DNA Designations

DNA-CP   DNA Certified Profiled   DNA-VP   DNA Verified Parentage

Miscellaneous Titles

CGC   Canine Good Citizen   TT   Temperament Test

About Paula McDermid

Ms. McDermid acquired her first Australian Shepherds in 1980 and has been devoted to the breed since that time. Under the kennel name "Bainbridge," she produced many champions, obedience, herding, and agility titled dogs. Among those beautiful and talented Aussies were two superstars:

> ASCA CH Steal The Show of Bainbridge, Best of Breed winner at the 1986 Australian Shepherd Club of America National Specialty.

> MACH4 U-ACHX NATCH4 ATCH-SP ADCH C-ATCH U-CH Chukker's Brumby Bainbridge AKC ASCA CD STdc ATDds HSAds TN-O WV-N TG-N JHD-S NF RN CGC. Awarded Most Versatile Aussie at the 2004 United States Australian Shepherd Association National Specialty.

Ms. McDermid's success as a breeder earned Bainbridge Aussies the "Hall of Fame" designation from the Australian Shepherd Club of America (ASCA).

Ms. McDermid served for nine years on the Board of Directors of the United States Australian Shepherd Association (USASA). Her positions included Vice President, Director, Newsletter Editor, and Chairperson of the Health and Genetics Committee (H&G).

Her greatest achievement as H&G Chairperson was the advancement of genetic health testing of Australian Shepherds. She spearheaded the establishment of the first Aussie epilepsy research program at the University of Minnesota's College of Veterinary Medicine. From 2007-2011, Ms. McDermid directed the expansion of genetic health testing at the USASA National Specialty, developing it into an important annual event.

Ms. McDermid began judging Australian Shepherds in 1986 at ASCA specialty shows and earned the title of Senior Breeder Judge. In 1995, she became the second Australian Shepherd Breeder Judge to be approved by the American Kennel Club. She judges AKC and ASCA shows across the United States, and FCI Australian Shepherd specialty shows in Europe.

www.ingramcontent.com/pod-product-compliance
Lightning Source LLC
Chambersburg PA
CBHW040328300426
44113CB00020B/2682